Wendy Harmer is one of Australia's most versatile and much-loved entertainers—broadcaster, author, journalist and stage performer.

As a stand-up comedian she performed at the Melbourne, Edinburgh, Montreal and Glasgow Mayfest Comedy Festivals, in London's West End and at the Sydney Theatre Company. As a broadcaster, Wendy enjoyed huge popularity leading Sydney radio station 2Day FM's top-rating breakfast show for 11 years and at ABC Sydney radio, rated highly in the morning and breakfast shifts from 2016–2021. She has hosted, written and appeared in a variety of TV shows including ABC's *The Big Gig*.

A prolific columnist for a host of magazine and newspaper titles, Wendy is also the author of eight books for adults including her bestselling novels *Farewell My Ovaries*, *Love and Punishment* and *Nagging for Beginners*, a 'how-to' guide for women. She has also written two teen novels and multiple books for children in the *Pearlie in the Park* series.

Wendy and her husband Brendan live with their two children, Marley and Maeve, on Sydney's Northern Beaches.

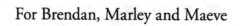
For Brendan, Marley and Maeve

WENDY HARMER

Lies My Mirror Told Me

A frank, funny, fearless memoir

ALLEN&UNWIN

SYDNEY·MELBOURNE·AUCKLAND·LONDON

Allen & Unwin
Cammeraygal Country
83 Alexander Street
Crows Nest NSW 2065
Australia
Phone: (61 2) 8425 0100
Email: info@allenandunwin.com
Web: www.allenandunwin.com

Allen & Unwin acknowledges the Traditional Owners of the Country on which we live and work. We pay our respects to all Aboriginal and Torres Strait Islander Elders, past and present.

 A catalogue record for this book is available from the National Library of Australia

ISBN 978 1 76011 208 0

Set in 13/19 pt Adobe Garamond Pro by Midland Typesetters, Australia
Printed and bound in Australia by the Opus Group

10 9 8 7 6 5 4 3 2 1

The paper in this book is FSC® certified. FSC® promotes environmentally responsible, socially beneficial and economically viable management of the world's forests.

Contents

Prologue

Ever since the ancients peered into surfaces of polished obsidian or shards of reflective mica hung on mud walls, we have consulted mirrors seeking deeper truths. In themselves, these shiny objects are inert and meaningless, until we endow them with supernatural insight into our vanities, yearnings and self-delusions, asking for confirmation or denial.

Asking a mirror for honesty? Deceptive, lying bastards of things.

Tricksters. Would not know 'truth' if they saw it. As the surrealist artist Jean Cocteau once observed: 'Mirrors should think longer before they reflect.'

I've rarely regarded my face in a mirror without wondering: *What if?* Not out of self-pity, but with an abiding curiosity about where life might have taken me if I hadn't been born with this unfinished face of mine.

Looking back at me, in my furthest memories, was a girl, and then a young woman, tilting her chin to present a brave, defiant face to the world, even when she would rather have hidden. I'm proud she didn't.

Contemplating my reflection in the mirror now, at almost seventy, I see the contours of my face softening and sagging. Perhaps I am way past consulting a magic looking glass for any new revelation.

But tracing the old, scarred tracks of tiny stitches connects me to times, places and people that may otherwise have been long forgotten.

And to the mirrors. Too many mirrors.

Let's face it.

They've always been the wrong place to look.

*

It's a rare thing to experience your parents sharing with more than a million strangers exactly what they thought of you on the day you were born.

Not sure I can recommend it.

On Monday, 7 February 2005, ABC TV's much-loved program *Australian Story* went to air with an episode that had been promoted all week: 'Comedian Wendy Harmer bravely reveals a set of photos showing the facial deformity she was born with . . . Locked away in the archives of the Melbourne Children's Hospital for nearly fifty years, the confronting photos were retrieved for *Australian Story*'s profile of the writer, broadcaster and stand-up comedian.'

As the familiar theme music played and the episode titled 'Operation Wendy' began, I was clutching a velvet cushion to my face—the last flimsy protection between me and the revelations my mother and father were about to share with the world. They'd never spoken to me about those first days.

The producers had unearthed my baby photos—black-and-white images I hadn't known existed were about to be shown on national television.

Beside me on the couch were my husband Brendan and our two small children—Marley, aged seven, and five-year-old Maeve.

What would they make of this strange, alien baby with a ragged opening where her mouth should have been and her huge, alarmed eyes?

We were all about to find out.

*

Excerpt from the program transcript of 'Operation Wendy':

Jessica Rowe—Presenter: Hello, I'm Jessica Rowe, a news presenter in Sydney. Tonight's program is about a friend of mine, a woman who was once warned she'd never have a career on stage or in front of the camera. But despite being born with a severe facial deformity, Wendy Harmer went on to become one of Australia's best-known performers and the highest-paid woman in radio. This is Wendy Harmer's *Australian Story*.

Graham Brown (Wendy's Father): When Wendy was born, to see her for the first time, she had virtually a huge mouth and she had a little button of a top lip which was fused to her nose. So, it was a huge hole in the face. Disastrous-looking thing.

Margaret Wicks (Wendy's Mother): Graham came in that night. He was pretty upset, and he said, 'I don't want you to see her. I've told the doctor you can't see her for seven days.'

Graham: It was a shock. Margaret was 17 and I was 22 at the time, healthy, and we couldn't believe it.

Margaret: Finally Dr Martin came in and brought me in a textbook, and she was one of the most severe cases of bilateral cleft lip and palate that he'd seen.

Graham: I had a fox terrier pup born with a cleft palate and I had to drown it. Wendy's condition was such that if she were not a human, she would have been put down. Thank God we didn't. It was the last of our thoughts. We loved that kid just the same.

Margaret: I looked at her and the first thing I thought was, 'Oh, my poor little love, you are going to have such a hard road here, and I don't know what to do.'

Graham: It was a hard-love approach that we gave to Wendy. Wendy could be loved and not mollycoddled. And so we said, 'Well, she's got to be toughened against the slings and arrows of outrageous fortune,' and that's the way we operated. We knew no better. And, in fact, I doubt if a therapist could have devised a better scheme.

Wendy: And there was a thing that my mother used to do, too. When I would come home from school and say, 'Oh, the boys have been picking on me,' she would say, 'I want you to go and stand in front of the mirror and when you can find something to complain about, you come out here and tell me.'

Margaret: So she went off with a tear in her eye. She said, 'I've got nothing to be sorry for.' I said, 'Right.' So, then I sat her down. I said, 'Darling, when you grow up and you have more operations,' I said, 'you will be just as beautiful as anybody else. It's just going to take time.'

Sixty years later, my mother admits that lesson in front of the mirror was 'brutal'.

1

The dream couple

My maternal grandparents, Ted Wicks and Rita (nee James), eloped to escape their families' disapproval.

Rita's people were Protestant and had come to Tasmania from England in the 1850s, settling around Scottsdale. Ted's were Catholic and had made their home in Deloraine.

The children of that era goaded each other with chants:

Proddy dogs
Sitting on logs
Eating maggots out of frogs.

Catholic dogs
Stink like frogs
Jumping out of hollow logs.

This ancient religious enmity was to prove disastrous for the Wicks daughter, Margaret Elsie, and eventually for her eldest daughter, me: Wendy Gai.

My grandparents had two children together—Rex and then Margaret—but by 1940, when my mother was just two years old, they'd separated. Rita was banished to the mainland and lived in Melbourne. Divorced. A disgrace. Big brother Rex lived with the Catholic side of the family in Deloraine. Little sister Margie was sent to her Protestant grandparents in Longford. They lived just half an hour away from each other in central northern Tasmania, but rarely met. My mother's early days were mostly spent as an only child. As she recalls: 'One day a man wearing a tuxedo was at our house and I was told, "Margie, this is your father." He gave me a shilling.'

She remembers her grandparents as 'very, very strict', but kind enough to a little girl they had no idea what to do with. They were from another era, almost Victorian in their outlook: 'Grandad James was the stationmaster in Longford, and I can't quite picture his face, but I do remember the shiny buttons on his uniform.'

Nanna James was a straitlaced, god-fearing woman. Mum was forbidden to make friends with any girls who had older brothers. She remembers her grandmother as a distant figure, rather like the Queen: 'When Nanna died, she appeared at the end of my bed wearing a wreath of white flowers and with the same sort of regal smile. She was calling, "Goodbye, Margie. Goodbye, Margie."'

Young Margie Wicks' days were routine. Off to school early. On weekday afternoons, working in the back vegetable garden until dark; on weekends, the front flower garden. (Her bedroom was off limits in daylight hours.) Bath once a week in the washhouse. Church twice on Sundays and then cake. That night, a treat: listening to a mystery play or, even better, a comedy, on the radio.

Always reading, reading. Devouring every book she could find. 'Where's Margie, the bookworm?' her grandfather would inquire.

'At school I was the odd kid who lived with old people. I was terribly shy and they thought I was a snob. I was just afraid of everyone and everything. A very wary child. I didn't have many playmates.'

When Mum was eleven years old, her mother Rita met Joe Scott, married him, and they settled in the Victorian country town of Woodend. Mum pestered Nanna and Grandad to let her go and live with them, and they agreed.

She was off to the mainland. Off on a grand adventure!

At fifteen, she was engaged; at sixteen, married; and soon after, pregnant with me.

In photos of her holding me as a baby, she's wearing her school jumper.

*

Woodend nestles in a valley in the Macedon Ranges, an hour's drive north-west of Melbourne, not far from the famed setting of Joan Lindsay's novel, *Picnic at Hanging Rock*. This is Dja Dja Wurrung country. Colonised by goldminers, Woodend was a small rural town like any other when my parents' paths crossed there in the 1950s.

From Rita's house, Mum took the bus to Kyneton High School ten miles up the road, where she got 'very good' marks in her exams. 'I must have had an accent, as everyone asked where I was from when they met me. Nanna and Grandad would always stop me if I didn't speak properly, as a young lady should, *my dear.*'

One day she came home to find Rita had pulled her out of school and got her a job as a machinist at the Lincoln Mill, where many of the women in Woodend were employed. She was on piecework, sewing high-end underwear—petticoats, brassieres and girdles. Her wage was five pounds. Rita took three of them. Mum was a fast worker, especially on shoulder seams and over-locking, and could sometimes make nine quid a week. Rita took six. Margaret has few kind words for her mother. She almost always refers to her as 'Rita' and the name is brittle in her mouth: 'Unfortunately, she was a grasping little woman. All she wanted was money, money, money. And everything she got she spent on cigarettes and clothes.'

Working at the mill in Woodend, Margaret experienced inde-pendence for the first time. Money of her own. Horse riding with new girlfriends to Hanging Rock for picnics (from which they all returned!). And there were the flicks: 'I adored the movies. I was in love with James Mason.'

When my father—a student teacher at Ashbourne, six miles down the road—roared into town astride his cherished Ariel Twin 500cc motorbike, he may as well have been sent by Columbia Pictures.

She was fourteen. He was twenty.

*

In 1932, the year of my father's birth, Australia was in the pitiless grip of the Great Depression. Almost a third of Australian workers were unemployed. Some 60,000 families were on the 'susso' (government sustenance payments); 40,000 men had taken to the road to hunt for work.

As the children of that time chanted:

We're on the susso now
We can't afford a cow
We live in a tent
We pay no rent
We're on the susso now.

My paternal grandfather, Fred Brown, was a fruiterer who sold his wares to the grand homesteads on the sheep stations of Victoria's Western District. During the height of the Depression, he was reduced to hawking the empty hessian bags the produce had come in. He is remembered by my father as 'English to the backbone and with the morals of a Methodist minister'.

Fred's wife Nellie (nee Walker) was from Irish stock and 'an artistic and proud woman'. They married in Horsham in 1927 and went on to have eight children in all.

When my father, Graham, their third son, arrived, Fred and Nellie were living in the tiny settlement of Skipton on the banks of Mount Emu Creek. Fifty-two kilometres south-west of Ballarat (or thirty-three miles in the 'old freight'), the name Skipton was imported from the market town in Yorkshire.

Old English 'scaep' (sheep) and 'tun' (town). Sheeptown. Literally! This colonial outpost was renowned for its production of fine merino wool. In the Depression years, when Australia's exports of wheat and wool were flattened by the collapse in global demand, Victoria's Western District did it as hard as anywhere else in the nation.

Although Skipton's population has never boasted more than around 700 souls, it did produce one famous son. Henry Bolte attended the primary school where my father later went and became Victoria's Liberal premier for a record seventeen years, from 1955 to 1972. Melburnians will know his name well from the Bolte Bridge, which spans the Yarra River. Until the day old Fred Brown died, every time he saw Bolte on television, he would stiffen in his lounge chair and bark: 'That bastard still owes me twelve quid, seven shillings and sixpence!' The grievance, according to family lore, dated back to a dispute over a fundraiser at the Skipton footy club, and I never heard my father refer to him as anything but 'that bastard, Bolte'.

The house Dad was born into on Blake Street, Skipton, was rented 'for the magnificent sum of five shillings'. No water or electricity laid on. Tank water, kerosene lamps, a wood stove. No radio or books, save for a world atlas and a yearly *Boy's Own Annual*, which Dad read 'from cover to cover, time and time again'. Instead, he and his brothers revelled in the outdoor life, with 'dogs and ferrets and chooks and ducks and cows, and there was a horse across the road we rode every summer'.

His uncle Jack Walker and aunt Anne were their neighbours, and had six children. Sometimes there would be twenty kids in the Browns' yard, attracted by the fragrant bounty in Pop's shed, where he stored the fruit and vegetables he bought in Ballarat and was again delivering to the surrounding sheep stations.

'There were kids galore,' Dad recalls. 'One day our parents went away and all the neighbourhood kids came around and we devoured a whole box of bananas. The old man went crazy!'

Pop Brown was also working a five-acre lot with fifteen milking cows and sending the produce to Ballarat by bus as a way of dodging the dairy inspectors. The family had all the milk and cream they could wish for: 'We lived off the fat of the land.'

And then there were the rabbits. Millions of the bloody things. Dad spent every weekend rabbiting with big brother Bill, a box of ferrets, a gun and their dogs—Boyo, Brownie, Ginger and Razor Blade. The dogs were a crossbreed of fox terrier and whippet: 'Foxywhippets—a dog that's born to chase rabbits.'

Despite the privations of the times into which he was born, Graham relates his early years as a classic 'boy's own adventure', unfolding in chapters of unlikely escapades and miraculous escapes, with a cast of outlandish characters.

(Thanks to my younger brother, Phil, I have hours of my father's recollections recorded on video. They were made a decade before Dad died, and so I'm able to quote him directly, in most instances.)

Frustrated in his ambition to become a professional runner— 'just not quite good enough'—instead he played Aussie Rules football. Every significant date in my father's life is cross-referenced with where he was playing or coaching footy.

Which team. The position he played in. By how many points the match was won or lost.

*

When my parents met in 1953, they became, in my father's words, 'Woodend's dream couple'.

If you were to cast them in a Hollywood movie, they look like they go together. Margaret, at a tiny five foot one, is a finely made, pretty, elfin thing. Her dark hair is cut in a fashionable bob. Her eyebrows are plucked pencil-thin, her lipstick a bold shade.

Graham is movie-star handsome. His luxurious coal-black hair is combed into a gleaming quiff. He's five foot nine with a lean body, match-fit after years as an athlete.

A graduate of Ballarat Teachers' College, young Mr Brown had done the rounds of a few one-teacher schools before he landed at Ashbourne. (It remains a family joke, told through gritted teeth, that in our entire lives with my father we only once lived in a good-sized town. Usually just that *bit too far* out of one.)

'So, I was up and down the main street of Woodend on this bike. The new boy in town,' says Dad.

Mum, knocking off her shift at the mill, saw him fly by most afternoons and was impressed. 'I sometimes walked out towards Ashbourne, a few miles out, hoping to hear his motorbike coming or going.'

He remembers with unnatural clarity the moment he met my mother. It was the day his Ariel Twin came to grief.

'I'd lent the bike to this fellow. He had no idea how to handle a powerful bike. And BANG! He snapped the chain, broke the chain case. All the oil ran out. And I had to get a screwdriver to undo the chain case to fix it.

'The only person around there at the time was this little girl, fourteen years old, who said: "My stepfather's got a tool kit." She led me through to her house and gave me this screwdriver.

'Well, that was my first introduction to her. From there on, everywhere I appeared, she'd turn up. She admits to this day, she chased the pants off me.'

As Dad tells it, Margaret ran away from her mother and step-father soon after, and was missing overnight. She turned up at his school the next day.

When he returned her to her mother, Graham told Rita: 'Look, this young girl is too nice to be running away from home. I'll become her guardian, if you like. And her mother said, "Oh, that'd be alright." And from then on, Margie was my girl. Everywhere I went, she went.'

Like, in the same house—*everywhere.*

Graham, in need of accommodation, was taken in as a boarder by my grandmother and paid her seven pounds a week. Which Rita was most pleased about, according to my mother.

'And, of course, as my girlfriend was in the same house, she and I had a great relationship,' says my father.

Relationship? Yes . . . well. A local schoolteacher living under the same roof with your teenage daughter? Who should be in high school?

Mum: 'We started having sex when I was fifteen.'

Me: 'How come you didn't get pregnant until after you were married?'

Mum: 'Just lucky, I guess. I'm not sure. I really didn't associate sex with childbirth. Nanna never talked to me about those things.'

Me: 'What the fuck were you all thinking?'

Graham and Margaret went to bush dances, the pictures, parties, motorbike races and on shooting expeditions. There were trips to go swimming or to nearby towns for football matches.

Football. Always, the football.

'I was playing footy for Woodend. We won a flag in the Riddell League, in '54,' says Dad. He had a car, a 1927 Oldsmobile Tourer, which he'd modified so the front seat could be folded back and serve as a spacious bed on weekend camping trips. 'What fun we had in that!'

There are snapshots of my mother in a series of arty and risqué poses. In a fetching swimsuit. Topless, her modesty preserved by a fallen log. In a cute blouse and shorts . . . aiming a gun.

The young couple bonded over books they'd read. A shared love of music and comedy—they adored *The Goon Show* on the radio. They were well-suited to each other. Just not suited, in any way at all, for the travails ahead of them.

By this time, Fred and Nellie Brown had left 'Sheeptown' and were living in Trevor Street, East Ballarat. My grandfather worked an allotment, growing peas and potatoes, and delivered them in his truck. He bartered his produce for meat, fish and anything else the family required.

Graham and Margaret would frequently blart the fifty miles down the Midland Highway to Ballarat in their 'old girl'—top speed 60 mph, happier at 40 mph. And if the wind was up and threatening to blow off the canvas top? Mum, laughing, recollects one trip where she stood up all the way, gripping the cover as they crawled along at 20 mph.

On their visits to Ballarat, my mother would find herself in a raucous household of twenty-somethings and teens—Dad's younger siblings. My auntie Elise lives in the old house in Trevor Street to this day. The youngest of Nanna and Pop's eight children, she remains the only reliable narrator of those times in the Brown household and tells tales with great wit and humour that has us both in stitches. Elise remembers my mother joining the fray for Saturday night dances at St Patrick's Cathedral hall or swimming at the old Eureka Stockade pool where Dad had spent summers as a kid: 'Margaret was such fun to be with. She laughed *all* the time. She was embraced by the family with open arms and included in everything.'

In the Christmas holidays of 1953, Mum and Dad announced their engagement.

*

My father often joked that he married my mother 'to get rid of her'.

This was partially true.

As the marriage date loomed, Margaret says she sat in the corner at country dances wearing her engagement ring (set with the world's smallest diamond, which cost precisely £22.10), while my father, always the show pony, chose the prettiest girl in the hall to steer around the floor. He fancied himself an excellent dancer. Of course he did. And poor Mum—who could play the violin, piano and was a lovely singer—didn't quite make the cut.

'He'd just be off and I'd be forgotten for the rest of the night. I had an insight that it was going to be like this for the rest of my life,' says Mum. 'And I didn't want that.'

So much for the 'dream couple' of Woodend.

Graham and Margaret's romance was cooling and they were thinking they might delay their wedding when, a few weeks before the end of the school term in 1954, the Victorian Education Department sent my father a letter.

A. Very. Important. Letter.

One of many such letters sent by the omnipotent, faceless 'department' that was to move our fractured family around the state like a piece on a chessboard.

For my father it was exciting: 'I had applied and got my first permanent appointment—to the primary school in Tarraville.'

His future was sorted. He would have his own school and arrive there with a new wife in tow. The wedding planning resumed in earnest.

My mother's foreboding was increasing by the day: 'I wrote to my father back in Ulverstone and pleaded with him to come over to the mainland and stop it all.'

When she told Rita what she'd done, her mother was livid.

'She had a plan to not only get rid of me, but thought Graham would have a salary and she would be able to borrow money from him when she cried poor.

'My father rang Rita and said he was coming. Rita told my father she'd ring the cops and stop him. So that was the end of that little saga. Mum pushed me into it.'

*

On 15 January 1955, on a scorching-hot morning, Mum and Dad were wed at the Presbyterian church in Woodend.

Mum hoots with laughter at her memory of it: 'When the minister said, "You may now congratulate the bride," your father reached out and shook my hand! I whispered, "I think you're supposed to kiss me."'

She did get her kiss from her leading man; she was a happy and excited bride.

When friends and relatives asked: 'And will you and Graham be starting a family, Margie?' she answered: 'Oh no! We're going to breed whippets!'

'Two weeks later I was at the other end of the world. Tarraville.'

She could cook one thing. Vegemite soup. 'A teaspoon of Vegemite in hot water.'

Soon enough she had thirteen dogs . . . and two children.

*

Even in 1887, Tarraville was described as a town 'well past its peak'. Its heyday was in the 1840s, the era of 'carrying', when food for oxen and horses was grown in the district and the town was a centre for blacksmiths, wheelwrights and saddlers.

Situated on the mouth of the Tarra River in Gunai country, and named after Charley Tarra, an Aboriginal guide, it was once the largest settlement in Gippsland. Its lustre faded when nearby Port Albert brought in the gold prospectors from Europe and China. Then the railway came and finished off the port, too.

These days the place (population 80 in the 2016 Census) is mostly known for fishing. Which is exactly what it was renowned for when my parents fetched up at Tarraville School No. 615. If there was a more remote teaching outpost in Victoria in the 1950s, you'd be flat out finding it.

The newlyweds' move to Tarraville unfolded as a ridiculous circus.

Dad took Mum to the Myer department store in Melbourne. It was like Aladdin's cave. They chose pots and pans, bedding, a lounge suite, floor rugs and 'Lord knows what else' on hire purchase—all to be delivered by train to the nearby town of Yarram.

Dad's Oldsmobile Tourer was loaded to the gunnels with the rest. Birds in a cage, dogs, a cat and the precious motorbike. (Think of the opening titles of *The Beverly Hillbillies* and you won't be far wrong. Although Rita wasn't loaded on top.)

My father relates a 'humorous' moment along the road: 'We got down towards Yarram, and Margaret's hat blew off. We had no windows in the old Tourer at the time. And the hat went sailing along like a glider, way down in the valley, and she started to cry.'

Mum remembers this too: 'It was the only hat I'd ever owned and matched my wedding going-away suit. It was so pretty, that hat. Your father just said, "Too bad—the cows have probably eaten it by now." I was really upset.'

'Anyway, she soon got over it,' Dad says.

Forget the gun; I would have killed him with my bare hands.

A perfectionist with timetables, fixtures and team rosters, Dad seems to have royally stuffed up every time he carted the family's goods and chattels to a new school residence.

He was informed that the house he and his new bride had been allocated was a modest dwelling on Roberstons Beach, down a sandy track from the school.

'No power or hot water,' Mum remembers. 'No neighbours. I was in the washhouse with the scrubbing board, taking the skin off my hands.'

After a week camping in an empty kitchen on seats taken from the car with a few blankets, Dad got his brother Bill to take his truck to the Yarram train station looking for their missing furniture and returned with a 'great big cardboard box, all wrapped up and rail stickers all over'.

'We said, "Oh, here's some stuff. Great!"' says Graham. 'We unwrapped it feverishly. What was it? A bloody mirror! No use to anyone!'

I think of my mother staring into that mirror and wondering what she'd got herself into. Dad declared his new situation 'magnificent'!

'We used to be able to go out and catch flounder. Six dozen flounder was nothing to us overnight. We got garfish, occasionally sharks. In half an hour we could come back with a four-gallon container full of king prawns. We had an old copper out the back and we'd cook them up and we'd sit there and eat prawns till daylight.'

'Life in Tarraville was quite lonely and yet exciting,' he reminisces.

My mother had been told that, if she planted parsley, she would not get pregnant.

That was very poor advice.

2

Running like bandicoots

Mirror in rear of school hall
Warncoort School No. 2218
Princes Highway between Birregurra and Irrewarra
Western District, Victoria

It's our Christmas concert.

I am six years old. I am an angel.

All the parents are here and we're going to sing a carol.

My daddy is the teacher and we have been practising.

Mummy has curled my black hair and tied it with ribbons. She made me a long white dress and a wire halo with tinsel on it.

I look pretty. Just as pretty as the other girls.

There's a boy behind me with only his tiny arms and legs sticking out from a big, round shape painted brown with black spots. It looks like an old potato.

Where is his head? How did he even get in there? How will he eat supper if his arms are too short and he has no head? He's yelling that he can't see where he's going . . .

OH NO!

*

WHOOSH! Unexpectedly, the curtain went up, revealing to the assembled in the Warncoort schoolroom a flight of baby angels still in their underpants. My first stage appearance was laughed at, and I remember being mortified and doing my best to hide.

The curtain was quickly brought down and the concert began.

The boy had landed the starring role in the school's production of *The Magic Pudding: Being the Adventures of Bunyip Bluegum and His Friends Bill Barnacle and Sam Sawnoff*—the beloved Australian children's book written by Norman Lindsay in 1918. A classroom classic and crowd favourite. He'd been cast as the famous cut-an'-come-again Puddin', encased in a giant sphere of brown papier-mâché. The 'black spots' were, of course, raisins, and he played his part to thunderous applause. We angels recovered and sang our little hearts out.

Who knows? Maybe the die was cast back then on that small wooden stage. Being revealed half-nude to a waiting audience is a familiar anxiety dream for anyone in the entertainment business, no matter how long you've been a performer. You forget your lines. The microphone doesn't work. You turn up in an entirely different show from the one you rehearsed for. People laugh when they shouldn't. Or there's dead silence where there should be laughter.

Can't say I wasn't warned.

*

Warncoort Primary School, first built in 1897, sits on the stony, windswept Victorian Volcanic Plain. The Western District.

Memories of that place remain bright and brilliant. They come to me in expanses of vivid colour.

There are four of us kids now. Me, Phillip Douglas, Noel Vincent and our new baby, Helen Louise. We go everywhere together. Today we are running up a paddock ablaze with yellow daisies under a vault of endless blue sky.

A whippet or two races ahead, bounding through sunburned grass. We're heading to an old cypress tree in the windbreak we call 'the aeroplane tree'. We find our special low-hanging branch, clamber onto it and pretend it's taking us to far-off lands.

We bounce too hard, fall off and tear back to the swings, the slide and monkey bars, laughing all the way. The school playground is all ours when the other kids go home.

Sometimes we lie on the warm earth, hold hands and watch the clouds go by.

I've never lost the yearning for the 180-degree skies of my childhood. I love the flat country. Where the land stretches almost to infinity, featureless, you look to the sky. The shifting cloudscape is your world and there you can conjure dragons, castles, fairies, lions and elephants.

When the wind blows up and threatens to untether your feet from the earth, you believe you can fly. I was sure I could . . . if I tied a cape around my shoulders, spread my arms wide and found the exact spot where the wind was windiest.

I couldn't quite pronounce my name, Wendy Gai, when I was small. In her letters to me over many years, my beloved grandmother, Nellie Brown, always addressed me as 'My Dearest Windy Day'.

*

A year before the Browns arrived at Warncoort School in 1958, the remains of the abandoned railway siding were demolished. The train hadn't stopped there for years.

The town of Colac was eight miles away, too far for my mother to walk (to this day she has never held a driver's licence or learned how to swim), but at least there was a telephone in our old twin-gabled weatherboard school residence, just across the neat yard and asphalt playground.

My father possessed a rare talent for finding some of the most isolated schools in Victoria to house his wife and children. He had driven us up from Tarraville in the May school holidays after applying for a 'compassionate transfer'. In his words: 'Margaret had felt the loneliness of being down there on her own at Robertsons Beach, Tarraville. It was just a little holiday shack area and she only had one neighbour, who was a Scottish woman. She was a bit of an old bag.' (Lizzie wasn't much company for a teenage bride. One piece of sage advice: 'Och! Margie! Be careful noo. One day I was puttin' ma scones in t' oven and ma womb fell oot.')

Only months after my parents' arrival, Mum had received the news that her stepfather, Joe Scott, had been killed in an accident while working with the State Electricity Commission. 'Got blown apart with an explosion down a hole,' as Dad put it.

My mother believes he took his own life.

*

I was born in Yarram Hospital, about a fifteen-minute drive from Tarraville, in October 1955. Margaret had turned seventeen in June.

My mother named me Wendy for the character Wendy Darling in J.M. Barrie's *Peter and Wendy*, one of her cherished childhood books. My middle name, Gai, is for my father Graham, who was always known as 'Gay' to his family.

I spent the first two weeks of my life in hospital, fed with an eyedropper. A slow drip, drip, into the hole where my upper lip and palate should have been. 'That caused terrible wind; you screamed day and night. And you were so hungry when you came home,' Mum recalls.

At the age of ten weeks, I was taken to have my palate repaired at the Royal Children's Hospital in Melbourne and then returned to Tarraville. More screaming. At three months old I went back to have my face patched up in rudimentary fashion.

It would stay like that for fourteen years.

After my birth, Mum says she felt like an 'outsider looking in' whenever they visited the Browns. She had overheard a discussion about my cleft lip and palate:

'So where did *that* come from? There's nothing like that in *our* family.'

'It must be because she's *Tasmanian*.'

After that, she didn't much care to visit: 'It made me feel guilty all my life. Like there was something wrong with me.'

Guilt and shame.

The revving twin engines of my mother's life.

*

There should have been six children, my mother tells me. She's surprised I haven't remembered this revelation, half-heard, from a long time ago, but she has never been good with telling me the detail of what happened when, much less why.

Margaret miscarried between me and Phillip.

'The night before, I had abdominal pains. By morning I was screaming and had started to bleed. You were in a canvas pram beside the bed, and I fed you and then I begged your father: "Don't leave! Something could happen to both of us."

'He got on his motorbike and went off to school. He said: "You'll be okay."

'I wasn't. I fed you, but the pain got worse, and I managed to grab a towel and hold it between my legs and this great thing fell into it. I was terrified.'

Margaret pushed me in the old pram up the two miles of sandy track to the nearest neighbour, across the road from the schoolhouse. '"Hazel! My stomach's fallen out. Quick. Look. Go get Graham!" I was taken to hospital and the doctor brought in the foetus in a kidney dish to show it wasn't my stomach or any other internal organ I'd lost. It was a baby.

'He said it was a boy; I'd been five months pregnant and I didn't even know. I was in shock. It didn't seem real. I just wanted my stomach back in. I had to get home and cook Graham's tea.'

Phillip was born in 1957: 'A great little boy, until he was about five months old,' Dad recalls.

Again, my mother ploughed the rickety old pram through the sand—two of us in it, this time—to Hazel's place, calling: 'Phillip's sick!'

My father was fetched from the school.

'And I went across the road and had a look at him, and he was lying on a pillow. He was very limp and pale,' says Dad.

At Yarram hospital, baby Phillip was diagnosed with meningitis. 'You'll be lucky if he survives,' the doctor warned.

He was raced 137 miles by ambulance to the Royal Children's Hospital. The siren on the ambulance was broken, and when the vehicle hit Melbourne they were stuck in traffic, going nowhere.

'We were supposed to have a police escort, such was the seriousness of it,' says Dad.

At the hospital, Phillip was given half an hour to live.

'He had meningitis and septicaemia. They put transfusions in his ankles, and they virtually pumped all his old blood out and put new blood in him. And within a couple of weeks he was jumping around like a monkey. He was so fit.'

Mum says Dad's present to her, after she survived this trauma, was a 'nice lightweight axe'.

*

By the time my mother became pregnant again, we had moved from Tarraville to Warncoort. She had made a firm decision not to have any more children. 'I'd just made up my mind, and thought that should do it.'

This didn't work any better than the parsley.

On the first day of 1959, Noel was born in Colac hospital. He had a cleft lip, and my mother and father were shocked. The 'Tasmanian Curse' had struck again.

A mere fourteen months later, Helen came and my mother couldn't bear to see her: 'I'd been having nightmares and I was sure Helen would be born with half a face. A nurse came into the ward with this bundle, all wrapped up, just a little face peeking out. I thought it must have belonged to the woman next to me. 'I turned and said: "Ooh, that's a lovely baby." The nurse touched me on the arm and said: "Margaret, it's *your* baby." I said, "No, it's not!" And we argued for a while. They had to work very hard to convince me she was mine.'

That was not the last of it. Another year or so went by and Mum was doing the laundry when the dreadful cramps came. She was familiar with this pain by now and knew it was too early.

'Graham wasn't answering the phone, so I rang a local farmer half a mile away to get him out of the schoolroom and take me to Colac hospital.'

Fifteen minutes after she was admitted, Mum was wheeled into theatre and operated on for an ectopic pregnancy.

The next morning, the doctor told her: 'We have given you a tubal ligation . . . tied your tubes. We think you have been through enough.' He did this without asking my mother's permission.

'I was distraught. I cried and cried and cried for days,' says my mother. 'I wasn't a woman anymore. I was barren after that.'

At the age of twenty-two, Margaret's childbearing days were over. But she had done well, according to my father: 'My mother had four in six years, but Margaret had four in four years. So the early breeding is a feature.'

From then on, the only 'breeding' they did together was of dogs.

*

The name Warncoort is an abbreviation of Tarndwarncoort. The name was shortened by the Victorian Railways in 1889 when it wouldn't fit on the metal sign to designate the modest station on the line between Geelong and Colac. In the language of the Gulidjan people it means 'up and down like a bandicoot running', a lyrical description of the low, undulating stony rises on the plain.

A grassy woodland threaded with creeks, lakes and marshes, both freshwater and salty, for untold millennia the place was bountiful for the locals. Emus, bustard, cranes, herons, geese were hunted. There was meat from kangaroos and possums. Freshwater mussels were collected from the stony shores of Lake Colac, fish and eels were abundant.

Far from being nomadic, the Gulidjan people (also referred as Kolakngat), are recorded as living in a collection of *wuurns*—stone dwellings made cosy with wallaby skins. They tended their fish traps, and in summer the women headed out and cultivated crops of yam daisies.

It's also recorded that between 300 and 350 Aboriginal people were massacred in the fourteen years from 1834 to 1848 during the colonial invasion of Victoria's Western District. It must have been many more. Aboriginal sites were razed, their inhabitants driven off, hunting lands fenced and woodlands levelled for livestock.

The fate of the traditional owners is an all-too-familiar story of dispossession, but for the Gulidjan people it seems to have happened exceptionally quickly. In 1839, the Wesleyan Methodist Missionary Society warned that Indigenous people in the district were at risk of becoming 'extinct'. Just three years later, the missionaries reported that 'most of the natives are dead and others are dying'. They cited venereal disease and low birth rates as the cause.

Some drifted into the larger settlements of Colac, Geelong or Ballarat, their lives blighted by disease, alcoholism and unending sorrow for the loss of culture and traditional life. Others found work on local farms: cutting thistles, digging potatoes or washing sheep. A few were engaged as seasonal shearers, their descendants noted in journals as being paid in rations of clothes, flour, sugar, tea and tobacco.

After 60,000 years, they were almost gone from the volcanic plains, and with them the running bandicoot and dancing brolga.

*

There were around twenty children in the Warncoort school-room when I was there in the 1950s, and many of them had the surname Dennis.

In 1840 three Dennis brothers moved from Cornwall to Tarndwarncoort, where they still live, six generations later. Here they developed Australia's first new breed of sheep—the famous Polwarth. One-quarter Lincoln, three-quarters Merino, hardy, and good for both meat and wool. The family now invites visitors to 'Tarndie', a handsome stone homestead and one of the oldest in Victoria: 'One family. One flock. Since 1840' is their calling card.

At Warncoort school we little white lambs assembled around the flagpole on Monday mornings, saluted and recited:

I love God and my country.
I honour the flag.
I will serve the Queen
And cheerfully obey my parents, teachers and the law.

Then we marched up and down the asphalt. Soldiers for the Commonwealth!

*

I can't pinpoint the precise day when I started school. From the age of four, when Mum was busy with the younger kids in the house, I'd wander across the yard to where Dad stood at the blackboard with his chalk and duster.

It was like that for all four of us. We learned to walk and talk in schoolrooms. Grew up swallowing dictionaries, literally.

The obligatory portrait of the Queen oversaw orderly proceedings, which hadn't changed much in half a century in that country school and many others like it. Every day the children greeted my father with a singsong, 'Good morning, Mr Brown,' and I'd enjoy a rebellious moment, muttering, 'G'day, Dad.'

When I was big enough, I got my very own wooden desk. I loved its worn, creaky lid and china inkwell, my pen and nib. How grown-up I was to be in the same room as the older kids. From the large windows there was a view of rolling paddocks and sheep ambling by, the perfect spot to daydream when lessons for grade six seemed to go on and on.

Brother Phil also recalls the day he claimed his own desk: 'You felt a bit superior because you could look down on the preps sitting on the floor on a mat.' His favourite time was in winter, when Dad would take the bottles of milk every school child was issued with, heat them in the urn and make hot cocoa: 'We'd drink it from mugs. It was perfect.'

I can't remember anything about the old residence. For me, the schoolroom, full of books, bats and balls, paints, pencils and paper, was home. A warm and comforting place.

I'd sometimes find myself carting the younger kids across the yard when Mum was calling them indoors. In one embarrassing episode, Helen toddled into the classroom in the nude to the sniggers of the older boys, and I was sternly directed to cover her up and hustle her out the door.

The life I describe seems impossibly archaic now, but it was old-fashioned even then.

We were on the cusp of the 1960s. A time of huge cultural change. Not in the backwater of Warncoort. In the classroom, it was still Just After the War.

The *First* World War.

*

According to the set of Victorian Readers we studied, published by the Department of Education in 1928, the past thirty years hadn't happened. It's extraordinary to think that the readers my father was teaching from were the very same books he'd learned from in his own schooldays back in Skipton. But, then, he was only a couple of decades older than me, I suppose, and change in 'the department' was glacial in every way.

There were eight readers, dating from the days when there were eight grades in primary school and a high school education was only for the wealthy. I have the complete set. They're fascinating relics and, viewed through modern eyes, a hair-raising compendium of racism and misogyny.

The Victorian Ministry of Education's 'committees of teachers and inspectors' set out their thinking in the preface to the *Eighth Book* (for older children):

TO THE TEACHER: The young readers are to begin at home, to be taken in imagination to various parts of the Empire, to Europe, and to the United States of America, and thus gain a knowledge of their rich heritage and acquire a well-founded pride of race.

'*A well-founded pride of race*'. This has a familiar ring to it, espoused by today's scourge of extremist white nationalism.

The books are a curious stew of random ingredients from the Western canon and it's hard to believe they were compiled for children. Poems, essays and play extracts from Shakespeare, Milton, Wordsworth, Shelley, Dickens, Tennyson, Coleridge, Byron, Thackeray, Browning, Kipling and Kingsley. Stray verses from the *London Punch*, the odd nugget of wisdom from Euripides. A continental dash of Tolstoy, Cervantes and Hugo, and from there to the USA for Lincoln, Longfellow and Whitman.

Lots of moral lessons by 'Anon' for no apparent reason. Within a few pages of the *Sixth Book*, students are invited to contemplate *The Death of the Dauphin*, *Young Lochinvar* and a folk tale 'from the Hindu'.

The contribution from woman writers is vanishingly small.

The Australian content—which makes up a quarter of the offerings—is national myth-making on an epic scale set against the backdrop of the success of British Imperialism. The theme of triumphant conquest of 'Terra Nullius' is all-pervading.

We hear from explorer Sir Thomas Livingstone Mitchell, late of Scotland, who, in 1836, writes from Pyramid Hill in central Victoria:

The scene was different from anything I had ever before witnessed—a land so inviting and still without inhabitants.

As I stood, the first intruder in the sublime solitude of those verdant plains as yet untouched by flocks or herds, I felt certain of being the harbinger of mighty changes there; for our footsteps would soon be followed by the men and animals for which the land seemed to have been prepared.

Of this Eden it seemed that I was the only Adam . . .

'*Still without inhabitants*' . . . and yet, in that same book, an essay titled 'The Old Inhabitants' furnishes illustrations of throwing sticks, nulla-nulla and boomerangs. Another tract describes in great detail the ritual of corroboree. Aboriginal people are depicted as either 'savages', 'primitive', 'feeble minded', or possessed of almost supernatural powers of observation that the white bushman cannot comprehend.

When it comes to either the condemnation or glorification of war, it's the same confusion. On one page, sorrowful lamentations on the carnage of conflict and futile waste of young lives; on the next, the blowing of celestial trumpets for those who made the 'ultimate sacrifice'.

My father was always ambivalent about commemorating ANZAC Day. Five of his uncles served in the armed forces. Great-Uncle Harry came home with post-traumatic stress disorder—or, as it was called then, 'a case of the ta-tas'. A family anecdote, often told, describes how Harry once threw himself bodily to the footpath in the main street of Ballarat when a car backfired, thinking it was enemy shelling. Another uncle died of alcoholism, a legacy of his wartime trauma.

The 'bush' itself is a romanticised character, both its virtues and terrors extolled in many titles: *A Lover of the Bush*; *Christmas in the Bush*; *Lost in the Bush*.

(I'm reminded here of a line from one of my stand-up routines, explaining the meaning of 'the bush' to an American audience: 'It's, like, not just ONE bush. It's not like we all stand around it and say: "Well, there's the Australian bush. It's a bewdy, isn't it? And there's a hundred kids lost in it and it's always on fire".')

When it comes to women's roles in the bold project of Australia, the message is clear. Women are to stay home and wait with patient stoicism until their menfolk return from their heroic feats of exploring, droving, mining for gold, cutting timber, shearing sheep or battling bushfires with not so much as a wet hessian bag to save a flaming hut or haystack.

And yet, for all the questionable content in the Victorian Readers, I'm sure they were the source of my father's enduring love of poetry. The books invited further reading of the 'classics', and he took up that invitation with alacrity.

He always prided himself on having a ready quote from John Donne, T.S. Eliot or John Keats and was never happier than when fielding a question from me on a high school poetry assignment. I well remember the excruciating to-and-fro he had with one of my teachers on the *true* meaning of Keats' 'Ode on a Grecian Urn' . . . with me in the middle.

Dad was a master of the oral tradition. Gave wonderful speeches and relished any chance to orate in his precise syntax and clear, booming voice that could reach the back row of any school assembly, town hall, sports club or bar. He could recite many classics by heart, although he favoured the works of Australian authors for the impromptu performances he was often called on to deliver at parties and barbecues.

Once heard, his recitation of A.B. 'Banjo' Paterson's 'The Man from Ironbark' was never to be forgotten. *'And "MURDER! BLOODY MURDER!" yelled the man from Ironbark.'*

In a tiny country schoolroom on a drowsy summer afternoon, sitting at a wooden desk, my six-year-old body levitated.

A favourite story of my father's was that I learned to read without much input from him: 'You went on holiday to your grandmother Rita's house when you were about five, and when you came back you could read!'

I assume this must have been from sheer boredom.

What strikes me most in the first, second and third readers I studied is the celebration of fantasy—mostly tales of European origin. They imbued me with a deep and abiding love of fairy lore, myths and legend. I lived half in the world around me and half in the magical world of beautiful princesses and handsome princes in ivy-covered stone towers. But, tellingly, most often I cast myself in the role of the witch—too ugly for polite society, banished, but possessed of magical powers and intent on bending everyone to her will.

I really did come to believe that I could make things go my way if I just concentrated hard enough, like Roald Dahl's Matilda. Looking back, it was a vain wish for power over events in my young life that spiralled way out of my control.

My favourite time in the classroom was Tuesday afternoons, when the schoolroom would be quieted and my father would tune in to the ABC radio program, *Singing and Listening*.

Again, I marvel that in the late 1950s and early 60s we were learning songs about 'Mr Sambo', pickin' cotton and weird

European folk ditties about 'little drummers and one-eyed cooks' and Andulko, a goose girl from Czechoslovakia.

I can still sing these songs, word-perfect, if asked.

Luckily no one ever does.

*

Two shadows always loomed. The long arm of the government authorities, away in distant Melbourne, always found us. No matter that where we lived was barely a dot on a map.

The Victorian Public Works Department was our nemesis: a malevolent overlord that condemned our family to endure holes in the floor, broken water pipes and fractured windows. We once waited four years to have the flaking walls in our house painted. The colours available were government green, government cream and government charcoal for the trim.

I came to think of the Education Department's dreaded school inspector every bit as unwelcome as 'the red-legged scissor-man' who lopped off children's thumbs. The inspector visited once a year, unannounced . . . or so he may have liked to think. In reality, the entire district knew he was on his way, thanks to the efficient workings of the Bush Telegraph.

Dad would be up the night before, swearing and in a filthy mood, as he prepared the school accounts, his work programs and student reports. The fences were to be stock-proofed, the flagpole in working order.

On the morning of the inspector's arrival, the phone would ring with the news that his car had been spotted—every farmer in the district knew his numberplate—and that he would be at our school within the hour. There would be a flurry of activity. An emu parade to pick up any litter, the flag run up the pole, and us kids threatened with blue murder if we stepped out of line that day.

It was the element of surprise in which the inspector most delighted. Walking in the door, pointing to the timetable and announcing: 'Mr Brown! You should be teaching grades three and four comprehension at this particular hour!'

Dad recalls one fabulously zealous individual who, fed up with his whereabouts being detected, parked his car over a hill and crawled through the long grass on his stomach, commando-style, to catch the school bell ringing three minutes late.

One principal Dad knew of hadn't kept any records for the whole year and was so panicked about the inspector's visit that, rather than being caught out, he burned the entire school to the ground.

Totally got away with it, too.

*

Warncoort School closed in 1971 with a dismal enrolment of eight pupils.

In the 'Kennett Revolution' of the 1990s, 350 Victorian schools were closed and 7000 teaching jobs lost. Many of those one- and two-teacher country school buildings were left empty, then robbed, vandalised and demolished.

That really did break Dad's heart but, to his eternal credit, he wasn't bitter. He understood that dwindling enrolments sounded the death knell for those tiny schools. He knew it was about economics. What he could not abide was the careless obliteration of memory and history. In Warncoort, the school was where locals gathered. It was the meeting place for the Young Farmers' Club and where the mothers came to play cards. It served as a polling booth.

As Dad told me not long before he died: 'Often in those rural settlements, the hall went, the football and cricket clubs went, and small schools ended up storing the honour rolls of the men who lost their lives in the war, the football trophies and the bowling club records. Then the school got shut down, and everything ended up in someone's shed, then down at the tip. There's not even a plaque or any memorial to their families. Just a few photos in someone's album.'

I visited Warncoort some years back and there was nothing to denote where the school or the house had been—every pipe, tap, rainwater tank and scrap of asphalt had long gone. Also gone were the red geraniums my mother planted and of which she had been so proud.

She recalls those days in Warncoort as mostly happy ones. 'I had four kids to play with and, really, I was just a kid myself.'

The remoteness of the place was often petrifying. A few times when she was home alone with us, my father off playing footy and with no idea when he'd return, she heard footsteps on the verandah. She suspected it was couple of Dad's mates she had no time for. Fetching the gun from the top of the wardrobe, she let off a warning shot through a window and shouted there was more where that had come from.

'The bitch is mad!' they shrieked and ran for it.

In 1962 my father applied for a transfer to Camp Hill State School in the boom town of Bendigo in Central Victoria. We were to live in a real, *proper* suburban street with neighbours either side, just over the fence. A corner shop, a tram, a five-minute walk to the White Horse Hotel and a start for Dad in the Eaglehawk reserves!

It was another version of Henry Lawson's description of the drover's wife: 'Her husband is an Australian, and so is she. He is careless, but a good enough husband. If he had the means he would take her to the city and keep her there like a princess.'

It's not long before his 'princess' jumps from the tower.

3

Tunnels and towers

Mirror on wooden dressing table
Sandhurst Road
California Gully
Bendigo

I am looking, looking. And I can see why the boys at school called me 'eagle beak', 'flat face', 'pancake head' and 'Wendy the Witch'.

I'm ugly. It's true. My face *is* flat. As if I walked into a door in a cartoon. My top lip is wonky and I have only stumps of upper teeth going sideways.

I look horrible when I smile.

Do not smile!

The boys made me cry, but if I tell Mum that, she will get mad at me.

So, I am going to say I've got nothing to be sorry for.

Even though it's a big fat lie.

And she knows it.

*

I was eight years old when I stood facing that mirror. Mum was twenty-five. It's not the first memory I have of looking 'different' to other children, but it was the first time that difference was named in ways that were meant to hurt.

*

To the neighbours we must have looked like the model family when we moved into our new house in the 'burbs of Bendigo. The handsome schoolteacher father, the very attractive homemaker mother, and four lovely, well-dressed, well-behaved children with good, old-fashioned country manners.

Soon, The Mother would go missing. The Father would lose the plot. The Children would go feral and roam the neighbour-hood doing exactly as they pleased.

If elderly Mrs Ristrom with the lilac tree or the respectable Ewer family who lived next door to us had known what lay ahead of them, they would have moved out before we got there.

*

Graham had scored a coveted position in one of the most pres-tigious schools in regional Victoria.

Camp Hill State School No. 1976 (originally named Sandhurst) opened in 1877 with an enrolment of 1290 pupils. It's an extraordinary edifice, regarded as a triumph of Neo-Gothic architecture and set high on a hill overlooking Rosalind Park in the centre of the city.

The locals fancy it as their very own Hogwarts. With its soaring spire, belltower, magnificent clock, grand rows of lancet and bay windows picked out in white against red brick, all set on a foundation of bluestone, it dominates the skyline.

This—ladies and gentlemen, boys and girls—was my new school! As far away from that one-room, weatherboard Warncoort school as my small self could imagine.

Camp Hill was one of 600 architectural gems built in Victoria in the late nineteenth century by the newly formed Victorian Department of Education. 'Marvellous Melbourne' was flush with cash from the gold rush and expressed its enormous confidence in the future with the Education Act of 1872, declaring that free, compulsory and secular primary school education be provided for all children. (How far we have strayed from that noble ideal—now with one of the most privatised systems of education in the developed world!)

Henry Bastow migrated to Tasmania from England in 1860 and became the architect and surveyor of Victoria's Education Department. He developed a set of building templates, most in the Gothic Revival style, and tweaked them as required. From the inner-city Melbourne suburbs of Footscray, Caulfield, St Kilda, Collingwood, Carlton and Prahran to the golden towns of Ballarat, Daylesford, Maryborough, Beechworth and Clunes, his beautiful buildings were a public expression of prosperity and unbridled civic pride.

In the heyday of the diggings in Ballarat and Bendigo, there was only one field in the world which yielded more gold—and that was California. Our new address, echoing those days, was Sandhurst Road, California Gully. There were mullock heaps and labyrinthine dark tunnels from old mines directly over our back fence.

We were on the ancient lands of the mighty Kulin nation, although, as it was for all the places I lived, I cannot recall ever encountering a child with that proud heritage.

They had been erased.

*

My odd face hadn't been a problem until I attended Hogwarts . . . er, Camp Hill Primary School.

I'd arrived in the playground a happy enough kid. During my time at Warncoort there had barely been enough of us to pick teams for a game of 'tippety runs', but now there were hundreds of children pelting around the playground as if someone had stuck a flaming stick into an ant nest. Cruel boys who followed me around at playtime and lunchtime and called me names. I could have done with a spell from Wendy the Good Little Witch, my favourite character in the comics I collected. One that picked up my tormentors and dropped them down a mine shaft.

Surely the fact that Dad was a teacher should afford me some protection. 'I'm telling on you! You're going to get into trouble!'

I shouted as I fled indoors, up an ornate wooden staircase, searching frantically for my father in the maze of staffrooms, offices, classrooms and broom cupboards.

When I found him, there was a firm: 'You have to fight your own battles. I can't do that for you. Now, off you go, I'm busy.'

At home my mother's 'brutal' lesson taught me there was no sympathy to be had there either. There was no one else to appeal to. Nothing to be done but get on with it.

I prefer to say I was 'teased' or 'picked on' rather than 'bullied', even though by modern definition bullying is what it was. The name-calling was intended to wound. But what's also implicit in the description of 'bullying' is a power imbalance—whereby the tormentors have more approval among their peers than the victim. And power over me, I resolved, was something those boys would never have.

I had a few witchy tricks up my sleeve.

*

A recent comment on social media took me by surprise: 'Well, it's okay for you, Wendy. Not everyone is as confident. You've got resilience. Lucky you.'

Never thought I'd see the day when hard-won 'resilience' would come to be regarded as 'luck' or some kind of privilege. But here we are.

Babies are not born 'resilient'. It is not a genetic trait. Yes, some are born predisposed to experience stress more than others, or there may be an underlying neurological disorder that makes the ability to form and maintain relationships much harder, even impossible. But 'resilience' is a positive, adaptive response in the face of adversity and developed over time.

More and more scientific evidence tells us that there's one factor, above all, that makes the difference between a child who can adapt and one who cannot, and that's a stable and committed relationship with a supportive adult.

At school, with my father as a teacher, I had that semblance of stability in my early years. I'm well aware that this protected me from the worst of it, even though his mantra of 'deal with it' was drilled into me. When I read heartbreaking accounts of those who have suffered shocking, traumatic bullying, I think: *Dad would have stopped that.* Relentless, daily emotional and physical abuse over years at school was not going to happen to me. In that way I *have* been lucky.

As a child, I expended a lot of mental energy forging a tough carapace that the taunting would not pierce. My favourite literary heroine was Jane Eyre, who'd triumphed over so many privations through rigorous and resolute mental discipline. Knew her worth.

I developed an arsenal of strategies to cope. I ignored the nasty comments, walked straight past those loathsome boys into class and kept my head down.

I became vigilant, watching for those who had the potential to become an enemy or an ally. There was safety in numbers, I figured, so I found a group of girlfriends who were a bit daggy, like me. Kind and loyal. Not the glamorous, popular 'A' group, but girls who loved school, did well at their studies and were never in trouble. Individually we could have all been targets at Camp Hill—the ones of Chinese descent, the too-tall ones, the too-fat ones, too-skinny ones, the shy, awkward ones, the 'brainy' ones—but together we were an anonymous collection of all-sorts. Not worth bothering with. I'd found my doughty tribe and stuck with them. And they stuck with me. This became the modus operandi for my entire school life. I never had trouble making friends. I was always, despite everything, optimistic and outgoing. Trusting. Never a 'loner' or an 'outsider'. One school report from primary school days notes: 'Wendy is a good student, but she talks too much'. My supply of naughty jokes, wry observations and gossip stood me in good stead.

There was one more thing that was required, I decided. A boyfriend. That would put an end to the mockery. And I found one . . . Greg. He had a head like a melon, with a big thick fringe of sandy hair above chubby cheeks, twinkly eyes and a wide smile.

Sometimes we'd sit together under the peppercorn trees at lunchtime. It wasn't a romantic connection; rather, we recognised each other as kindred spirits, and Greg—bless that boy—decided he would be, if not a *real* boyfriend, my sturdy bodyguard. The skinny rat boys had a go at calling us 'Fatso and Flat Face'. Greg smashed them in one go. Job done!

If my father wasn't there to offer a hand to pull me out of miserable situations, he was behind the scenes, pushing me out front. One Christmas, a combined school choir was to sing in the vast, vaulted space of Sacred Heart Cathedral. I was chosen as a soloist for one of the carols. This can have only happened through my father's intervention.

On skinny, trembling legs, I piped, '*There's a star in the east on Christmas morn . . .*'

The throng of children behind me responded, '*Rise up, shepherd, and follow.*'

The echo of those voices ringing up, up to the heavens remains one of the most thrilling moments of my life on a stage.

Phil remembers my father putting a lot of time and energy into making sure my diction was perfect, determined I wouldn't have a trace of impediment to my speech: 'We'd all be sitting there, choking down our peas, and you'd be reading from the stupid newspaper at the table. You were always Dad's special project.'

Dad's ambition for me was to be Australia's first woman prime minister.

Missed it by a mile.

*

In Bendigo—when it wasn't footy season—there were camping holidays to the beach or the banks of a river to go fishing. (I'm sure I learned about the basics of sex in caravan parks. You can see right through canvas with a good light behind it.)

There were Easter holidays in the Grampians. Weekends visiting Auntie Pat, Uncle Tom and our four cousins. Dad's sister and her husband were both teachers too, and they moved around the state between towns like we did.

Sometimes they were the ones to visit us. It was open house at Cal Gully and often we'd get back from a trip to find Auntie Pat and her crew, or our aunties Elise and Barbara, settled in the lounge room with a cuppa, watching TV. I always loved that about the Browns: you could arrive unannounced, eat them out of house and home, and they'd return the favour. Country-style.

Then there were Dad's *interminable* Sunday drives. It was sometimes announced that there wasn't any money for a summer holiday, so instead we would be going on lots of *drives*. Groan. The outstanding feature of my father's Sunday drives was that they rarely had a destination. He would just tear along the road until the petrol gauge showed half full, then turn around and drive home. If the lunch Mum packed had to be consumed by the roadside or on a median strip, then so be it. If there was no animal to be hunted, fish to catch or the promise of a blazing fire, was there really much point to the whole expedition?

In those days, the state of Victoria wasn't big enough for the four of us kids, let alone the back seat of a Holden FC. And the bonhomie of a game of BP Spotto only lasted so long.

It would start out nicely enough. 'Oh, a motorbike—Spotto! Tick that off. Look, a green car—Spotto! Tick that off.' But before you were ten miles down the road: 'Oh, a big, fat, ugly pig sitting right next to me! Tick that off.'

Dad would be swiping at the back seat with his free hand and roaring, 'Will you kids sit still in the back and stop kicking my seat!'

That's the domino effect of a Sunday Drive. It starts with a kid whacking his sister and ends with an FC wagon up a gum tree.

Mr Brown took the opportunity to make our trips *educational*. Forever pointing out fascinating species of eucalypt, fern or native grasses. And, even more frustrating, he was always spying fauna that we, squashed in the back seat, had no hope of seeing.

Dad: 'Look up there, kids. There's a koala in that tree.'

Us: 'What tree, Dad? Where?'

Dad: 'Just there . . . the mother with a baby on its back.'

Us: 'Where's the mother with a baby, Dad? Where?'

Dad: '*There!* Up there, near that hawk's nest. Are you kids bloody *blind*?'

When he was utterly pissed off, he'd screech the car to a halt and shout: 'Right, you can get out and walk!' Then he'd hurtle up the road and around a corner, so the car was out of sight.

I was once left in the middle of a rainforest on a winter afternoon. Instead of running up the road, wailing like a big baby, I stood my ground and waited until he reversed enough for me to see the tail-lights. Then I ran.

We'd arrive home late, the four of us ratty and tired, and Dad would say, 'Well, wasn't that a great day? Just goes to show we have everything you need right here in Victoria!' Ignoring the fact that if we'd lived in Britain we could have almost driven to Scotland, with something more interesting to see on the way than deserted farm sheds, a dry creek bed, boring rock formations, stupid, dumb, fucking sheep . . . and zero koalas.

Tall tales of Dad's Sunday drives became one of my earliest stand-up comedy routines. The audience, as they say, 'related' and always laughed their heads off.

I hadn't suffered alone.

*

My mother's recall of the day she tried to kill herself is a 'blur': 'I was totally, physically and mentally worn out. There was no one to go to. I'd come to the end of the line and I just wanted it over.'

My father's memory of this particular day, as you might expect, begins with where he was playing football.

'One day I was playing footy for Eaglehawk and I left to go to Rochester, or somewhere up the line. It was about August, approaching the finals, and we went up on a bus.

'I got home and the kids are all dressed up in Margaret's clothes and there was no sign of Margaret about. And I said, "What's going on?" And they said, "Mummy is having a sleep."

'So I went into the bedroom and she's having a sleep, alright. She's knocked down several, or many, sodium Seconal. This was likely to happen. I knew she'd been taking more than the prescribed dose earlier on.'

Being the eldest, I have more vivid memories of that day than my siblings do.

Our mother had called the four of us into the bedroom, where she was lying on the bed, and said: 'If I don't wake up, call Daddy.'

This was very strange. Why wouldn't she be waking up? She always woke up. Who would make our tea? Dad never made our tea. Anyway, he was at the football. How could we call him? We didn't know where he was any more than she did. None of it made any sense.

She said we could go into her wardrobe and wear any of her clothes and jewellery. (Why would she do that? She was always careful with her things and didn't let us touch them.) Then she gave us all some money to spend at the corner shop on anything we wanted, even lollies. (She never gave us money, especially for lollies. She never had any money to spare.)

As Phil, Noel and Helen raced up the street to the corner store, whooping with excitement, I trailed behind, dragging my feet. There was something not quite right, but what? I wasn't sure, but knew it was something bad. Should I go back and wake her up? Mum had sounded sleepy and she wouldn't be happy if I disturbed her, so I decided I'd better not.

The next memory I have is of my father carrying her limp body out to the car and banging her head hard on the doorframe as he tried to manoeuvre her into the back seat.

I watched the car back out the driveway. Saw it disappear down the road.

After that everything goes to black.

My father takes up the narrative: 'She was unconscious. I took her straight to the hospital, rang her doctor and he said, "I'll meet you there." So I took her into emergency. It turned out that she had taken an overdose. She was rescued. They pumped her out or whatever they do.'

From there she was transferred to Dana House in Ballarat, where she stayed for some weeks. Then, rather than returning to us in Bendigo, the doctor was adamant she go to her mother's place in Tasmania instead.

She stayed away for seven months that first time. Then returned. Left again. I have no recollection of the dates but my father is a reliable source of the timeline.

'Well, she used to write all the time and I wrote back to her all the time. She came back at Easter the following year. She stayed in Bendigo with the family for fourteen months.

'And then, on her birthday in June 1967, when she was turning twenty-nine, she suddenly disappeared. Margaret at this time was working at Welmar Shirts in Bendigo, near Eaglehawk. So I rang there. They said, "Oh, she left mid-morning."

'I couldn't work it out at all. I rang around all known associates and friends, neighbours, whatever. No one knew where she was, so we notified the police. Thought she might have topped herself as she had attempted suicide before.

'About eight p.m. they reported that she was safe. They said: "She's with her mother in Tassie."

'She claims she doesn't remember a thing about that day,' says my father. 'I don't know if that's the truth or not. Now, when I speak to Margaret, she says it was either get out or die. So that really explains it, doesn't it?'

'So then there we were four kids and me.'

*

I have a very clear memory of that day. I'd hidden behind the couch in our lounge room so I could leap out and sing 'Happy Birthday!' I waited and waited there, but Mum never came home.

(Since that day I have had a deep, pathological hatred of 'surprises'. I read the last page of every book. Attempt to divine the contents of every wrapped present. Many years later, my agent and husband, aware of this, were secretly approached by

'This Is Your Life' hosted by Channel Nine's Mike Munro—the set-up an 'ambush' by loved ones, colleagues and a studio audience. They immediately declined, knowing I would have tunnelled my way out through the floor.)

In my father's taped recollections, he says that, when his wife left him, he was 'devastated . . . I couldn't believe it.' But is anyone truly blindsided when a partner leaves? I mean, apart from in Hollywood movies, when it's later discovered the wife or husband is working for an international drug cartel, or as an undercover operative for the CIA, or has been abducted by aliens. Seems to me there are *always* clues. And that's why we're watching the movie. To see what was missed that we surely would have noticed.

Margaret denies taking more than the dose of barbiturates prescribed by her doctor. Says she only ever used them for sleeplessness. In the sixties, along with benzodiazepines, marketed as Valium, they were handed out like sweets to housewives suffering from 'nerves'. Mum was never referred to 'social services' for her mental health—as if there was such a thing at that time in a country town.

My father had a wife and four children, but often lived life as if he were a single man. His timetable during footy season went: school on weekdays, a night (or two) of footy practice and club meetings. Friday Pie Night. Saturday was Game Day—wherever that took him—before finishing up the weekend with what was euphemistically called A Pleasant Sunday Morning; i.e. a restorative piss-up. More beer and more mates until he came home that afternoon and fell asleep in front of the television.

Monday it started all over again.

Meanwhile, my mother's life was chaotic. Four children to see off to school in the morning. Sometimes the power would be cut off because Dad hadn't paid the bill. Kids to get to bed, and never knowing when her husband would come home or how many stray drunken fools he'd bring with him.

'There was never any money for anything. Everything was on the tick at the local store. There were always debt collectors at the door. He never came home from footy practice,' she remembers.

Margaret also says that my father belittled her, undermined her self-confidence. Seared into her memory is a day when she was standing on the front lawn in Bendigo wearing a summery playsuit.

This *is* a story I have heard. Many times.

'You should have been a boy,' Graham told her, and then took inventory of her physical flaws: 'Your lips are too thin, your shoulders are too broad, your breasts aren't big enough, your waist is too thick, your hips and thighs are too narrow and your knees are too knobbly.'

That my mother is able to recite this litany many decades later is testament to how callous his words were, how much they hurt. They led to a lifetime of battles with her body image. In her mid-eighties she still diets, although she has always been petite.

Not the least of my mother's accusations is that my father was a serial philanderer and, in their marital bed, always harassing her, demanding sex. That's why she took to sleeping with a weapon—a gun or a knife—under her pillow, she says. 'I just wanted love from your father. A cuddle was all I needed. I've never had that sort of affection, my whole life.'

I cannot recall my father ever gathering me in his arms in a show of tenderness.

He could do 'funny'. One of his comedy turns was to emerge from the shower with his wet hair combed into a part in the middle and a moustache drawn on with an eyebrow pencil—his impression of the man on the label of the Worcestershire sauce bottle.

He could do 'practical jokes'—he once gave Noel a Sao biscuit with slices of Velvet soap on it instead of cheese. (Which was *not* a 'joke' at all.)

He could do 'facts'. Plenty of those, you only had to ask.

But 'cuddle'? That was never his style.

My mother had always missed Tasmania: the mountain views and morning mists she adored as a child, the lush greenness of the place. She admits that the pull towards home had always been 'very, very strong, like an umbilical cord had been cut'. Bendigo was the worst place she'd landed. She often complained that it was too hot, too dry and horribly flat. I always think of her as being rather like the sad dormouse in the A.A. Milne poem 'The Dormouse and the Doctor' who is prescribed the cure of chrysanthemums yellow and white, but is always dreaming of a view of geraniums (red) and delphiniums (blue).

There's no point now in me apportioning blame, although they've pointed fingers at each other. I've stopped trying to understand what transpired between Margaret and Graham throughout the sixty years of their relationship. The status of their association was always opaque, both to us and to their subsequent partners. We never knew if and when they were in contact with each other. The careers and relationships of their children, and our daily doings, including the birth of their grandchildren, were the subject of many letters to and fro, and long phone calls later on. I know that much.

My mother visited the mainland for the occasional birthday and for all our weddings, but there was never a time when our family of six was together without an attendant crowd gathering around a cake blazing with candles and a drink in our hands.

Probably wise. A family therapy session would have ended with blood on the walls. We kids could have all done with an honest reckoning of the past but, deprived of it, we patched each other up as best as we were able.

The walking wounded.

Before my father died at the age of 83, my mother regularly made the trip from her home in Launceston to where Dad lived in Lara, outside Geelong, staying with him for months at a time. By now they were both single and, apparently, happy to take up where they had left off, decades ago. I had to get used to saying 'Mum and Dad' in the same sentence and, after so long, that was deeply weird.

In my calls to them, they'd pass the phone back and forth. My mother would still chide my father for his parsimonious habits and he remained exasperated by her extravagance.

There they were, together again, laughing and telling stories like newlyweds.

Then they'd part, with lurid accusations and recriminations.

Then reunite.

I give up.

4

The Famous Four

Mirror in girls' toilets
Camp Hill Primary School No. 1976
Goal Road
Bendigo

I don't have to lie to my mother anymore. She's gone. I don't know if she's ever coming back.

And there's plenty to complain about.

There's a reason why children ask their mothers: 'Mummy, what happened to that little girl?' and their mothers say, 'Come away. Shoosh, now.'

Or when my friends say: 'If you didn't have that, you would be really pretty.'

Or when grown-ups say: 'You know that children born like you are given the most beautiful eyes? You have beautiful eyes.'

All the better to see you staring at me with your sad face.

Why do grown-ups have to lie?

*

My father recalls our new situation without Mum cheerily. 'They adapted like ducks to water. The kids were left pretty much to their own devices . . . and they didn't do anything wrong. They were able to get their own breakfast and cut their lunch, things like that, or go and buy their lunch and make their own beds. There were all kinds of good things they could do.

'And I don't know how they were able to do that, because they were thrust into a position where anything could have happened. They could have become lawbreakers. They could have become vandals. They could have been anything. But no, they were all very good. None of the kids ever got into any trouble. They've never been belted. They've never needed to be chastised or anything like that, and they were all so close together.'

And I don't know how they were able to do that . . .

My mother, despite all she had to deal with, had been diligent in teaching us good daily habits, like brushing our teeth and making our beds. At the dinner table, a sharp WHACK! across the knuckles with a butter knife for the crime of a fork held upside down, or chewing with one's mouth wide open, was enough to instil a lifetime of table manners. OW! I feel I owe Great-grandmother James for these painful lessons.

And I owe my father for this one: 'It's "*May* I leave the table, please?" not "*Can* I?" Yes, you *can* leave the table at any time. You have the ability to do so. But have you been given permission? That's the question.'

Honestly, it would have been easier for him just to say 'no'. But he never let even the slightest opportunity to teach logic and self-regulation go by. It was maddening.

The Church of England was my mother's chosen denomination for the Sunday morning service. The Brown children were always 'well turned out'. Hats, handbags and gloves for the girls. Collar and tie, with shorts or trousers and neat jackets for the boys.

At one Sunday School lesson on the Last Supper, I took a penetrating look at the seating arrangements at this famous repast and saw there were no women sitting at the Lord's table. I silently made up my mind that from then on, I wouldn't be singing and clapping along.

*

Whatever I hadn't been taught by my mother, I learned at Brownies.

Every week I'd diligently shine my badges with Brasso, carefully iron my stiff brown calico dress, fasten my leather belt, knot my yellow tie, don my yellow knitted beanie, and walk to the hall in Eaglehawk.

It was my pilgrimage to a place where I could find 'order' and 'rules' that made some sense of my world that had no boundaries. Friends chafed at the restrictions their parents imposed: Where were they going? Who were they were seeing? What time would they be home? I always envied them.

'Look! We are the jolly pixies . . . Helping others in their fixies.' At least, that's how I remember the song for the six pixies of the 2nd Eaglehawk Brownie Pack. At every gathering of the Brownies, we held hands, danced and sang that sweet little ditty with enormous joy. (The gnomes rhymed with 'homes'; the elves with 'ourselves'. The fairies cheated, if you ask me; 'And we're the Fairies shining bright. Trying hard to do what's right.' No wonder no Brownie pack I ever encountered had leprechauns.)

While Dad did his best, there were just some things he couldn't teach me. These were the skills I learned sitting on the wooden floor in front of a red-and-white-spotted papier-mâché mushroom. How to sew on a button, lay a table, fold clothes, darn a sock, plait my hair.

Of course, more adventurous things were taught too—how to tie knots and set campfires—but it was in mastering the small domestic niceties I derived the most pleasure.

Some may think that teaching girls these dreary household tasks was somehow limiting to our potential, but later, when I became a mother with a family of my own, I still laid my table and sewed and folded with the kindly and reassuring voices of Brown Owl and Boobook Owl in the back of my head: 'Knives and spoons go on the right, forks on the left; glasses in a triangle; make a shank on the button by winding the thread.'

I had dearly wanted to graduate to Girl Guides but, with everything falling apart at home, didn't complete the set tasks required to attain my 'wings'. In a ceremony in a local park, a special path was marked out for those girls in our pack who would 'fly' up to Guides. A crowd of parents was there, applauding. While I was accepted, I had to 'walk' up to Guides—not *on* the path, but just *beside* it, on the grass. I felt inferior and never once attended a meeting of the Girl Guides.

In 2013 I was invited by Girl Guides New South Wales to speak at a fundraising lunch in the dining room at Parliament House in Sydney. At the end of my talk, you guessed it, I was retrospectively awarded a cloth badge—my precious wings.

In a room full of wonderful, supportive women, I sobbed like a big baby.

By the way, if you ever need someone to tie a reef knot or send a message in semaphore, I am that woman.

Although I might need a few days' notice.

*

Free to roam wherever we liked, with no parents watching out for us, we kids spent from dawn till dusk in the abandoned goldmining diggings over the back fence. California Gully and Eaglehawk were riddled with deep shafts, pitch black tunnels and towering mullock heaps from operations begun in the mid-1800s. In 1932 there were almost 2000 miners still working the Bendigo diggings and the last didn't leave till as late as 1959.

It horrifies me to think of the risks we took there. It must have been only sheer luck that we didn't perish in some ghastly mis-adventure. To us the place was wildly romantic, like something out of the American Wild West, where John Wayne rode in the deserts of Arizona, Utah or New Mexico with the blazing sun always set at High Noon. Peppercorn and willow trees overhung narrow paths between stony ridges. Tall cliffs exposed layers of sandstone and slate; below them were bottomless sliding drifts of fine, yellow sand and grey, pulverised clay.

We scrabbled away, digging tunnels and underground cubbies. Our best-ever cubby was huge—big enough to fit all of us, plus the two kids from next door, who were part of our gang. We gouged niches in the clay walls for candles and dragged below a few bits of old furniture to sit on. It was a magnificent construction but, looking back, if it had collapsed, it would have suffocated all of us.

Sometimes we'd get up at dawn, pack tomato sandwiches and bottles of orange cordial for a trek to the Badlands of Eaglehawk. Spend the day climbing the grandest mullock heap of them all, sliding down the slopes of shattered stone on sheets of corry iron.

We didn't have horses, like they did in *Bonanza*, but in one memorable escapade, Phil convinced our daredevil brother Noel to ride a rickety pushbike over the edge of a cliff. Phil had calculated that if Noel went full pelt off this three-metre-high precipice, he would land in the branches of a willow tree and then—*ta-dah!*—execute a safe landing in a pile of sand. Ever the entrepreneur, Phil had gathered a group of eager punters, who stumped up five cents each to watch the dazzling spectacle. Noel, on the borrowed pushbike and with a cape tied around his shoulders, went at breakneck speed and flew like a bird . . . for a few feet. Then went down like a shot duck.

There was a roar of excitement—this was money well spent!

Bad luck for the poor kid who owned the bike, its wheels now square and spokes sticking out like a handful of toothpicks.

He'd been warned of the risks, was paid his fair share of the box office, and that was that.

Noel walked away unscathed, a legend in his own lifetime.

*

Question: What's the most important element in truly memorable childhood adventures?

Answer: An enemy!

For us it was the three boys who lived up the street. They were tough, mean and lean. One of them was a teenager! They fired slingshots at old Mr Womby's horses. Threw rocks at us. Chased us through the old diggings on their pushbikes.

We had girls in our posse and weren't a match for the trio physically, but we were more clever. We'd spend hours down at the creek, fashioning mud balls with a sharp stone hidden inside, hardening them in the sun and then stashing our ammo in secret strategic locations on the cliffs.

Noel and Helen were excellent shots. Could fire off a slab of shale that curved through the air and hit a target with phenomenal accuracy. Phil and I managed the supply lines. All we had to do was to lure our foes into position up a cul-de-sac for a full-on surprise attack, pelting their stupid heads from above.

We hauled an old car bonnet up into a tree to serve as a lookout so we could see them coming. The boy next door, who was a bit older than us, nicked a roll of steel cable and wired the bonnet, upside down, to a branch.

Those boys discovered it. They couldn't cut the cable to the bonnet, so they left a pile of their human shit in it. They returned the next day, chopped down the entire tree with axes and set it alight in a bonfire.

Our enemy was ruthless.

One day we were ambushed; the four of us had let our guard down on an overgrown track. The boys chased and herded us into a shallow mining pit. We cowered there, looking up at them silhouetted against the sun, taunting us as the evil fiends they were. We'd be bashed up, for sure.

We didn't know it, but Dad, on his way to the White Horse Hotel up the road, had spotted the commotion. He snuck through the undergrowth, bided his time, and then burst from a clump of banksia, roaring bloody oaths.

The Man from California Gully!

'Got one kid in a headlock, threw a bike ten feet and the rest scattered,' Phil recalls with relish.

They didn't bother us much after that.

*

As every nostalgic parent or grandparent will say of the fifties and sixties: 'We made our own entertainment.'

We did too, when we weren't in front of the TV watching *Batman*, *I Dream of Jeannie*, *F Troop*, *Get Smart*, *The Beverly Hillbillies*, *Petticoat Junction*, *The Flintstones* and the rest. The woodshed was our own little theatre, where we staged plays we'd written or held gigs for our band styled after The Beatles, bashing away on upturned rubbish bins or strumming cardboard guitars. Our father was always charged a premium price to watch.

One particularly fun game Phillip and Noel devised was Fire Brigades. Not a lot of rules—you set fire to the tall grass in the empty lot behind our house, then try to put it out with sheets of Masonite . . . until your father sees it's about to burn down Mrs Ristrom's lilac tree, and her house, and puts it out with the hose.

*

In summer Dad dropped us off at the Bendigo Olympic swimming pool when the gates opened in the morning and picked up again when the gates closed. We were permanently sunburned and always peeling huge sheets of dead skin off our legs and arms. I reckon every freckle I have can be carbon-dated to those blazing hot, endless days at the Bendigo pool.

Dad was an excellent swimmer and had decided that, out of all of us, I had the potential to excel. I put in a lot of hours swimming up and down. Down and up. I still swim a tidy freestyle with Dad's instructions in my head, and he was still teaching swimming into his seventies. The boys were later encouraged in football and Helen in Little Athletics. Sadly for Graham, none of us pursued a career in sport. He would have dearly loved one of us to bring home a gold medal.

He would swing by the pool to give us lunch money to spend at the kiosk and, if there was enough of a crowd there, take the opportunity to give a master class in diving off the ten-metre platform. Ever the show-off, he loved the 'oohs' and 'aahs' when he climbed the diving pool ladder and, with a somersault, executed a perfect entry into the water, causing hardly a ripple.

One exploit lives in infamy: the day he mistimed his dive and landed with an almighty *THWACK!* He exited the pool with his stomach a throbbing shade of magenta after his epic belly-whacker. Gathering his dignity, he strode across the concrete as if entirely unaffected.

Of course we made sure he never, ever lived it down. He always laughed when we sent him up, without mercy.

He knew that we knew that he could be a ridiculous man.

It was our shared secret.

*

In his low moments, Dad told us we might have to go to an orphanage; even be split up if he couldn't cope. We were determined that would never happen and whispered about it late at night under the blankets.

I said: 'Do you know that, because we are brothers and sisters, we all shared the same view inside our mother's tummy for nine months? We are the only people on earth to have seen that. Isn't that an amazing thing?'

We agreed that it was. We would behave, look out for each other and no one would split us up. Ever. We would stay together until death, we vowed. For almost sixty years of my life that was true, until our darling Noely-Poley left us.

In my self-appointed role as the mother of the house, I tried to keep things from descending into chaos.

I took to ironing Dad's shirts for school, timing myself by the clock. Collar, sleeves, front left, front right, back—I got it down to three minutes per shirt and put them on hangers. Five shirts in all, one for every school day.

In the football season it wasn't unusual for my father to take off on a Friday night and not come home until Sunday morning. The four of us were left to fend for ourselves. One night I scraped together a meal of dry Weet-Bix spread with Vegemite. That's all I could find in the cupboard.

Often, we'd tell Dad the debt collectors were at the front door, and Phil remembers him 'taking off like a hare' across the backyard and vaulting the fence. He wasn't there on the day our furniture was repossessed. Lots of stuff he'd bought on hire purchase—bedroom settings and lounge furniture—hoping Margaret would appreciate his efforts and stay. But he hadn't kept up the payments. A Big Truck from the department store rolled into the driveway and some Big Men barged into our house and carted our stuff out the door. I howled for them to stop and bring everything back, to no avail.

There were times in Bendigo when I felt utter despair. I just could not see a way out of our predicament. As hard as I tried, dirty dishes and clothes piled up. The house was a wreck, Mum was gone and I never knew when Dad would turn up.

Instead of running away into the bush or catching a bus to nowhere, I had 'suicide' in my vocabulary as an avenue of escape, and it presented itself as an option. Like my mother, I just wanted it 'over and done with'. It was something I'd seen close up. It didn't look that difficult.

You could even do it in bed.

But my exit plans were rather more dramatic. I climbed on the garage roof one afternoon and jumped, landing on the concrete driveway with a painful thud. Sprained my ankle.

Lesson learned. Suicide was a lot harder than it looked.

One freezing night, the rain pelting down, I curled up like a worm around a post in the back fence, hoping to bury myself in mud and be at one with the elements. Just dissolve. I was rescued by my brothers. They were hopping from one foot to the other on the back porch, shouting: 'Wendy! Come inside. Right now!'

Who would look after those three kids if I wasn't there? I crawled back across the grass, sopping wet, to my bed.

In recent times, Phil has told me of all the things I did to keep us together. 'You made sure we had clean clothes, got up in the morning and got dressed for school. Made sure there was milk, eggs, bread and butter. Dad didn't ever see what you did, but you took on a lot of responsibility and it made a huge difference.

'We struggled in a lot of ways. You were our surrogate mum.'

His generous words touched me in a way I hadn't expected. When the tears stopped, curiously, I felt as if a load I hadn't known I was carrying was lifted. I *had* tried my best, but hadn't thought anyone had noticed.

In the next sentence, Phil was quick to remind me that he was once cast as 'Face Ache', the King of the Goblins, in a school play and I called him that for years.

Sorry about that, Chief.

*

My father was on a reckless trajectory.

He held down his teaching job, but on weekends it wasn't unusual for him to have thirty mates in the backyard guzzling on an eighteen-gallon keg well into the night. That's where all the money went. Spent on grog.

They'd be feasting on yabbies he and his mate Eric poached from local dams. The writhing haul was brought home in bulging sugar bags and boiled up in the old copper in the laundry. We kids would sit on the back steps shelling yabbies for hours. I'd make sure to stash some in the fridge so we could have yabby sandwiches for our school lunches. Deluxe!

(I still can't go to a restaurant and order yabbies, knowing I'll get a measly six of them on a fancy plate with gourmet tarragon sauce. Pfft! They should be eaten by the dozen, warmish, out of a bucket, doused in salt and brown vinegar.)

If yabbies weren't on the menu, Uncle Bill, a gun shearer, would bring mutton, kangaroo or rabbits from the sheep stations where he was working in the bush. Dad's best mate and favourite drinking partner, he could tell a terrific yarn. My brothers were sometimes farmed out to him on school holidays, staying in shearers' camps where life was rough and ready.

Phil remembers: 'One night, totally hammered (not that you could ever really tell with Uncle Bill), he called up the dogs to feed them. Five out of six turned up. He whistled for the other one a few times, but it never showed. He grabbed a shotgun and headed down the back paddock. Noel and I heard the shot.

He came back carrying a dead fox terrier and said, "No sense having a dog if it won't come when you call it.'"

When Mum still lived with us, she had sewn me a beautiful white broderie anglaise top and linen flares to wear at an Eaglehawk High School social. It was my first year at Eaglehawk High—a short pushbike ride from Cal Gully. I'd felt like the belle of the ball. With her gone, and a Christmas party on my social calendar, I was sent off with Uncle Bill to buy a new outfit. We came home with a plain navy-and-white-striped A-line cotton shift with a zip up the front. I hated that dress and later burned it in the backyard incinerator. I never, ever forgave Uncle Bill for buying it.

I longed for the company of older women.

My aunts, Elise and Barbara, often visited us from Ballarat and, when school holidays came, they took me away to stay with them, Nanna Brown and her sister Great-Auntie Claire.

These were the best of times for young 'Windy Day'.

5

Windy Day and the Fairies

Bevelled mirror in dark wooden mantelpiece
The 'girls room' (once the 'good front room')
Nanna and Pop Brown's house
East Ballarat

If there is a God, I ask only one thing: Please do not give me big bosoms like Auntie Barbara and Auntie Elise.

I'd really like to be as beautiful and popular as them one day, but their bosoms are just too big.

Thank you.

*

I did end up with Great-grandma Walker's generous bosom.

'Skinny legs, big boobs. Runs in the Brown genes. Sorry, Wen,' hoots Auntie Elise.

I have twenty-eight first cousins, by my count, and the Walker bosom has been randomly bestowed. Elise reminds me of two of my cousins. Sisters, one of them was small-breasted and became a renowned ballet dancer, while 'the other copped the bosom and had to go into choreography'.

Whenever my father's sisters—Patsy, Barbara and Elise— were together, they told hilarious tall and true stories. Laughed and laughed. Cups of tea, or glasses of beer and wine, were nursed as the old photographs came out and I could see the spot that I, the black-haired, odd-looking kid, occupied in my sprawling family. Any child loosed from their moorings knows the suffusing warmth and deep comfort that 'belonging' brings.

My aunts are resourceful, independent types who have applied themselves to overcoming life's travails with good humour and an open mind. I'd like to think those qualities are in the genes.

Auntie Pat was a commanding figure—statuesque, beautifully spoken with a deep mellifluous voice, artistic and, as a teacher librarian, extremely well read. Her siblings would say she was 'bossy and opinionated'. The same charge was always levelled at me by my siblings. It's exactly the reason I adored her and why, until her death in 2020, I often picked up the phone to ask her advice. Both she and Auntie Elise were stalwarts of the Ballarat theatre scene. Perhaps that runs in the genes too.

When I was younger, I had often visited Nanna and Pop Brown's house on Trevor Street with my parents, and even then the small wooden house seemed ancient. To fire up the single gas ring in the kitchen took a shilling in the slot. The walls were papered and, through the cracks, you could see the hessian underneath. The ceilings were improbably high. Vast.

It was a bugger of a house to keep warm in bitterly cold Ballarat winters. Visitors had to first thaw out with their arses to the open fire in the lounge room before they could utter a full sentence.

By the time I knew him, Pop Brown had suffered a series of strokes. He moved slowly with the aid of a walking stick and was constantly shooing people out of the way so he could cadge a skerrick of warmth from where he sat in his armchair.

Before his illness he'd been a big drinker and was thoroughly unpleasant when he'd had too much. I remember him as a gruff old man, but tolerant of his many grandchildren running all over the house and backyard. When my brothers were little, Pop spun a fantastic tale of how, in a locked corner of the woodshed, he was building a rocket ship he'd soon take to the moon! Phil and Noel were desperate to break in and see it, but never did catch a glimpse. A family visit always ended with Pop standing unsteadily on the back step, waving his stick in the air and challenging us to a race to the back gate. When we kissed Nanna 'goodbye', she secretly pressed a silver coin into our hands.

When I was older I went to Trevor Street by myself during school holidays and shared a room with Barbara and Elise, then in their twenties. On Friday and Saturday nights I'd curl up in my bed in the corner, peeping over the top of the eiderdown as they transformed into the most exotic creatures I'd ever seen up close. Teased hair, black eyeliner, pink lipstick. I'd breathe in the

intoxicating scents of perfume, powder and hairspray and almost
swoon with happiness. It was the pure dose of grown-up femi-
ninity I'd so been missing.

They were madly social, always off to dances and parties.
I remember their fashionable suede boots and how sometimes
Auntie Barb would knock up a new miniskirt on the Singer
sewing machine. I marvelled that she used only one yard of
material and, if she bent over, I could see her bum!

Cousin Billy Brown had the room down the hall. He was the
son from Uncle Bill's first marriage. Bill's wife had left him when
Billy was one year old. Auntie Elise says she handed him over to
my grandparents with the parting words: 'Here, I'm giving him
to you. I'm going.'

Nanna Brown raised eight children of her own and grandson
Billy. To bring in a wage after Pop's first stroke, she worked the
late shift at the Ballarat Orphanage, caring for the toddlers. She'd
retired by the time I fetched up on her doorstep during school
holidays, and you'd think she'd be heartily sick of small people.
Instead, she lavished 'Windy Day' with affection and I soaked up
every moment. She was a very important figure in my young life,
as the best grandparents are.

Her children called her 'Mother', 'Nel' or 'Noel' (my brother
was named after her). Nellie was a handsome woman, more petite
than her daughters. Sometimes she borrowed their boots or a
rabbit fur coat to wear for an outing and cut a glamorous figure.
She wound her long, snow-white hair into a generous bun on
the top of her head. I never did see how she created this splendid
confection; her and Pop's bedroom was strictly out of bounds.

Every morning, Pop shuffled up the hall to take her tea and toast in bed; he'd make it with his 'good' hand.

My nanna was firm but fair. She was made of tough stuff, didn't brook any complaining or self-pity, and spoke in a low, even tone that I found instantly calming. I felt safe with her. That's what it was.

She spoiled me with my favourite dessert—jam roll with vanilla ice cream. Sent to the corner shop to buy a bottle of milk or loaf of bread, I was free to spend the change on musk sticks, chocolate freckles, a bag of cobbers or a pink coconut ice cream on a stick. And I didn't have to share with anyone. It was all just *heaven*.

Auntie Elise says I was a 'normal' kid who loved to perform, sing and play with puppets, and 'totally unaffected' by my 'harelip'. It's true that when I was at Trevor Street with Nanna I barely thought about it at all.

Nanna Brown was a magical being and cast her spell on me. I'd been reading *The Lion, the Witch and the Wardrobe*, and in the gloomy bedrooms at Trevor Street there were imposing, dark wooden wardrobes that I wished I could slip through to the snowy landscapes of Narnia for adventures with Queen Lucy the Valiant and Prince Caspian. No such luck, but with Nanna Brown as my companion, that plain old weatherboard house and modest garden became enchanted places.

She taught me ballet steps, a smattering of French words, indulged my deep love of fantasy and wove elaborate stories invented especially for me. There were sweet-faced fairies dancing at dusk in the flower garden and a mischievous brownie who lived behind a thick curtain . . . if only we were quick enough to catch them.

There were tram trips up Victoria Street to Lake Wendouree and the shady spot known as 'Fairyland'. We'd sit together on a bench at the lake's edge as Nanna pointed out water sprites flitting through the reeds.

'There goes one just now, Wendy. Did you see it? The sun shining on its lovely wings.'

'Yes, I did, Nanna. I saw it. It was beautiful. There's another one! Look!'

I was perhaps too old to believe in fairies. But I *did* believe. No surprise that I would go on to write my own series of fairy stories, *Pearlie in the Park*. Hurly Burly! Stars and Moonbeams!

Years later, as a young teen, I questioned my Nanna more deeply about these fanciful fairy sightings. She confessed. 'It's the gardeners. They collect the wings from dead dragonflies and tie them to the reeds with thread from spider webs so that, when the wind blows, small children can imagine they see fairies.' I was satisfied with this answer . . . until a few years later, when I realised my darling grandmother had fooled me again.

My first crush was on Cousin Billy, conveniently in the same house. Just a few years older than me, he was tall, lean and handsome, with a swept-back lick of sandy hair, a roguish grin and quick wit. If Billy could have ignored me traipsing behind him making big cow eyes, he surely would have, but he was stuck with me.

He'd fang down the precipitous hill to the Eureka Stockade on his homemade skateboard to meet his mates as I tore after him shouting, 'Billy . . . Billy, slow down!'

He never did.

My adoration of Cousin Billy had been my secret, but I soon realised he was too rebellious and grown-up for timid me. It was slightly disturbing because he was related, but an experiment with 'romance' on training wheels.

One Christmas morning we woke to find he'd got up before us and opened every single present under the tree. Nanna, rarely angry, was furious. Billy was crossed off my list. The list with only his name on it.

My first attempt at a crush. Crushed.

*

Other times I'd stay with Great-Auntie Claire and Uncle Bert at their farm in Bamganie, near Meredith, an hour by car and almost dead south from Ballarat.

This was a proper farm. A rambling homestead with a huge kitchen garden, lots of chooks, geese and, in a pen near the house, always an orphaned lamb or two to be bottle-fed. Paddocks and sheep as far as you could see. The property boasted its own shearing shed.

Great-Auntie Claire was a tall, broad-shouldered, industrious, no-nonsense country woman, the backbone of rural Australia, like so many generations of women before her and since.

In a corner of her kitchen was the walk-in pantry. A sacred space.

The pantry was dim and mysterious, lit by a single globe, with shelves from floor to ceiling. And every shelf was full. The fruit from the garden was glacéd, pickled, preserved, made into relish, sauce, chutney, curd, butter, marmalade, cordial, jam and jelly. On another shelf there were potted meats and herb-infused vinegars. There were biscuits in tins, slices in trays, sponges under lace covers, pies in deep dishes and tantalising jars of coconut ice and toffees . . . way out of reach.

The pantry was also home for saved paper bags, string, corks, rubber bands, candle ends, jars of leftover soap and the trusty Fowlers Vacola bottling outfit. If I could choose any place from my childhood to revisit, it would be that pantry on the farm among the tall jars of peaches, tins of ANZAC biscuits and bunches of drying lavender.

I would busy myself collecting eggs, harvesting the kitchen garden, taking 'smoko' to the shearing shed and learning the basics of sewing on the treadle Singer under the direction of Great-Auntie Claire.

I know exactly where I was on 3 February 1967. Sitting on a branch in a mulberry tree at the farm and listening to the old Bakelite radio that sat on the kitchen windowsill. It was the day they hanged Ronald Ryan, the last man to be executed in Australia.

Victorian premier Sir Henry Bolte owned Kialla, a neigh-bouring property, and the debate over capital punishment was all over the news and a topic of heated conversation at Claire and Bert's dining table, with me listening intently.

As a kid, I wasn't naive about death—I'd seen too many rabbits shot, fish gutted or chickens running around in the backyard, headless, when Dad took to them with the axe—but it seemed to me that knowing the *exact* time of your death would be too much to bear for any human. Ryan's fate haunted me.

Ryan was sentenced to hang for shooting a prison guard while attempting to escape with a fellow inmate. It had been widely expected that the sentence would be commuted. When it wasn't, there was national uproar and an estimated 18,000 people marched in the streets in protest. Newspapers, churches, universities and lawyers campaigned to spare Ryan's life. Seven of the jurors in the case wrote to Bolte's cabinet pleading for mercy. One said later: 'We didn't want the rope. If we had known Ryan would hang, I think we would have gone for manslaughter.'

But Bolte was determined he would have his execution, and at 8 a.m. that February day, Ronald Ryan was led to the gallows in Pentridge Prison. When asked by a journalist what he was doing at the precise moment Ryan died, Bolte responded: 'One of the S's, I suppose. A shit, a shave or a shower.'

In 2017, as a columnist for the *Sunday Telegraph*, I wrote of how that execution had stayed with me: 'Be thankful you are no longer able to pull the lever or load the gun yourself. Be grateful you never have to look into the eyes of a condemned man. Many a brave soul has been undone by the experience.'

Bolte was to turn up like a bad penny in our lives. In '68 he said of schoolteachers campaigning for better wages and conditions: 'They can strike till they're black in the face. It won't make any difference'.

I wonder if 'that bastard, Bolte', long dead now, still owes the Skipton Football Club twelve quid, seven shillings and sixpence?

*

Auntie Elise sent me a family tree of the Browns with a covering note: 'All English/Irish Aussie families need a convict ancestor.'

In our family it was my great, great, great (something) grandfather, William Langham, born in 1810 in Kingsland, London. At the age of twenty-one as convict No. 674 he embarked from that place in 1832 on the ship *Lord William Bentinck*, sailing to Van Diemen's Land. Convicted of larceny for stealing a coat, he was transported for seven years and eventually, as a free man, settled in Ballarat, working as a brickmaker, carrier and labourer on the goldfields.

(In 2007, I was approached by the producers of the TV show *Who Do You Think You Are?* It was to be the first series on SBS adapted from the wildly successful BBC show of the same name. Would I like to be on it? I airily dismissed the notion, saying: 'Oh, no. My family is *so boring*. It's the same story as so many others. English and Irish potato farmers, workers on the goldfields. I don't think anyone's done anything very interesting.' They took me at my word. I would like to take the opportunity here to apologise to all those in my extended family tree for this deplorable lapse of judgement.)

*

At the end of 1967, Dad informed us we were leaving Bendigo.

He had a new position, as headmaster at Selby Primary School No. 4685, just outside Belgrave in the verdant hills of the Dandenong Ranges. He wanted to make a fresh start. I'd just turned twelve and was ready to leave the place behind too.

Dad and Uncle Bill totally stuffed up our arrival. That was a given.

'We made a miscalculation on our departure. We were supposed to go to the bank on the second of January, but for some reason it was a bank holiday, so we had no money. And in those days you couldn't just go to any branch to get your money. You had to go to the branch where you did your banking, and that was back in Bendigo.

'Brother Bill and I, we had no money for a beer. So we pooled what we had in our pockets, went and bought a couple of flagons of Marsala and some Coke. And that's what we drank for about a week. And don't ever let anyone tell you it won't bring flies because they came in their thousands.'

We kids left behind our gruelling five-year war of attrition in the Badlands of the old mullock heaps. In Selby it was day-long rambles in Sherbrooke Forest, climbing mossy rocks in creeks cascading into ferny, foggy gullies and spotting lyrebirds darting between towering stands of mountain ash and stringybark. No more *Bonanza*. Now it was *The Adventures of Robin Hood*.

The wooden school with gabled roof, dating from the 1950s, was just outside the gate from the residence. A few houses were dotted here and there among dense trees. Our house was nothing flash; I never did live in an Education Department house that boasted an indoor dunny. But at least this one was on the septic and actually flushed.

Again, unsupervised, we had our share of hairy exploits. As the famous Puffing Billy train steamed over the huge wooden trestle bridge down the end of our road, we'd dare each other to stand on the tiny wooden emergency platform cantilevered off one side. With a sheer drop of thirteen metres to the gully below, we'd screech with fear and excitement as the train rumbled past, shaking our teeth and bones. Sometimes Phil and Noel would hitch a ride on the back of the train, jump off at Emerald Station and spend the day swimming at the lake.

If one day the old Puffing Billy had run off the rails, careened down an embankment and ended up a flaming wreck, it would have been the perfect metaphor for what happened next.

Sometimes, late at night, I heard the mournful song 'The Carnival is Over' by The Seekers emanating from the lounge room, played on repeat. I knew my father was deeply unhappy but, as a teenager by now and with my own theatrical scenarios of love and loss to indulge, there was nothing I could do to help him.

Dad opened the doors of our home to all comers. 'We used to have beautiful parties. They'd be forty people in that little house and it'd be jumping off the ground,' he reminisces, although some of his guests, he admits, were 'on the shady side'. He was in with a bad crowd. Some ex-crims; some still practising and yet to be apprehended. Dad stored their stolen goods or helped them evade the police who came knocking. One visitor was a notorious bikie, king of the local roller derby circuit. Others were 'alternative' types—artists and drifters. They were all big drinkers, raucous and wild when they got going.

Dad loved his 'party tricks' and devised all kinds of contests of physical strength for amusement, but his favourite turn was as amateur hypnotist using a black-and-white spiral he'd drawn and attached to a record turntable. He experimented with post-hypnotic suggestions that incited pandemonium. From our bedrooms we'd hear cheers, roaring arguments, then savage fist-fights and women screaming.

For us it was a waking nightmare. We kids would barricade ourselves inside one bedroom, terrified, as drunks banged on the door at 4 a.m., shouting at us to wake up and join the mayhem. Phillip remembers pushing the cupboards and beds against the door to keep us safe. I feared they'd break it down and molest me and Helen. We'd huddle together in a corner as, just outside the door, the party raged, squalled and our house heaved until dawn.

We'd get up in the morning to a house strewn with empty bottles, broken glass and splintered furniture. Pick our way through the debris and go to school.

So freaked about where this was all heading, I went back to church. On Sunday mornings I walked up the hill to the old stone All Saints' Anglican. Maybe it was the painted sign outside that spoke to me: *In 1939 the church was a sanctuary for women and children during the bushfires.* I've no idea what the congregation made of the young girl sliding shyly into a pew up the back by herself and sobbing throughout the service.

How Dad managed to turn up for school and do his job is, again, a mystery—a testament to his physical fitness and work ethic, I guess—but less than a year after landing in Selby, and now in his mid-thirties, he knew something had to give. As he says on Phil's tape: 'I'd been wondering how I was going to handle these kids running around.'

As if *we* were the problem?

Enter our 'housekeeper' Alison. My father eventually married her and she officially became my stepmother in 1987. It was a Victorian Education Department stipulation that only a legal spouse could access his superannuation in the event he died before she did.

His second wedding was a ceremony at the Maryborough town hall, with Auntie Elise and Cousin Billy as witnesses. A counter lunch at the pub and then back to school, finishing at 4 p.m. for my father's last day in a classroom.

'I beat the department's rules by about an hour and a half,' he brags.

*

The word that always springs to mind when I think of my stepmother Alison is 'martinet': a person who is happiest when they are inventing rules for others to follow and devising elaborate punishments for when they don't.

Our household was in desperate need of order, and if anyone was going to wrench that order out of chaos, it was Alison. She was ceaseless in her activity in the house and garden. Vibrating with an agitated, dangerous energy, like an electrified bull ant, she was unlike anyone I'd ever met.

I was thirteen when Alison gatecrashed my life, and in the years I lived in the same house with her it was rare to have an exchange that wasn't purely transactional or openly hostile. For all the time we knew each other, she never once rang me nor I her. I haven't the slightest idea of what made her tick or why she took up with my father and stayed with him for three decades. Why they never had children together.

Alison was in her early twenties, about ten years older than me, when Dad engaged her on $15 a week, plus expenses, to work in our house in Selby. She'd been a nanny in Tasmania before she came to us. Within months she went from being the 'house-keeper' to staying overnight and then sharing my father's bed. They kept their new status secret. We took to snooping in Dad's room when they went dancing and worked out for ourselves that they were a couple. Sometimes, in silent protest, we'd turn Alison's prized framed portraits of Elvis Presley, newly installed, to the wall—just to signal that we knew what they were up to.

During my mother's courtship with my father, she complained of being abandoned as he chose the prettiest girl in the room as his dance partner. That wasn't Alison. Brown-haired, about the same height as my father, slim and thin-faced, Alison was neither pretty nor plain. Not exactly dowdy, but conservative in her dress, she made most of her clothes by hand, mostly in darker, 'serviceable' colours; I can't remember seeing her in anything as flamboyant as floral.

Alison sat somewhere on the spectrum between the shy heroine governess in *Jane Eyre* (without Jane's intelligence and generous nature) and Grimm's overtly wicked stepmother in 'Snow White' (without a poisoned apple). As a friend once described her: 'Like Mary Poppins without the charm. Or Mrs Doubtfire on a No Good, Very Bad Day.'

Alison's parents lived in a village in the Dandenong Ranges not far from Selby. Her English mother ran a household that was strict, conservative, but close-knit. Alison's moth-eaten template of elaborate rules and punishment for how children *should* behave, considering our history of self-management—or 'running wild, like savages', as she liked to say—was doomed from the start.

We had been taught to boldly question *everything* and *everyone*. This was quite out of the realm of Alison's experience. And she did not care for it, at all.

In the house, Alison would go at a task in a frenzy, almost as if in a trance, showing us hands red-raw and bleeding after a day scrubbing floors or bathroom tiles. Then she would turn around, cook dinner and do laundry late into the night.

If the boys hadn't chopped wood for the fire as directed, Alison would march up the yard—even in the dark or during a thunderstorm—and maniacally chop it herself, afterwards presenting her blistered palms in reproach. She had a strong suit in 'martyr'.

Every morning we'd be woken at six thirty as Alison, wearing her wooden Dr. Scholl's clogs, swept the hallway vigorously, her hard shoes *clack-clacking* on the floorboards, her broom urgently *knock-knocking* on the skirting boards outside our bedrooms in loud rebuke.

Her proficiency in every kind of craft was remarkable for someone entirely self-taught—knitting, sewing, crochet. One look at you and she could draft a pattern for a dress and make it that day. I spent many hours standing on a table being stuck with pins as she fitted and hemmed a garment. A life-sized voodoo doll. I'm a handy knitter, seamstress and embroiderer— I thank Alison for that, at least.

A fair cook, too, Alison served a few staples of stolid, traditional English fare: toad in the hole, fish pie, curried sausages or lamb roast. A specialty of her mother's was Ki-Si-Min—beef mince, shredded cabbage, a packet of chicken noodle soup and Keen's curry powder. That's about as exotic as it ever got. (I never encountered anything as 'Continental' as an olive or garlic until I left home.) A rare treat was chicken marylands in white sauce with tinned pineapple. We ate it up. We were hungry kids. Delicious yo-yos, jam drop biscuits, caramel and coconut slices appeared in the cupboard. There was fresh fruit in the bowl on the kitchen bench.

Almost overnight our lives were transformed. Dad's wild parties ceased. There was food on the table for breakfast and dinner. Lunches packed for school. Clothes laundered and ironed. Our wandering caravan was back on track with our basic physical needs catered for.

Then, ominously, rosters of duties and lists of 'dos and dont's' appeared in the bathroom, laundry and on the fridge. We were to have TWO biscuits each or ONE helping of baked slice per day. ONE piece of fruit. The allocated portions were carefully counted and noted. To guard against any pilfering when she was out of the kitchen, Alison would wind a few strands of her hair around the knobs on the cupboards—a dead giveaway if they were broken. The bins were forensically inspected for extra banana skins or apple cores.

One day she discovered some Twisties were missing out of a packet and we were lined up in the lounge room and the thief ordered to confess or else our 'privileges'—watching television or seeing friends—would be stripped from all of us.

Phil cracked under the pressure and was 'sent to Coventry', a peculiar punishment thought to date back to seventeenth-century England, meaning he was to be ostracised and ignored. If you spoke to the shunned person (who was not to be addressed by name or in any way acknowledged), you were punished too.

At the breakfast table it went like this . . .

Phil: 'Could you pass the butter, please?'

Noel: 'Yeah. Here you go.'

Alison: 'Who are you passing the butter to, Noel?'

Noel: 'Phil says he wants it for his toast.'

Alison: 'I'm sorry, I don't know anyone by that name at this table.'

Any one of us was under threat of this treatment. Turning us against each other was a favourite technique to gain control. Noel and Helen, being younger, were more easily manipulated. We had always been so close, and I found this tactic particularly devious.

Every week, one child was chosen to accompany Alison and my father on a Saturday morning outing to the shops in the nearby town of Belgrave, where there would be a treat of an ice cream, cake, toy, cosmetic, magazine or some reward we dearly wanted. We were to compete for this excursion. All week we were either 'in' or 'out', our progress marked on a chart. Life with Alison was like a never-ending episode of *The Hunger Games*.

There were constant arguments because Alison refused to be challenged over any outlandish statement she might make, and she made bizarre claims on a range of arcane subjects. This, we suspect, was because she felt intellectually inferior to Dad and strove to prove she wasn't.

'How do you know that? Where's the proof?' we'd ask, exactly as we'd been taught. Alison saw even the mildest query, uttered with genuine curiosity, as a challenge to her authority, and would react with incandescent rage. Out of a clear blue sky an object would be hurled, aimed with intent. Once, without warning, it was a heavy coffee mug that smashed into my elbow while I was watching television, unaware there was 'incoming'.

Just to make any confrontation even more frustrating, Alison also claimed to have a photographic memory of everything we'd ever said or done. 'That's not what you said last Friday afternoon when you were in the kitchen. I remember exactly.'

We took our many grievances to our father, and he responded: 'Give Alison a bit of leeway. Try to see it from her point of view.' Dad was still spending too much time at the pub and left everything to her. Our litany of complaints fell on deaf ears. We battled on without him.

The psychological abuse was mind-bending. I often confessed to and apologised for stuff I hadn't done, just to make life easier. Anything to avoid being in Alison's 'bad books'.

I have no doubt Alison found her situation stressful. Trying to corral us four kids who'd been looking after ourselves for so long? It must have taken every ounce of her indefatigable energy and an iron strength of purpose. I can understand, and forgive, up to a point . . . but not past the point where her relentless verbal and physical abuse turned our house into a warzone.

Being whacked on the legs with a hairbrush by my mother was one thing. Alison's unexpected, open-handed 'SLAP!' that left my cheek red and stinging was another entirely. A slap across the face can only have one purpose: to humiliate.

She was as far away from our shared family values as anyone I could think of. Didn't find 'so-called humour' funny. Was prudish and narrow in her cultural tastes, reading only horror novels and listening to fifties rock'n'roll. Fine as far as that went, if she hadn't actively denigrated the books and music we loved as 'rubbish'. Alison had little appreciation for anything beyond the purely practical and I don't recall hearing any conversation between her and my father beyond work-a-day arrangements. I never witnessed any physical affection between them, although they were quite social and perhaps their circle of friends saw another side.

Alison faithfully supported my father in all his endeavours for three decades, but ran a home that was increasingly unwelcoming to us. It wasn't unusual to hear from her in later years: 'We're not doing Christmas. Don't come.' It was the antithesis of everything my father had known growing up in the hospitable, open-armed Brown family.

As an adult, I once asked my father: 'Why Alison? Was it love? Why?'

He ducked the 'love' question and answered: 'I promised Alison that, if she would look after you kids, then I would stick with her until the end. That was the bargain I made.'

Was the 'bargain' worth it? It's true we didn't end up in that orphanage, but the 'Alison Years' had a profound impact on the trajectory of our young lives. Still in our teens, I went off and got married. Phil was kicked out and couch-surfed. It took a long time for us to recover and achieve some equilibrium.

Did my father have his misgivings about the pact he'd made? We think he did.

'Sure, she brought the control and discipline he thought we needed,' says Phil. 'But he didn't realise how determined she was to break our free-thinking spirit. I think he came to regret that.'

Maybe that's why he didn't marry her until he felt he had to. Maybe it was she who hadn't wanted to marry him.

6

The monkey bus

Hand mirror
Hospital bed
Preston and Northcote Community Hospital

I look even worse than I did before.
    My mouth is sewn together.
    I can't talk.
    What have they done to me?
    I will NEVER be beautiful.
    They are, all of them, liars.

*

The nurses hadn't let me see my face for a few days after the operation, warned me that I wasn't a 'pretty sight' with my face still swollen. 'Prepare yourself for disappointment,' they said in soothing voices, even as the doctors who'd come by to peer at me

96

declared it to be a 'wonderful outcome' and really 'one of the best surgical repairs of its type' they'd ever seen.

The train tracks of dozens and dozens of tiny stitches under my nose were prickly to my exploring fingers. But why could I feel them on my chin too? And why couldn't I move my lips to talk? It was strange. Frightening. What did I look like? I needed to see. I was grown up enough to handle it.

I was almost fifteen. It was *my* face!

When, finally, they gave me a hand mirror to look . . . I gulped in despair, turned my head to the pillow and wept.

Then, when the nurses were gone, I took up the mirror, looked, and looked again. What did the doctors see that I couldn't?

*

Around one in every 700–800 babies in Australia is born with a cleft lip, cleft palate or both. A common congenital condition, it's not known exactly why at the six-to-eight-week mark of pregnancy, there is sometimes a glitch where the normal fusing of the lip and palate fails. For some there is a genetic link; for the rest it's a complex interplay between chromosomal and environmental factors.

Numerous studies have linked an increased risk due to various toxic chemicals or even 'organic dust' from hay or livestock, which is common on farms. But all the papers I've read conclude 'more research required'.

Of one thing we can be sure: a 'harelip' is not caused by a witch assuming the form of a hare and bounding across the wooded, dusky path in front of a pregnant woman, cursing the baby in her belly so it is born with the 'Devil's Mark'. The term 'harelip' originated around the fifteenth century, descriptive of the mouth of a hare or a rabbit. Just like the words 'retarded' or 'spaz' or 'cripple', 'harelip' is an offensive term.

In essence, it's saying that someone has the face of an animal.

*

I'm proud to be recognised as part of the 'cleft' community and 'represent' on the national stage, although it took a long time for me to feel comfortable with it.

In my *Australian Story* episode I travelled to Fiji to highlight the work of Interplast with a group of volunteer reconstructive surgeons who travel to South-East Asia and the Pacific to repair cleft lips and palates. Their motto is 'to humanise a child'. In the medical clinic in Suva, hopeful parents had brought their children to be assessed for surgery. Some had driven a hundred and fifty kilometres to get there, queuing for hours before the doors opened. The need was immense. Heartbreaking.

In mothers' arms were squirming babies with deep fissures from their mouths to their noses and I saw myself as I was born. Others were teens with the same flat, squashed nose and scarred lip which had been patched up at birth and who had waited all the long years for more surgery as I'd done. They hid in the shadows and couldn't meet anyone's eye. Old superstitions regarded them as less than human, often not even worthy of an education and their chances of finding a wife or husband remote.

I was struck by the words of one doctor who worked in cosmetic surgery back in Australia and she told me how rewarding it was to work with Interplast. 'The patients here are always grateful for their results, with cosmetic surgery they never are.'

When I was young, I never saw any women who looked like me in magazines, on TV or at the pictures, and certainly never cast as a heroine or a romantic lead. I did see one American actor, Stacy Keach, who had a cleft lip; but he was a man and so could hide his thin scar with a moustache. That was it.

Recently, I found a website that lists 'celebrities' with clefts and found my name there along with Joaquin Phoenix and Jesse Jackson. Although the site notes that 'she speaks with a lisp'. (I don't.)

And if you're planning to uglyshame me on social media and go all medieval on my arse?

It's 'harelip'.

Not 'hairlip'.

Get it right.

*

When I took up that hand mirror in the hospital, the sight was overwhelming at first. *So* many stitches in the wounds, still red and angry. Was this the best I'd ever look? It was not the instant transformation from 'witch' to 'princess' I'd been hoping for.

It was disappointing, but fascinating too. I could now see why I couldn't open my mouth and why I could feel stitches on my chin. The surgeons had taken a portion of my lower lip, turned it upside down and positioned it under my nose to fashion a complete upper lip where there hadn't been one before. An ingenious patchwork solution, but one that I was in no way prepared for. I wasn't able to open my mouth to express my surprise and bewilderment at what had been done to me.

The surgical procedure is known as an Abbé flap after American plastic surgeon Dr Robert Abbé who pioneered it in 1898, and is, in effect, a 'lip switch'. (Although Italian surgeon Pietro Sabattini is recorded as first performing this operation, sixty years earlier, on a patient maimed by a sword.) Following the surgery, the lips are sewn together for up to a month as the graft establishes a new blood supply.

Hard to believe that I'd waited until I was in my mid-teens for my century-old operation. Every few years Dad and I had driven from the country to Melbourne's Royal Children's Hospital, where doctors had photographed my face and measured my head. Plastic surgery is an ever-evolving area of medicine, and when I was young it was thought that the facial reconstruction I required would be best done when my head had stopped growing. When would that be? No one could quite say. It was just 'not yet'. The trip home would be long and sorrowful.

I can't recall ever being apprised of any plan. How many operations would it take to make me look 'normal'? Would the scars disappear completely? What could I expect?

Again, no one seemed to know—or, if they did, I can't remember them ever telling me. These days, not only are clefts picked up by ultrasound in the womb, but most corrective surgery is completed before a child's first birthday.

*

I shouldn't have been allowed to roam freely on that plastic surgery ward, but I did. I poked my head into various rooms. To teenage me, it was a Carnival of Horrors.

I saw the man who'd tried to kill himself by putting a gun in his mouth but succeeded only in blowing away half his jaw, and what was left of it was horrifically mangled. The little boy whose back had been burned from his shoulders to his waist, leaving a molten purplish terrain. Others with flaps of grafted skin in mismatching colours which made up a human quilt of pain and suffering.

It was nightmarish. All their plastic surgeries seemed to be attempts to patch their poor bodies after terrible, sudden and catastrophic injuries. At least I'd lived with my scarred mouth for as long as I'd been alive. I was grateful for that one thing.

As for how I now looked to others? Auntie Merle, renowned in our family for being made of strong stuff, visited me in hospital, took one glance and fainted dead away. She apologised profusely to the matron, blamed it on the stifling closeness in the ward and escaped for a breath of fresh air. Of all the visitors I must have had—all bearing bunches of flowers, cards and reassuring words—she is the only one I recall. It didn't augur well.

(For years afterwards, well into my thirties, I was plagued by weekly, freaky dreams in which I sensed someone standing over my bed, staring down, and I'd wake to find the room empty. Other times I'd wake up choking, attempting to regur-gitate clattering metal objects from my throat—cutlery, kitchen utensils, serving trays. The dreams were disturbing and constant. My mother, by this time working in nursing as a theatre assistant, suggested the dreams may have come from that first, long operation, where I'd swum up from the anaesthetic into semi-consciousness with tubes in my throat to help me breathe, and was then submerged again. This explanation made perfect sense to me, and overnight the nightmares disappeared. An anaesthetist friend told me her explanation was plausible.)

Sent home to Selby for recuperation and healing, with my mouth sewn in the middle until I went back for the next operation, I was to be fed liquids through a straw. *Strictly no solid food* or else my recovery would be compromised.

Phil, Noel and Helen figured out that, if they were careful, they could push a cheese Twistie or a piece of banana into the small openings of my mouth, either side of the stitches.

Right there, that's true love.

And we never did tell anyone.

*

With the stitches removed after the second procedure, I was keen to get back to life at Upwey High School. I'd enrolled there three years before in Form 2 as the misfit in the wrong-coloured school uniform (Dad hadn't got his shit together to buy me a new one after Eaglehawk High), but once more, I found my loyal tribe and was content enough in their company.

Was it raining or foggy, or was the summer sun already filtering through the gum trees on the morning I returned? I have no recollection. I stood on the gravelly edge of the road waiting for the school bus, which was advancing with every minute that ticked slowly, agonisingly, by.

But as for how I was feeling? That comes back to me with dreadful clarity. I felt like I might vomit on my black lace-up shoes. Every nerve ending in my body was prickling with fear and urging me to run. I thought of grabbing my schoolbag, hurtling back home to the safety of my bedroom, or taking a flying leap into the fern gully below and just disappearing.

I wanted to evaporate. Never to be seen again. Ever.

The daily school bus trip, winding down the mountain road from Selby to Upwey, through the wooded foothills and onto the flat, was always rowdy.

On every school bus, the seating arrangement is roughly the same. Zoologists have long documented dominance hierarchies in monkey tribes. Every monkey knows its place in these primate social structures which have evolved for beneficial behaviours in feeding, grooming and mating. Same on our bus.

The dominant males commandeered the back seat. The alpha females sat in the two rows in front of them. The nondescript rabble occupied the middle. And the front seats, under the nominal protection of the driver, were reserved for the misfits, the timid and the newbies.

During these twice-daily journeys up and down the mountain, I'd found myself a congenial spot in the middle with like-minded souls. Being ordinary was our greatest survival mechanism, but I'd also seen the middle-seat folk rise up as one if challenged. There was safety in numbers, so we were mostly left alone.

Still, there were small, daily humiliations to deal with. If you were sporting a dodgy haircut, had new glasses, a broken arm encased in pristine white plaster or were on crutches? You'd have to endure the taunts, and pray that at the next stop a new red-headed kid with a 'foreign' accent would appear and replace you as the object of attention.

That fateful morning, I wasn't getting onto the bus with a new haircut, specs or a broken limb. I had something infinitely more arresting. Same me, same uniform, same hair. No glasses or broken bones, but with an accessory no one on the bus had ever seen before, and neither had I until a few weeks earlier. I was getting onto the bus with a brand-new face.

The bus veered to the side of the road and braked on the gravel. The door opened. I braved the top step, then the second . . . and the third.

The driver nodded a welcome after my almost two-month absence from the usual pick-up spot. The timid newbies up the front saw me and sent sympathetic looks. I saw them with new eyes, too. I kept my head down and slowly paced down the aisle to the middle of the bus, where I always sat.

My usual seat was empty, waiting for me like a throne.

A girlfriend offered me a red frog lolly. No one mentioned my new face, and I sensed that all my unremarkable companions—the mostly silent majority—were bristling and ready to challenge any unkind remarks from the peanut gallery up the back.

They never came.

And I have never forgotten that kindness.

Thank you, fellow hairy primates!

*

When I was in high school, my Form 2 geography teacher took me aside after class for a talk. In his opinion, I idolised my father in a way that wasn't good for either of us.

This intervention (just guessing here) may have been prompted by my father's habit of recorrecting my already corrected homework with a thick red pencil, complete with annotations in the margins directed to my teachers, then instructing me to take the pages back to class. I can only imagine my teachers' seething annoyance. And as the funny-looking kid in the wrong school uniform, it wasn't helpful.

Dad completed many of my homework assignments and relished the stoushes over English literature. My maths was a complete write-off. Even he, regretfully, gave up on my pathetic efforts at numeracy. Despite, or because of him, I did well and got good marks in most subjects.

Me: 'Look, Dad, I came second-top in my year.'

Dad: 'Oh yes . . . Who came first?'

As a reward, he presented me with an alarm clock: 'So you won't ever be late.'

Not that I was ever late for the school bus. It took me away from Alison's steadily ratcheting war of attrition at home. I stayed overnight and weekends with friends whenever I could, although the privations imposed by one devout Dutch Calvinist family, their insistence on long hours of silence and their incessant Bible readings sent me to the telephone, pleading for rescue. Fifteen minutes later Dad was in the driveway, revving the getaway car.

It was at a girlfriend's house that I first encountered the startling phenomenon of menstruation when I saw her fixing a pad to a sanitary belt. I thought back to an incident where Dad had come rushing in from our outdoor toilet at Selby and said he'd seen blood. Who had been in there lately? It wasn't me. He thrust a book at me and muttered: 'Read these pages I've marked.'

I didn't. So when my sports teacher explained all in detail in the gym at Upwey, I wonder if she spotted Wendy Brown there in the middle row, looking like a stunned mullet.

Thankfully, she did not recommend growing parsley.

*

My dental treatment was ongoing. My mouth had been fitted with a metal contraption called a 'rapid expander' to widen my narrow palate so I could one day be fitted with upper dentures and have a proper smile. The nasty thing was wired to my back teeth and had a screw in the middle that was to be turned daily with a tiny key.

As I dutifully turned the key, my palate was widened by excruciating increments, causing a constant, aching pain in my facial bones and vicious headaches. I hated it.

One day at school I turned the key another notch, felt a shuddering, ominous 'CRACK!' and was convinced my skull had been fractured. I fled to the staff in head office, who calmed me down and assured me that—phew—my head was still in one piece. (If only I'd known then that my dental issues would not be resolved until I was in my twenties.)

*

All this while, Mum, working as a nurse in aged care in Tasmania, was sending me long, anguished, rambling letters in which she often expressed a desire to wade into the sea and drown, or jump off a cliff. Her decision to keep on living was a daily struggle, almost literally, between The Devil and The Deep Blue sea.

Her profound pain at leaving us, expressed in poetry and prose, was a lot for me to take on, understand and respond to. I couldn't let her disappointments pull me under when I was just learning how to swim in life's turbulent ocean, and so I tried to 'logic' my way through, as I had been taught. Eventually I fashioned my own buoyancy device and decided that she'd been incredibly brave to have chosen her own existence over staying with us four kids. She only had one life to live, and so did we. So to sacrifice her happiness for ours didn't make any sense. I often told her so. I don't know that she ever listened. I can't begin to imagine how she explained that she had four young children but wasn't with us. It must have been excruciating. I've never had the courage to ask her.

I also came to realise, even back then, that in some ways I was mothering my own mother. That she was the wayward child and I was the forgiving, patient, understanding one.

My father never spoke ill of her, apart from rare, frustrated outbursts when he couldn't decipher her often Delphic utterances. She read our tea-leaves when we were kids and has always put faith in apparitions, portents and omens. However, one day back in Bendigo Dad told us that she'd written with an offer to take Phil and Helen to live with her in Tassie. Noel and I would stay with him. I'd rarely seen my father angry, but he was angry this day and declared that would *never happen*. We four would never be separated. The damage was done, though, and I was left deeply saddened, thinking she didn't want me and Noel because we weren't as 'perfect' as Phillip and Helen.

I asked Mum about this only recently, and she insisted vehemently that Dad had misrepresented her. She explained her motives this way: 'I had no way of getting you two to hospital in the mainland. I didn't have any money. I knew you and Noel would be fine with him. I also thought it might shock him into getting his act into gear, stop screwing around and knuckle down.'

In my photo albums I have many, many photographs of the four of us kids in a row, embracing. Even as adults with children of our own, it became a family joke that whenever we were gathered, one of us would say: 'Let's get a photo!' I'm sure it was because, deep down, we needed evidence that we had stayed together and what a triumph of will that had been.

Wendy, Phillip, Noel and Helen—we were the 'Famous Four'. The perfect number (two boys, two girls) for tag-team wrestling, board games, bunk beds and swimming races.

My brothers and sister were unwavering and fierce in their defence of me.

Their love was deep, constant and sustaining.

*

I thought I might be a teacher when I grew up, like my father and Auntie Pat. In Bendigo, when school was out, I'd set up a classroom in the garage with a blackboard and chalk, and I'd be the 'teacher' with my younger siblings as the 'students'. Sensibly, they absconded as soon as they could.

Phil reckons it was my 'incessant, fucking annoying' reading aloud from newspapers that set me on the path to journalism.

At Selby, I'd determined that the neighbourhood was in desperate need of an august journal to document its momentous events for posterity—all the news, human interest stories and local sporting contests. I started a little newspaper and named it the *Greenwell Gazette*. ('Greenwell' being the road we lived on.)

After school and on weekends, when other kids were watching *Lost in Space* or *Bugs Bunny* on TV, I slaved over my newspaper. I appointed myself the editor-in-chief and press-ganged my siblings and local kids into being my staff reporters. I handwrote all the stories they gathered and even drew all the 'photos', mastered the duplicating equipment in Dad's school office, stapled the pages together and, in my other role as head of distribution, delivered them to our neighbours' letterboxes.

The *Greenwell Gazette* had four pages and a circulation of . . . five.

My first three editions went gangbusters!

One front page announced in a bold headline: POWER'S ON! It was a top yarn about the newly built house down the road that had finally been connected to the electricity. I ran a popular feature article about a lost dog that turned out to have been in the woodshed all along, and in the sports pages there were must-read reports of marble tournaments held in our driveway.

Flushed with success, I was ready to move on to scandals and exclusives that I knew would be red meat to my avid readers.

The eagle landed when a source told me that one neighbour 'Ray' (not his real name), had crashed his truck through his own front fence when inebriated, and had lied about it to the police.

What a scoop! My banner headline screamed: RAY WAS DRUNK!

And when that edition of the *Greenwell Gazette* was duly delivered?

I estimate it was only ten minutes later that there was a loud, insistent knock on our front door. And there was Ray, threatening to punch Dad in the face.

The *Gazette* was summarily shut down by its proprietor. But it had been a heady month in Australian media!

There are a few things I take away from that very first effort.

Number one: The power of the word 'allegedly'.

Number two: Ray wouldn't have given a rat's if I'd written 'allegedly' or not, he still would have threatened to punch Dad in the face.

Number three: Never reveal your sources. (Although I will divulge here, for the first time, that my 'deep throat' was one of Ray's children. And even if it sounds like I revealed my informant just now—note that I haven't named which of his kids dobbed him in, and he had a few of them. So, good luck with that, Not-Your-Real-Name Ray!)

*

At Upwey High, my English teacher, the wonderful Shirley Collins, recognised my passion for writing and took me under her wing. Our school's annual glossy journal, *Lyric*, was a compendium of tedious addresses from staff, life advice from prefects, sports results and . . . sorry, just nodded off there.

What we needed was a revolution! New media! With Mrs Collins' encouragement, I started a newsletter and named it *Cyril*. Geddit?

Fellow students were invited to contribute gossip, poetry, stories and cartoons. There was plenty of material to work with. A standout was the *real* no-holds-barred account of what happened on the school excursion to Ayers Rock. It must have been Mrs Collins' intervention that saved *Cyril* from being sued for defamation and shut down.

I'd co-opted a few mates to help edit, print and distribute my scurrilous rag (one *very special* front cover I drew was of a 'flower child' in a poncho), while the rest of our classmates were being flogged on the back oval playing sport.

Upwey High was one of many public schools that lacked proper facilities, so often our 'sport' was the dreaded 'cross-country running'. Lucky for me, I'd made the acquaintance of the notorious and beautiful ratbag Ponsford, whose blonde hair was tinged green from the chlorine in her family's pool. A most exotic creature to my eyes, she smuggled a flask of something alcoholic in her sports uniform and we'd hide out in a stormwater drain, then re-join the stragglers on the home stretch, faking exhaustion. Inevitably, we got sprung and so, no more cross-country running for us!

There was no downside to this punishment I was able to detect.

*

In 1968 I'd sat in the Upwey quadrangle with my friends, bereft because I couldn't go to Melbourne to see The Monkees. In 1970 my class visited the cinema to see *Woodstock* and life was never the same. Mind blown, man!

In that era, Upwey High had quite the reputation as a wayward, progressive 'hippie' outlier in the public school system. The senior students had their own home rooms where they could smoke(!). The boys were allowed to wear their hair long and some came to school with ponytails or plaits. (There was a story about them, with pictures, in one of the Melbourne newspapers, which was thrilling.) The first-year students' curriculum was divided into terms studying Earth, Wind, Fire and Water. A quite sensible approach, if you ask me.

Around this time my father came home from foraging at a local junk shop with a record player and some vinyl LPs he thought I might enjoy. In the pile were, improbably, Cream's *Wheels of Fire*, The Jimi Hendrix Experience's *Are You Experienced*, the Rolling Stones' *Out of Our Heads* and *The Beatles*, aka 'the White Album'. I doubt my father had the slightest clue he'd bought me four of the most seminal albums of the era. They'd probably ended up in that junk shop as an act of domestic revenge by an ex-lover or were dumped there by an outraged parent.

Our 'housekeeper' Alison didn't like me playing those unsavoury records in the house, so they went with me on babysitting jobs and, when the parents were out the door, I'd blast Jimi Hendrix and imitate his sexy growl . . . *yeah, you know what I'm talking 'bout.* I can still recite the absurd lyrics of Cream's 'Pressed Rat and Warthog'. Know the 'White Album' backwards.

But it wasn't the eroticism of Jimi or the surrealism of Cream that really spoke to me. Among the pile Dad brought home was the eponymously titled *Joan Baez*, a collection of traditional folk songs recorded in 1960, and it was these songs of injustice, sung with so much heart and soul, that stuck and stayed. I played that record over and over for years as my brothers pounded on the bedroom wall, begging for sweet relief.

(Much later, in my twenties, I was a stalwart of the local folk music scene at the Rainbow Hotel in Fitzroy. I travelled to festivals and sang with anyone who'd have me. A journo friend from that time recalls: 'You were *so* into folk music. I bet that's one thing people don't know about you.' When I was performing stand-up comedy with Richard Stubbs in the late eighties, he threatened to throttle me if I sang so much as one more 'Hey, nonny, nonny' in his presence.)

At Upwey High, summoning every atom of self-confidence I possessed, I tried out for the role of Fiona in the school production of the musical *Brigadoon*. I was passed over for Melissa, Miss Goody-Two-Shoes, who couldn't sing half as well as me. It was because I wasn't pretty enough, I was sure.

Offered a role in the chorus, up the back, I declined it and, out of sheer spite, didn't go to see the show. Truly, if only given the chance, my rendition of 'Waitin' for My Dearie' would have had everyone in that school hall on their feet, applauding. In awe!

I can only marvel that I thought I could pull off the romantic lead with no actual front teeth.

*

My facial scars were healing and fading. I was settled at Upwey High, with a circle of friends I trusted. My carefully curated persona as a cheeky rebel who challenged authority suited me. Not quite one of the 'cool' kids, but in their outer orbit. I felt more and more self-assured.

Then Dad came home and told us we were moving again.

This time to Freshwater Creek.

In the middle of fucking nowhere.

7

From Woodstock to foxtrot

Broken mirror
My bedroom
Anglesea Road
Freshwater Creek schoolhouse
Victoria

Oh my God!

What has she done?

Everything's on the floor. All my clothes pulled out of the wardrobe and the drawers.

There are no sheets or blankets on the bed; it's just a bare mattress.

My posters and pictures are ripped from the walls.

All my make-up, my jewellery, my hats, my shoes, my books, my records—*everything*—in a huge pile in the middle of my bedroom.

Who does shit like this?

I have to get out of here.

Far away from her.

*

'I've got a bone to pick with you, Wendy.' Alison was waiting at the front door when I got off the school bus. When she said those words, crossing her sinewy arms and fixing me with a malevolent stare, I knew it spelled trouble. This time she'd found a pair of bloodstained period undies I'd forgotten to put in the wash, so she'd wrecked my room in some kind of psycho frenzy.

'Now you put everything back where it was. And say you're sorry!' she hissed and slammed the door. The cracked mirror was dumped on top of the pile, many of my posters torn and ruined, treasured ornaments chipped or broken. Of all the punishments she'd exacted, this was the worst. A total violation of my privacy. A hateful act.

But I was trapped in that house with her. There was nowhere to go.

*

Freshwater Creek is on the main road between Geelong and the southern Surf Coast. When you're driving, it's just at the point where the kids in the back seat start chanting: 'When are we gunna get there?' and you're thinking: 'Christ, there better be a beach at the end of this.'

Today, you won't find the old Freshwater Primary School No. 256. It's gone, just like the school at Warncoort. I sometimes wonder if the evidence of my early years has been put into some kind of witness protection program.

When we arrived there in 1971, there was only the school, a petrol station and, away across the flat paddocks, an old wooden community hall, a bluestone Lutheran church and a cemetery. It was fifteen kilometres outside Geelong. I was well and truly stranded.

Many of a certain age will remember the Freshwater Creek signpost because it was home to what could have laid claim to being the world's ugliest tourist attraction—a ten-metre-high giant Tarax soft-drink bottle made entirely of . . . 17,000 empty Tarax soft-drink bottles.

In the seventies, families speeding south down Anglesea Road on their way to magnificent beaches stopped at this 'outstanding attraction': VISIT THE GIANT TARAX BOTTLE AND SPIRAL SLIDE. WALK UP THE INSIDE OF THE BOTTLE AND SLIDE DOWN THE OUTSIDE—GREAT FUN FOR EVERYONE!

I was often inside, earning some pocket money selling tickets to the monstrosity and its accompanying display of 'old and rare bottles'. I fantasised about taking to the lot with a sledgehammer. (There's some debate about whether the giant bottle was ultimately hit by lightning or just fell down in the late seventies or early eighties. Either way, it was not a moment too soon.)

We were back on the plains originally inhabited by the Wadawurrung people, who once moved across a vast swathe of country as the seasons dictated. Again, the displacement of the traditional owners of the land had been breathtakingly swift after millennia of habitation. The squatters came, and by 1861 the Wadawurrung were allocated a mere acre of land by the missionaries. Their number was counted as six males and one female.

The country places I lived in as a child always seemed to have a lonely, melancholy air about them. Back in Warncoort, when I walked the green paddocks dotted with sheep to a friend's house on the horizon, it all felt strangely empty. I have come to understand why. The people who had always lived in these landscapes had been driven off after colonisation and took with them the ancient stories and songs which imbued every rock, tree, animal, flower and even the starry night sky with meaning. The ancients who had sung the world into being were gone.

I was on arid land, stripped of understanding.

When we got to Freshwater Creek, the adjoining properties were home to a small piggery and hobby farms. A few old, larger holdings ran sheep and cattle.

Our weatherboard place dated from 1883 and was finally condemned a century later in 1984. It was rescued and moved to the Waurn Ponds campus of Deakin University as part of a collection of 'historic Australian buildings'. 'Historic' because it was the last school in Victoria which housed the classroom and residence in a single structure.

Stepping out our back door, you turned right and in a few paces were in the tiny schoolroom with its lofty ceiling and classic wooden-framed, thirty-six-paned windows. There was no way little sister Helen could be late for class; she could see the school door from her bedroom—a shoebox-sized walled-in section of the back verandah.

Dad and I visited the restored building at Deakin. I was astonished that six of us had ever called it home and that it had survived its journey without splintering into pieces. It was later carted off again and used as an extra classroom for a local school.

My father remembers the day we arrived at Freshwater Creek. 'I walked into the pantry and went straight through the floor-boards and down to the ground underneath. It was a bit of a dump.' A classic Graham understatement.

No family should have been condemned to live in that house. The wind howled across the Western Plains and blew dust through every crack in the walls and up through the rotting flooring. Birds nested in the roof and infested the house with mites. Paint flakes drifted from ceilings. Taps were old and rusted. Either open or closed, the windows stuck fast. Freezing in winter. Stifling in summer.

No matter how much energy Alison expended on incessant scrubbing and sweeping and cleaning, there were too many of us crammed into those miserable rooms in that falling-down dump. I believe she came to regard the four of us as her primary obstacle to achieving the domestic order on which she so prided herself, so she became dispirited and increasingly vindictive.

One incident Phil relates is particularly disturbing: 'There was the famous "roster" of tasks we were all assigned, and one of them was to feed the cat. It had just had a litter of kittens, and I'm not sure who it was that failed their feline care duties, but one night, while we were all eating dinner at the kitchen table,

Alison went on a huge rant about how "careless" and "useless" we were because the cat needed extra care.

'She stormed out the back door of the house. About fifteen minutes later she marched back in, held up a dripping-wet bag and said we wouldn't have to worry about the kittens anymore. She'd drowned them in a tub in the outdoor laundry.

'We were horrified. You and Helen burst into tears, and Noel and I ran to Dad, who was watching TV in the lounge room, and told him what she'd done. He came into the kitchen and told us that we'd have to be more responsible and then he retreated.

'I think he had a fight with her in the bedroom later that night, telling her she'd gone too far. I remember the whole house was on edge for days.'

By this time, Dad was shepherding Phil and Noel, both handy players, in a local football league which, happily for him, took him out of the house. He also pioneered a pool competition based in the Waurn Ponds Hotel—meaning he was still spending many hours at the pub, drinking and yarning with his mates.

I can't remember ever seeing my father drunk. He was absent for long hours and, when he came home with more than a few beers on board, he could talk the leg off a chair. He was opinionated and bombastic, often told funny stories, but was never belligerent or violent. I cannot recall him ever suffering a hangover or even contemplating giving up the drink. He didn't imbibe alone and rarely touched wine or spirits. For him it was always about the companionship he found in bars, clubhouses or backyard barbecues. And beer just made it all . . . *better.*

Meanwhile, Alison, left at home, berated me. 'YOU are the problem in this family. YOU always have been. YOU are the reason your father drinks and never comes home.

'It's because of YOU!'

*

Culture shock—defined by Kalervo Oberg, the anthropologist who coined the term in the 1950s, as 'the anxiety that results from losing all our familiar signs and symbols of social inter-course'—accurately describes my state of mind when I got off the bus at Oberon High School.

When I was picked up by the school bus on the main road at Freshwater Creek, the kids in the back seats were impossibly blond and beautiful with bright-red tattoos of Mercurochrome on their knees and elbows from where they'd tangled with rocks and reefs. This was the surfie tribe from Anglesea and Torquay. There was a smell I came to identify as lemon juice and peroxide. It was mixed in a potion and bleached their hair to shades of caramel, honey, gold and platinum. They were so alien to me they may as well have been elves from Rivendell. Then there were the kids from the local farms, tanned from working outdoors, open-faced and smiley. The thirty-minute bus ride was chatty and relaxed. They didn't pay me much attention, for which I was grateful. I couldn't see any of this lot bogging off for an illicit ciggie behind the train station or collecting petitions against the Vietnam War like the kids from Upwey High had done.

Was this a good or bad omen?

The real thud came when I stepped off the bus at Belmont—in those days an outer southern suburb of Geelong made up of new housing estates. At Upwey the school grounds had been green and leafy; some of the buildings, dating back to 1937, were substantial and had a bit of history to them. But if I'd thought the name Oberon—the mythical King of the Fairies—implied there was some magic to be found at my new school, there was none. Established less than ten years before I got there, Oberon High was an uninspiring collection of ugly low-rise buildings plonked in a dry, barren field, with a few straggly gum trees the only shade.

The last two years of my schooling would be spent in simmering rebellion against what I saw as ridiculous rules—the strict enforcement of correct uniform—and endless, tedious assemblies. Upwey High, where the teachers and students had cooperated in a rudimentary form of democracy, had ruined me for Oberon and its pointless authoritarianism. I did not like it one bit.

I campaigned to establish a Students' Representative Council, and we had one win at least—those who wanted to opt out of sport were granted permission to spend their time in the library. Not that I disliked sport; I just reckoned we should have had the choice.

One evening we seniors were bussed into town to attend a political forum at Geelong College. Walking through the spectacular, manicured grounds and under ornate ivy-covered colonnades, I was dumbstruck. It was a world of privilege I hadn't known existed; for the first time I saw my education was 'second-class'.

During the forum, in a grand hall packed with students, I unexpectedly found my voice. In a Q & A on pollution, one of the politicians on the dais finger-wagged: '*You* should all do *your part* and put your orange peel in the bin.' Patronising arse! I was up on my feet before I knew it, challenging him about the noxious fumes spewing daily from the Shell oil refinery in Corio. This earned a huge round of applause and cheers.

I have no idea how the The Arse responded. I was so shocked by my audacious intervention that my legs didn't stop shaking until I was back on the bus, heading back to ol' 'Scrapheap High'.

For Phil and Noel it was rough going at the all-boys Geelong Junior Tech in Moorabool Street, right in town. The grounds were dubbed 'the prison yard' by the inmates, some of whom had grown up at the Glastonbury Children's Home in Belmont (formerly known as the Geelong Orphanage), where they had suffered abuse. They were, in their turn, violent. Sometimes my brothers got off the bus with bruises and black eyes.

One bastard of a teacher there dubbed Noel 'Lippy the Lion' (after the TV cartoon series *Lippy the Lion and Hardy Har Har*)—a vile slur because he had a cleft lip. The name 'Lippy' stuck and, although Noel was a brave kid, a scrapper who could look after himself, I knew he was sensitive to the insult. I was so angry on his behalf.

At Oberon High, once more, I found my spot in a convivial mix of friendly country and suburban gals who flew beneath the radar. Even managed to crack the surfie chick code and somehow ended up in a netball team called 'Shane'. We wore Hawaiian print skirts and necklaces of pukka shells. *Aloha!* I may have been the only brunette on our side.

As a feisty defence winger, I also played in a Saturday morning netball competition at a suburban court in Belmont. Dad would drive me there and back from Freshwater Creek. While Phil cannot recall any conversation he had with my father beyond 'Where did you boys put that spanner?' or 'You boys have rooted this!', Dad took the opportunity on those drives, just the two of us in the front seats, to impart his knowledge on religion, philosophy and world events. He'd read Rachel Carson's book *Silent Spring* and become convinced by her crusade against synthetic pesticides in the environment. I took it all in.

These were cherished interludes, away from the turmoil at home, but were almost overshadowed by the day he forgot to collect me at the end of my netball match and eventually, to my mortification, picked me up from a friend's house when it was getting on for dark.

No prizes for guessing where he'd been.

*

From Woodstock to Foxtrot. That's a neat summation of how my teenage social life unfolded at Freshwater Creek.

I fancied myself Janis Joplin-esque. But without anywhere to go to in my groovy outfits, I took to parading along the main road in my wide-brimmed purple floppy felt hat, embroidered vests and bell-bottoms, all adorned with feathers and ropes of beads. Rose-coloured glasses completed the look. My brothers thought I was crazy. The most attention I ever got was derisory comments shouted by the local farm boys speeding by in their utes.

One day Alison took all my 'hippie' clothes and nailed them to the back of my bedroom door as a punishment for . . . something . . . I don't know what. Phil remembers that he and Noel used pliers to extract the six-inch nails, but my precious garments were ruined.

It was a long way from Max Yasgur's dairy farm in Bethel, New York, and Woodstock's 'three days of peace and music' to the humble Freshwater Creek hall and the Saturday 'old-time' dance, an event scarcely changed since horse-and-buggy days. But, looking for any kind of social diversion, I would crunch my way across frosty moonlit paddocks to the hall to meet my dear friend Garry Scale.

Garry, as 'the only gay in the village', remembers me as his 'first-ever fag hag'. We'd met on the bus and clicked instantly. He was so funny, witty and handsome. We shared all the school gossip. 'You were so worldly to a lad like me,' he recalls.

On Saturday and Sunday afternoons I'd ride my pushbike to his family's hobby farm about three kilometres up the road, and we'd spend hours in his bedroom playing records, belting out show tunes from *Oklahoma*, *Carousel* and *Cabaret*. I've loved musical theatre ever since.

Garry had taken dance lessons in order to squire young women at debutante balls. We went along to the old-time Saturday dance with a cynical teenage attitude, planning to send up proceedings, but, despite ourselves, got into the swing of things; we always had a fun time and laughed ourselves silly.

Inside the hall, its walls adorned with historic plaques honouring those fallen in The War and photos of footy teams past, the floor was expertly polished. Small children skidded up and down the length of it, throwing up flurries of sawdust. When it was swept away, the surface was as slippery as an ice rink. In an anteroom, the wives of the local cow cockies set up the tea urn and laid on a lavish supper of homemade cakes with lashings of fresh cream from the farm. Delicious!

On long wooden benches either side of the dance floor we sat—the men on one side and the women on the other—eyeballing any likely romantic prospects. There were none for me. None for Garry either. The tennis sheds out the back, where the young blokes were hanging, smoking and drinking, was where the real action was, but we didn't dare venture out there in the dark.

The band took their places on the raised stage. Often it was Taylor's Orchestra, a popular four-piece, all in dinner suits and bow ties, which did the rounds of the country halls in the district.

Every new dance was grandly announced by the bandleader: 'Ladies and Gentlemen, the Bon Ton. Please!'

The Pride of Erin, Gypsy Tap, foxtrot, quickstep or a waltz were on the dance card. Literally. Their names, written in embellished script, were propped on an easel at front of stage. I dreaded the Progressive Barn Dance and developed a quick sideways step to evade the straying, sweaty hands of a procession of farmers older than my father.

From my specific, hand-drawn instructions, Alison had sewn me a mini-dress in royal purple embossed crepe with eyelets down the front threaded with white laces. A pair of white platform shoes, big and clumpy as house bricks, completed the look. My hair was straight and halfway down my back. In my eyes, I was looking fine. A vision of seventies glamour.

It was the night I debuted this ensemble that I accepted a lift home from a local farm boy named Lance. He drove his ute in precisely the wrong direction up a darkened dirt road, with me protesting all the way. In one sweeping motion he switched off the engine, turned and thrust his hand down the front of my dress. I punched him in the head, leaped out the door and trudged home, kicking at sheep shit in my clunky shoes and shedding furious tears.

Garry and I both escaped Freshwater Creek.

He went on to attend NIDA in Sydney, became a star of musical theatre and TV and, later, a teacher librarian bringing the arts to high school children. He remains a lovely friend.

*

School holidays were spent at Ballarat with Nanna Brown, or I'd go rabbiting with my brothers. Noel kept ferrets and knew where all the warrens were. Many hours were spent sitting on a rock or lying in the yellow, spindly grass, waiting for a bloodied ferret to emerge after it had feasted on rabbit kittens and fallen asleep underground. A gruesome business.

On Sunday mornings we'd ride our bikes to a waterhole and catch eels, skin them and fry them up for breakfast.

(In 2009 I was a contestant on *Celebrity Masterchef* and cooked rabbit in mustard sauce. Observing me joint a whole rabbit, judge George Calombaris declared my quick and efficient method expert enough to earn a place as commis chef in his kitchen. No greater compliment could have been bestowed! I was kicked out in the second round when I didn't add enough gelatine to the passionfruit jelly on Stephanie Alexander's fiddly, layered crepe dessert.)

*

The last two years at high school passed uneventfully enough.

My final-year exam results came in the mail in the summer of '72. They were average—with one exception: an A for English. I'd had my heart set on studying at university, but Dad told me, regretfully, we didn't have the money—just as his mother had once told him.

If my results weren't anything special, I could at least boast a *real* boyfriend who lived in *Melbourne*!

I'd met Michael Harmer at a dance in Geelong after I'd nagged my father to drive me there from Freshwater Creek one Saturday night.

Michael had a few things going for him. He was tall, with long dark hair, a beard, and looked rather like Roger Glover, the bass player in Deep Purple, one of his favourite bands. He was a sweet man, just a few years older than me, endlessly devoted to the girl he called his 'Angel Eyes'. Best of all, Mike had wheels— a Chrysler Valiant sedan he'd customised with lay-back seats and studded black vinyl interior.

He could take me places far, far away from Alison.

Mike worked at the Government Aircraft Factories at Fishermans Bend as a heat treater—bending metal into shape in blazing furnaces. He lived in Melbourne, but often visited workmates in Geelong's working-class suburb of Corio, so driving the extra distance to visit me in 'the sticks' was no problem.

Sometimes, when Mike took me to a party and it was getting late, I'd ring my father and ask: 'Should I come home now?'

Dad would answer cryptically: 'How can you tell if something is "over"? How "late" is "too late"?'

This was Graham the amateur psychologist teaching me to take responsibility for my actions. I see that now, but at the time I'd shout, 'Oh, bloody hell, Dad!' and slam down the phone. All I wanted was for him to set some boundaries, but, as usual, there were none. I was left to figure out life for myself.

Mike and I pashed madly in my bedroom while Alison banged on the door, shouting: 'I know what you're doing in there!' And we *almost* were. I was seventeen and at Mike's flat in Elwood when I promptly burst into tears because I was no longer a virgin.

When Mike suggested we set up house together in a flat in West Geelong, I accepted. At last I'd escape the hellish environment created by Alison. My God, how happy that woman must have been to see the back of me!

I celebrated my eighteenth birthday in that old schoolroom at Freshwater Creek. It was the last time I saw the place.

Dad was on the move again. A new school. Another reset.

He took Noel and Helen with him.

Phil wasn't invited.

It was the end of the Famous Four.

8

Ducks on pond

Wall mirror
Ladies' toilets
Geelong Advertiser
Ryrie Street

Look at you.

You're exhausted.

You've rewritten this stupid story ten times over now.

This is torture.

And LET GO of my skirt!

WHY is he grabbing hold of my skirt?

It's humiliating.

And if I hear them mutter 'ducks on pond' when I walk in the door *one more time* . . .

*

I'm told I was the first woman to be hired in the newsroom of the *Geelong Advertiser*, established in 1840. The first bird to land and fluff her feathers in more than 130 years.

When I started, there was only one other female on the editorial floor—the social editor, Evelyn Higginbotham, who dutifully recorded the ladies' lunches, weddings, fashion parades and fundraisers in the lively, provincial city scene. An older woman swathed in a shawl and hunched over a two-bar radiator in her cubbyhole office, she reminded me of Miss Havisham. She never spoke to me. I scurried by to the ladies' toilets at the end of a long, dingy corridor, often to mop up tears after a pitiless session at the subeditor's desk.

Bob Osburn, who also started as a cadet at 'the *Addy*' and went on to spend his working life in newspapers, remembers that newsroom as a particularly tough environment in which to learn the trade. Young journalists were routinely humiliated and lectured in front of the rest of the staff. It was a blood sport. The newsroom thrived on deadlines, competition and needless tension. We cadets were fresh meat put through the grinder. Instead of the chief sub telling us, 'Your lead's in the second-last par, bring it up the top' and putting the story in the 'holdable' basket for the next morning, or just spiking the whole damn thing, we were left to decipher increasingly obscure subbing mark-ups. Typing and re-typing until we were almost delirious.

It was like operating the Enigma machine in World War II.

The *Geelong Advertiser* was a broadsheet, published six days a week.

'It devoured copy,' says Bob. 'You wrote until your notebook was emptied. Every quote, background paragraphs, descriptive phrases—all made it into your story. It was nothing unusual to write twenty stories in a shift. Rarely was a story axed. A badly written story could always be salvaged. There were few who would give their time to help a cadet.'

'Ducks on pond' was a colloquialism I knew well from country life. Whispered across lakes and dams at dawn by one duck hunter to another, it was the signal to 'SHOOSH!' when game birds were settling on the water and any noise would startle, causing them to take flight and ruin the day's shoot.

I'd heard it used in shearing sheds as a warning that women were about—an admonition to keep blokes' secrets and moderate their language until the sheilas were out of earshot. Muttered in the newsroom, it meant: 'Watch out, she's coming.'

It should have been demoralising. Except this time they'd picked the wrong little black duck. I'd landed a job at a real, fair dinkum newspaper, my long-held ambition fulfilled.

I wasn't going anywhere.

Mrs Higginbotham, dedicated to her social pages (which accounted for a good number of sales of the paper), garnered little respect or attention from the all-male newsroom. One chief of staff could 'sense' whenever she stepped across the threshold to deliver her copy. 'He would rise from his desk, amble over to the newspaper files and drop the loudest, most grotesque and prolonged fart he could muster. Without fail, it sent her storming back to her nook,' says Bob.

I was undertaking the three-year Diploma of Vocational Writing at the Gordon Institute of Technology, where we took classes in writing poetry and plays; learned how to massage a public relations press release; cover a news event. It was a brilliant course. Writing every day. I revelled in it. I was chosen from a room of hopefuls in my journalism class for a start at the *Addy*.

I was green and nineteen when I entered the newsroom, and Bob remembers me: 'The first female newsroom journalist. Slim, with long dark hair, you quickly made your place.'

Imagine a scene that hadn't changed in decades. Drab green walls, not unlike a public hospital ward; no windows; a long desk with a row of black Bakelite phones. Wooden booths for the journalists—two rows of four, where you eyeballed the person opposite. Each cubicle was furnished with a heavy Remington typewriter, a bundle of copy paper and the mandatory ashtray. Within view, behind a low glass wall, sat the Chief Sub. Everyone could hear and see when some hapless individual was getting a bollocking for mistakes in grammar or spelling.

There was no direction on the finer points of how to improve your writing or frame a story. It was all to be learned through trial and error but, as it happens, a discipline very familiar to me.

I persevered.

One hulking Chief Sub took to correcting my copy with one hand and, with his other, he'd grab a handful of my jacket or skirt in his huge fist and wrench me close to his side, so I was captive and he had my undivided attention. (Long pants were officially outlawed for the young lady!) Somehow, I never took this to be sexual harassment, although it was embarrassing and demeaning. He didn't do it with the young male cadets. As the first female on the floor, there was no one to complain to.

'Go away and do it again,' he'd grunt and throw the copy back at me, leaving me to divine the meaning of his arcane scribbles.

As a copy girl and then cadet, my shift began at 4 p.m. It was all 'GO!' from the minute I clocked on. Monitoring the telex machines, tearing off reams of text from AUP and sorting them into baskets for news, sport, finance and features. Typing copy to go back up the line and writing 'fillers' from press releases.

I'd dash around on errands on my trusty pushbike. Picking up the weather map from the last Melbourne train into Geelong station, checking in at police headquarters in Gheringhap Street and placing a last phone call to the hospital. It all ended around midnight.

It's indicative of the pressure I was under that I'm still able to recall with a shudder one of the most stressful moments of my professional life. Racing across town on my bicycle to deliver copy for the 3GL radio six o'clock news bulletin, my groovy spiderweb-patterned tights became hopelessly entangled in the chain. Couldn't go backwards or forwards, and I was stuck in the middle of peak-hour traffic. Loyal 3GL listeners went without their news that night and I copped shit for it for weeks.

Despite it all, I thrived. There's nothing to match the full-throttle adrenaline rush of a newspaper office on deadline. The thrill of being the first to read the international bulletins off the wires was utterly addictive. Watching the journos and photographers sweat, swear and argue over the next edition was compelling, and I couldn't wait to get a 'round' to call my own.

As a lowly cadet, the two tasks I most enjoyed were compiling the 'News of the Past' section and writing the 'Old King Cole's Court' column. 'News of the Past' ran on a Saturday, featuring items from twenty-five, fifty, seventy-five and a hundred years ago, to be gathered from the newspaper archives. I escaped the mayhem of the newsroom, whiling away my time in the musty stacks, flicking through the fragile pages of original newspapers, some a century old, reading first-hand accounts of colonisation, bushrangers, crime and the mighty civic enterprise which established the thriving port for wool and grain exports.

The 'Old King Cole' page, lorded over by an image of the 'merry old soul' wearing his crown and calling for his pipe, his bowl and his fiddlers three, was full of colouring competitions, riddles and puzzles for the kiddies. It was now the early seventies, and this was weirdly arcane.

Every week I'd compose a short letter from the 'King' himself. I'd do my best to disguise that I was writing as a female teenager and try to sound a bit 'wise' and 'worldly'. But sometimes I just wrote whatever came into my head. The biggest mailbag I ever received was after advising my loyal subjects that a bait of curry powder on a bit of bread was a sure way to catch a fish.

In the seventies, all newspaper readers were regarded as 'subjects'. Newspaper editors were demigods. We journalists answered to no one except our bosses, and we had no idea who our bosses answered to in turn. All opinion writers were over sixty and male—an unspoken edict.

The only way readers could approach the fortified towers of the Fourth Estate was to write letters, but the angriest ones were never published. The mighty citadel was guarded by the gate-keepers and never breached.

*

'Shacked up' with Michael Harmer in West Geelong, I was only a short bike ride away from the *Addy*.

Just as men of my age get all nostalgic about their first cars and recall with misty eyes the zebra-striped seat covers, the gearstick topped with a billiard ball and the rear back door you could only open from the outside, I remember every detail of my first kitchen.

In the tiny one-bedroom flat—one of many in a nondescript blond-brick block—I was, at last, the mistress of my domain. It's where I debuted as a sophisticated hostess at the dinner parties we held for Mike's friends.

My galley kitchen was resplendent with a lime-green Laminex breakfast bar set with stoneware plates on raffia place-mats. Earthenware canisters sat on a shelf beneath a macramé wall hanging I'd made in the shape of an owl. I owned a full set of ramekins, Splayds, Arcopal tumblers, Pyrex casserole dishes, serviette rings engraved with signs of the zodiac, an electric frypan, a fondue set and bits and bobs of Tupperware. A bamboo blind above the sink, a round rice paper shade in the lounge room, purple corduroy-covered bean bags and a poster of my pop idol, Melanie, completed the groovy seventies ambience.

Home Beautiful should have preserved that kitchen as a museum piece for future generations. I'm sure today's young homemakers would be intrigued to see just how *special* burnt-orange ramekins can look on lime-green Laminex.

After a series of disasters with incinerated paisley oven mitts, shattered baking dishes, charcoal roast ducks, raw whole snapper and shrivelled shish kebabs, I hit on a dinner party menu which was a sure-fire winner: prawn cocktail for entree, beef burgundy with Spanish-flavoured Rice-a-Riso for main course and dessert of fruit salad with a dash of Grand Marnier. Let's not forget the after-dinner mints!

With Neil Diamond's *Hot August Night* as the soundtrack, and after a few bottles of Orlando's sparkling Cold Duck, the evening was swinging . . . until Mike insisted on playing one of his tedious prog-rock Emerson, Lake & Palmer albums or Mike Oldfield's *Tubular Bells*. I wanted to hear Joan Baez, Melanie or Steeleye Span, and we'd squabble over it. We didn't like each other's taste in music. That should have been a sign.

Over time, cracks deepened into chasms.

I can't remember exactly when Mike first proposed that we get married, but he asked me constantly after we moved in together. A deposit on a new home in a housing estate, holidays on the coast and saving for trips to England to see his family . . . he had our future, even the names for two children, all mapped out. 'Insert yourself here.'

I've often thought of the window to my state of mind at that time as being opaque, but I see now there's not just one window to peer through; it's a collection of small, mismatched frames.

A newspaper cutting reminds me that I took the lead role of Marigold in a student musical production called *The Sammy*

Sunshine Raggedy Ragtime Revue, which had been created by a bunch of lovely friends from 'the Gordon'. In what may have been a preview of things to come: 'The revue included some witty comments on the fourth university [Deakin] with Sammy in the role of the university's new vice chancellor.'

In another folder are my *Geelong Advertiser* articles. My review of an exhibition of the New York photographer Diane Arbus; a yarn about a war veteran who liked to dress as Santa and deliver toys.

In an old album are daggy souvenirs from road trips with Mike. A breakfast menu card from the Blue Gums Hotel Motel in South Australia; matchbooks from pubs in Queensland.

Two more minor surgical operations to correct and narrow my flat, wide nose had given me a profile, and I'd had a dental plate fitted. But I still clamped my lips together when asked to 'smile for the camera'.

Michael loved me as I was, and I had no doubt he'd always be faithful. Looking in the mirror, I asked myself: *Who else will have you? Maybe this will be the only offer you'll ever get.*

Just as alarm bells had been ringing for my mother right up to her wedding day, they rang for me. And, like her, I couldn't quite see my way out of it. If I broke up with Mike, where would I go? How could I afford my studies? Keep my job?

When I finally said 'yes', was I in love?

I'm sure I told him so and told myself the same.

But a memory I have, bright as day, is saying to two girl-friends on the eve of my wedding, 'Well, there's always divorce, right?'

*

I was wed at the Melbourne Registry Office in August 1975, three months shy of my twentieth birthday, in a dress I'd found in an op shop. A drab olive crepe mid-length number embroidered with tiny bronze beads and teamed with brown-and-tan cork platform shoes. My hair was a pageboy bob. There was no bouquet.

I cannot imagine an outfit less festive, unless I was being married during the London Blitz.

Brother Phil was one of three witnesses to the ceremony, which was followed by a pub counter lunch and a trip to Tasmania to visit my mother for a honeymoon. On meeting my new husband, she recalls, she told him: 'You're going to have a tough time with that one. She is a very, very powerful woman.'

Hah! Not so powerful as she liked to think.

Back at the *Addy*, home from holidays, I sheepishly confessed I'd got married and was informed by a managing editor that I could no longer keep my maiden name, Brown, and that from then on I would write under the surname Harmer. I was to be addressed in the office as 'Mrs Harmer'. There was to be no argument.

Because I began writing under that by-line, I never found an opportunity to change it back. I have no affection for the name you now know me by—no offence to the Harmer clan. My former husband was from Birmingham, and I'm a fallen, forgotten, tiny twig from a branch of his venerable family tree, established in England after the Norman conquest of 1066.

I'm just a plain, old Brown, from the Old English, meaning 'brown'.

*

A year after I started at the *Advertiser*, the new cadet intake included Rosita Dellios, an acquaintance from the Gordon. It was exhilarating to have female company in the newsroom. Rosita was tall, blonde and beautiful and conducted herself with a quiet, earnest reserve. Totally unlike me, but we instantly formed a resistance alliance of two. A sly cartoon of two old biddies in dressing-gowns and hair rollers yakking over a back fence appeared on the office noticeboard.

'It was hard working in an all-male environment where being a woman was novel and encouraged pranks,' Rosita recalls. 'We were working the night shift and were told to go to the docks to interview sailors from a visiting US submarine. We arrived but there was no one there. The place was deserted. So I think I said, or you said: "There's no point waiting any longer, there must have been a mistake. Besides, if anyone sees us standing here at night, they might think we're prostitutes." Returning to the newsroom we said there was no one there to receive us, and the staff—all males—burst out laughing, saying it was a joke.'

Ho, ho, ho! Hilarious!

However, like Bob Osburn, Rosita says she learned how to write, *really write*, at the *Geelong Advertiser*. As a young reporter, she was afforded the opportunity to interview Australia's first ambassador to China.

'The newspaper let me be the "China hand", which was very prescient of them as I ended up being a China academic at Bond University,' says Dr Dellios.

The 'City' round took me to the chamber of commerce, council meetings, social welfare outfits, theatres, museums and galleries. Whizzing around town on my ten-speed powder-blue racing bike, gathering any scrap of 'news' I could find, before hitting the office and writing feverishly. In 1976 I graduated to a billing as the paper's 'Industrial Writer'. Seeing my by-line up the front of the paper was intoxicating. I was hooked.

After my promotion, I began dropping into the office of the federal member for Corio, Gordon Scholes, and Trades Hall. It's fair to say that the Seamen's Union delegates, fresh from the docks in Geelong, hadn't ever seen a young, female reporter at their meetings. The first time I went, I took my place behind a table on the raised dais at the front of the hall. But proceedings were soon interrupted when some bloke stood and addressed the assembled: 'Ahem! Mr Chairman. Do you think we could get a front put on that table? The young lady's legs are distracting everyone here tonight. It's very hard to concentrate.'

Then, Lord Help Me, they debated the issue as I tried to wrench my skirt down to cover my knees.

Can't recall final tally of the vote.

*

At home, things with Mike were, inevitably, going south. He didn't care much for my journo friends, and what he saw as their incessant navel-gazing and office gossip. I was sick of his tradie mates and their plans for hair-raising adventures.

We spent many weekends in the wild, camping in tents or sleeping in the Valiant, as Mike—an accomplished free-diving spearfisherman—explored treacherous blowholes, deserted bays and windswept beaches.

One memorable afternoon, when they gathered for a fishing competition, the boys took me by boat to a remote bombie, where I was deposited on the bare rocks to act as 'shark lookout' while they dived. It was only at dusk, back on shore, with the campfire roaring and the first tinnies cracked, that they remembered me. I was collected from my rock—sunburned, thirsty and fucking furious.

Other days were spent in the hot, dusty, godforsaken surrounds of the Calder Raceway, barracking for 'Ford' over 'Holden'.

I believe I may be the only woman alive to have mastered the feat of balancing on cork platform shoes on scoria while carrying an Esky.

No wonder I was happier sitting in the car with my pile of books.

*

On my reading list, as for so many young women of the era, were Germaine Greer's *The Female Eunuch* and Erica Jong's *Fear of Flying*. I was coming to see just what a bad bargain I'd made. How limited and stultifying the future I'd signed up for.

My marriage shielded me from what I was sure would have been bruising rejections from men, but was Mike the only man I'd have sex with? I took up a small mirror, sat on the bathroom floor and, as advised by *Cleo* magazine, followed a step-by-step guide on how to masturbate to orgasm. Success! A revelation!

(Years later, during intermission at a glam event at the Sydney Opera House, I rocked up to *Cleo*'s founding editor, Ita Buttrose, and thanked her for the info. Said how much it had meant to a sheltered girl like me. She was taken aback, but replied graciously, 'My absolute pleasure, Wendy.' I hope I answered, 'No, Ita, the pleasure has been *all mine*.')

Rosita remembers that at the Gordon I'd shown off my engagement ring—a yellow topaz flanked by two diamonds.

'You seemed to be proud of it and what it meant. I congratulated you, but I remember being inwardly shocked, thinking, *But why would she want to get married?* It seemed like a bizarre thing for you to do.'

It was a 'bizarre' thing for me to do. *Stupid* also comes to mind. After I was married, Rosita remembers that in the office, I'd sometimes call my mother in Tassie late at night, and she'd find me upset and crying in the Telex room, a good place to hide.

I'd wanted to leave Mike for a long time, and my mother was urging me to, but I couldn't summon the courage. I knew he'd be terribly hurt. It was my mistake I'd married him. I should have been braver and said 'no'.

I told myself that the time and place to leave would present itself if I was patient.

In the summer of '76, everything changed.

*

Mike sometimes rode his bicycle to Fishermans Bend and back for work, a round trip of 140 kilometres. *I know. Crazy.* This particular Christmas he'd decided to tackle the Nullarbor Plain and ride 3375 kilometres from Perth to Geelong. Alone. *Madness.*

With him away for weeks, I threw a drinks party at our flat and invited my workmates from the *Addy*. Everyone left at a decent hour except for one senior member of staff who stayed . . . and stayed . . . and then made a lunge for me. As I ducked out of reach of his outstretched arms, he whined, 'But I thought you knew—I've always been a little bit in love with you.'

I've related this incident over many years as if it were a joke.

'A *little* bit in love?' I mean, he could have tried harder. Ha-ha! But it wasn't funny. His half-arsed declaration rocked my self-confidence.

In the office, I couldn't meet his eye and, as the months went by, found our daily interactions increasingly awkward. Was it my imagination, or was I being passed over for important assignments?

One afternoon, wearing trousers in open rebellion, I was using the heel of my shoe to bang a nail into the leg of a busted chair when he appeared in the newsroom with a visitor he was showing around. 'And here's our resident women's libber, *Mrs Harmer*,' he trumpeted in a sarcastic tone.

I remember the contempt in his voice. Rosita was there, she does too.

It wasn't the only reason to leave.

As Bob Osburn tells me: 'Most of the early seventies cadet intake left because the old grey brigade held all the senior positions. It was a newsroom roadblock. Jobs for life. If you wanted to develop your potential, you were forced to leave the newspaper and the city for metro publications, the best thing an ambitious young journalist could do. The metros craved hardworking young journos from the bush, actually trained them, and promoted them on merit.'

The day I departed, there was a presentation ceremony in the office.

A fellow alumnus from the Gordon, who'd started a year after me, was sent off with words of high praise. He was an 'excellent reporter' and 'going places'. He was given handsome bound volumes of the works of Henry Lawson.

I was told: 'Wendy, we're all going to miss your smiling face.' My gift was a presentation pack of Yardley's April Violets—bath cubes, talc and eau de cologne.

I hope whoever found them in the bin in Ryrie Street enjoyed my fragrant offering to the patriarchy.

9

Hold the front page

Ornate, wood-framed mirror
Lady Mayoress's office
Melbourne Town Hall

Look at you in this mirror, Ms Wendy.

You with the cyclamen pink streak in your dark hair, your flippy short skirt and black satin stilettos, striding across plush carpets in these sumptuous, grand rooms.

How did *you* get into the inner sanctum of Melbourne Town Hall, small-town girl?

Who let *you* in here?

Get back to the office.

Find an angle *The Age* or the *Herald* won't have.

Make headlines. Get another front-page by-line.

Set the hares running.

Let *them* follow *you*.

Like Dad says, whatever you choose to do, be the *best*.

*

I was single and a 'Ms' now. One day I'd just up-and-left my husband. The moment had come after I'd spent long hours curled up in a disconsolate ball on the kitchen floor. I couldn't stay a minute longer. 'It's not you . . . It's me.' I just had to go.

Told him he could keep everything in our flat, took some clothes and records, and went.

A stint in public relations for Geelong's Bethany Babies' Home and then on to Swinburne Technical College's information office in Hawthorn, Melbourne, proved I wasn't cut out for a role in PR. I missed the excitement of daily deadlines and the huge cast of diverse characters I'd engaged with at the *Addy*. Missed my clever journo mates, who'd educated me in politics and culture, expanded my thinking and my tastes. More than that, my 'nose for news' kept sniffing out mini-scandals that would have made good copy in the newspapers. Not quite the person you want in-house, banging out cheery press releases and staff newsletters. PR wasn't where I'd thought journalism would take me. Depressing.

In a move of epic stupidity, I succumbed to Michael's forlorn entreaties and moved back in with him in a dingy flat just down the street from Swinburne. I'd felt so guilty for leaving him.

Mike was a good man, loved and took care of me, but as a staunch left-winger and trade unionist—with every reason to dislike the press (especially one on the 'Industrial' round)—wasn't happy that I wanted to go back to daily journalism. He didn't issue an ultimatum, but the message I received was: *It's me or the newspapers.* He should have known he'd lose.

One last-ditch effort took us to marriage counselling. After hearing our laments, the therapist looked at us and said calmly: 'You're both young. You haven't got any children. Why on earth are you staying together? Give up.'

A very good summation of things, I thought.

Single again—this time *for sure*—I hotfooted it to Flinders Street and scored a job.

Visiting the family at Lucknow school outside Bairnsdale, in my battered old cack-green Volkswagen, I realised it was the first time I'd been on a country highway without a man behind the wheel, taking me somewhere or other.

Finally, I was in the driver's seat.

I wound down the windows and sang Helen Reddy's 'I Am Woman' to paddocks of startled cows.

*

In 1978, at the age of twenty-three, I was back in a newsroom. Not just any newsroom, but on the editorial floor of the mighty tabloid *Sun News-Pictorial* on Flinders Street, Melbourne!

The *Sun* and its sister afternoon broadsheet, *The Herald*, were the most influential newspapers in Victoria with astonishing circulations—the highest in Australia by a huge margin and sometimes even outselling comparable titles on Fleet Street.

The *Sun* was the newspaper I'd read aloud from at the kitchen table to improve my diction. As a kid I was a member of the paper's Corinella Sunbeamer club and entered its colouring competitions. Like generations of Victorian children, I earned a 'Herald Learn-to-Swim' certificate after completing twenty-five yards freestyle. An avid follower of Aussie Rules footy, and a dedicated supporter of the Geelong Cats, my father was never without a copy of the *Sun-News Pictorial*. Its sports pages were an encyclopedia on everything Aussie Rules and a bible for its followers.

It's almost impossible to describe the atmosphere in that newsroom, especially to younger readers who have never spent time in an office being constantly shouted and sworn at through a heavy fog of cigarette smoke. It was everything you've seen in old black-and-white movies—even down to the wild-eyed maniac racing the length of the chequerboard black-and-white linoleum floor tiles, waving a notebook and yelling: 'HOLD THE FRONT PAGE!'

The *Herald and Weekly Times* (*HWT*) building thrummed and our desks vibrated as the presses rolled day and night in the bowels of the building, with two daily papers operating from the same editorial floor. Four editions each. The first *Herald* subeditors would arrive at 6 a.m., mere hours after the stragglers from the *Sun*'s subs desk had packed it in.

Modern newspaper offices purr quietly as copy is sent back and forth by computer. Queries and replies are delivered with a soothing email 'swoosh'. Earnest conversations are held in low tones. But this was like the racket in a fish market. The *CLACK* and *DING* of pummelled typewriters. Cries of: 'COPY!' The persistent chatter of Telex machines. Heavy telephone books hurled at phones that rang shrilly on unattended desks . . . *THUMP* . . . *CRASH!* Reporters yelling above the din. Editors yelling even more loudly to get their attention.

I was in my element. Could not have loved it more.

I snagged a desk, a typewriter and a pile of blank squares of copy and carbon paper. From this vantage point, I surveyed the length of the newsroom. In front of me, the hive of *Herald* reporters was already buzzing by the time my 10 a.m. shift started. We *Sun* reporters were in the middle, with our Chief of Staff and his assistants sitting to my left behind a low, wooden, swing-door partition. Behind them was the maze of features staff and subs desks.

It was an adventure to navigate the labyrinthine layout and locate where the copy tasters, picture editors and photographic and sports departments were to be found. Then there were the offices of the star columnists, cartoonists, more specialist editors and the 'stringers' seconded from assorted news organisations. A long, carpeted corridor, the hushed surrounds of 'Mahogany Row', was where the executives were ensconced. I often visited the TV room; a cubicle where the copyboys and girls hid, trying to catch a moment's peace.

In Bruce Guthrie's excellent book *Man Bites Murdoch* (essential reading for anyone interested in Australian media machinations), he writes that in those days the *HWT* 'had a diverse share register and no real majority shareholder. In that sense, it was truly independent.' (The papers were merged to become the *Herald Sun* in 1990, three years after the acquisition of the *HWT* by Rupert Murdoch's News Corp.)

*

Every day I pitched story ideas to our Chief of Staff (COS), Don Baker. Tall, bearded, nattily dressed and with glasses perched on the end of his nose in an owlish manner, Don possessed a dry wit and an almost supernatural calm in the eye of a storm. He was endlessly patient with my pestering him for more space and by-lines.

I regard him as one of the most important mentors of my professional life. He rarely said, 'No,' but instead: 'You may have something here, Wendy. Come back when you've done some more digging.' An irresistible invitation.

Don says: 'I had so much help from chiefs of staff and editors in my early years in country papers that I just wanted to show my thanks by doing whatever I could to help others newer at the game than me.' He loved newspapers, and his passion was infectious.

After the *Addy*, I found the *Sun* to be surprisingly egalitarian. Not what you'd call 'diverse'—a concept no one had heard of back then—but women made up almost half of the reporting staff. Every year eight cadets were hired and Don recalls it was an 'unwritten rule' that four would be female. If you worked hard, you were given more responsibility and rose through the ranks.

I started on the general round with other junior reporters as a metropolitan 'D Grade'. Don had a list of stories to assign, and from day to day I never knew where I'd end up—on the deck of visiting naval ships; at tedious charity luncheons dining on rubber chicken; writing up school concerts; summarising keynote addresses from myriad 'experts' at conferences; covering protest marches and almost being trodden on by police on

horseback; or, alarmingly, heading to bushfires wearing my ridiculous high heels.

Sometimes I was sent to interview visiting major celebrities, with no research at all. None. That's why I remember the
withering looks I got from Peter Allen and Joan Collins, as if a
cockroach had just scuttled over the vanity units in their penthouse suites.

Recently, I cheekily asked Don what he remembered of
me as a reporter, and he kindly replied: 'The mention of your
name brings up a raft of memories. I'm thinking particularly
of one year when you were rostered on duty Christmas Day.
I was COS and there were a couple of other junior reporters on
board, and I vividly remember telling the picture editor Peter
"Torchy" Howell (and possibly you as well) that I didn't care
what happened that day—with you on deck we could handle
anything tossed at us!

'We knew you could ferret out a yarn and tell it. How we
loved coming across a reporter with your skills.'

Hello and thank you, *Geelong Advertiser*!

I often rang Dad to show off that I was on first-name terms
with his favourite columnists—the always-entertaining Keith
Dunstan and Aussie Rules legend Lou 'Louie the Lip' Richards.
I knew he was impressed, but he was never one for being impressed, so like many fathers of his generation he quickly changed
the subject. 'How's that car of yours going?'

(He was less impressed when, in 1992, I was awarded the
Douglas Wilkie Medal as the person who'd 'done the least for
football in the best and fairest manner'. A much-loved columnist

who took aim at Melbourne's obsession with footy, Wilkie established the Anti-Football League. His 'AFL medal' had been won by Harold Holt, Raelene Boyle, Barry Humphries and his mate Sir Les Patterson. The award ceremony included the ritual destruction of a football, and the year I won it I had the pleasure of putting a Sherrin through a wine press in the middle of the MCG.)

Sitting across from my desk were Paulie Stewart and Mark Trevorrow—two names you'll recognise from Australian entertainment. Paulie, sweet and mild-mannered, became the wild front man for the rock band Painters and Dockers, known for singles such as 'Die Yuppie Die', 'Nude School' and 'You're Going Home in the Back of a Divi Van'. Paulie was later awarded an OAM as a tireless advocate for the people of Timor-Leste and co-founder of the ska/reggae band Dili Allstars.

Mark is known now for his alter ego, the outrageous gay icon Bob Downe, and today is more flamboyant and sparkly and funnier than ever. Then—as the writer of the music column—Mark styled himself as 'Lord Rap' and nicknamed me 'Scoop'. He had tickets to every gig in town and was generous with them. Likewise, his stash of 'wait and return' cab chits. Leaving taxis to wait for *six hours* while he went to a gig may be the reason they eventually became rare as hen's teeth. He reckons the *HWT* bill for taxi dockets topped a million dollars one year he was there.

When Don Baker pointed out to Mark that he'd called in 'sick' for seventeen Mondays in a row, Mark replied, 'Well, I like to go out on Sunday nights.' In those days it was the only night

Melbourne's dance clubs hosted exclusively gay events. 'I wasn't about to give them up,' he says, indignant to this day. 'Don was gobsmacked.'

Sent to the sports department subs desk as 'punishment', Mark's fast, accurate editing and outrageous wit soon made him a favourite. He stayed there for a year before he gave in to the insistent seduction of showbiz. Journalism's loss. The glitter and polyester industry's gain.

It was a happy circumstance that saw the three of us together, gossiping and laughing uproariously, while we banged out copy on our battered typewriters with no inkling we'd all end up on stage.

*

Like most reporters, I served my time on the subs desk. The then editor, Rod Donnelly, remembers me as a feisty young feminist who objected loudly to the use of 'Mrs' and 'Miss' instead of 'Ms'. 'You kept us all on our toes in those days,' he told me recently at a reunion of old staffers. (I hear this comment as: 'Wendy. You were a total pain in the neck.')

Those were the days of hot metal composition by linotype operators. The fascinating documentary *Farewell, Etaoin Shrdlu* captures the last day the century-old technology was used at *The New York Times* in 1978. It lasted at the *HWT* until 1983.

In one realm, editors in shirtsleeves used rulers and lead pencils to mark up slips of copy paper in a state of quiet industry. A floor above, hot metal slugs were racked up and hammered into place by men in grey dustcoats and boiler suits working in sweltering conditions. They commanded giant machines, so deafening that sign language was often the best way to communicate. Both departments worked in concert, racing against the clock to deliver to the presses so the printed papers could be loaded on time onto trucks, trains and planes for distribution.

As a young woman on the subs desk, being sent into the domain of the compositors—to 'the stone' to sign off pages before they went to the presses—was nerve-racking. It was confronting to insist on making changes to pages with grimy men operating linotype machines that used vats of molten lead heated to 535 degrees Fahrenheit to set the type.

The first country edition went 'off-stone' (to bed) at 10.30 p.m., then the three 'metros' at 1 a.m., 2 a.m. and the 'final' at 4 a.m. To pass the time between editions I'd bring out my knitting, which raised eyebrows on the all-male desk. I'd clack away like a modern-day Madame Defarge.

As the night wore on, there were games of corridor cricket—using rolled newspapers as bats and scrunched pages as balls—singalongs started in earnest and the beer fridge steadily emptied. The *Sun* Subs Club was infamous for intoxicated, outrageous behaviour and I joined in happily. There were weekly awards handed out for the most excessive, intemperate acts, culminating in the awarding of the annual 'Roscoe'—Roscoe being a tatty, stuffed galah on a perch that my drinking mate Peter Klages—a down-table sub from Brisbane—had found in an op shop. He'd fetch the bird from a cupboard every night to oversee the raucous gathering as we sang and drank the joint dry.

One 'Roscoe' was awarded to a journo who, the worse for wear, had fallen asleep on the giant rolls of paper in the loading dock and narrowly missed being put through the printing press . . . or so the story goes.

Like every workplace where the inmates work long, unsociable hours, we developed a gallows humour—none more so than the denizens of police rounds. Peter corroborates a yarn that became folklore. Every year the journos from the round would run a sweep on the final tally of the Victorian road toll. This particular year, it was won by a journo from *The Age*. He left the celebratory piss-up and was promptly hit by a car. Legend! (Only his pride was injured.)

I had a brief moment on police rounds but, after an all-night drinking session at a St Kilda nightclub, found myself driving a couple of detectives back to Russell Street headquarters across the Punt Road Bridge during morning peak-hour traffic, squinting into the sunlight.

Too hardcore for me!

*

My first 'proper' round was on transport, working initially with senior reporters Barry Donovan and Ben Ainsworth until it became my own. Cuttings I have from that time report the opening of the West Gate Bridge and the era of TAA, Ansett and Bizjet. PETROL MAY HIT $1 A GALLON, reads a headline from 1979. 'It will take the price of a litre of petrol to 22.78c a litre, or $1.03 a gallon'!

Next stop was the Melbourne Town Hall round, or 'Clown Hall' as it was dubbed by a succession of reporters who'd worked there. It was complete luck that I arrived around the same time as new Lord Mayor Irvin Rockman. Handsome, charismatic and dynamic, he was a gift to a young reporter. 'Brash new-money, young Toorak millionaire, high-flying businessman, luxury hotelier, three-times-married, father-of-six, renowned under-water diver and celebrated photographer' is how Irvin Rockman CBE was remembered after his death from cancer in 2010 at the age of seventy-two.

Those of us who worked the Town Hall round in his tenure—among them, Bruce Guthrie from the *Herald* and Janne Apelgren from *The Age* (who later married and have managed to stay that way for almost forty years now)—would tap on his door to find him with his feet up on the mayoral desk and operatic arias blaring. He was always forthcoming with a colourful quote.

In between wives at the time, Irvin ('Please don't call me Lord Mayor') often gave us the run of the vacant office customarily occupied by the Lady Mayoress. Here we could write or change our clothes. Luxury compared to the cramped reporters' room which, Bruce recalls, 'was the size of a bathroom and we could hear each other breathing. Hopeless if you were working on an "exclusive".'

Soon Clown Hall would put my by-line on the front page for weeks in the infamous stoush over the 'Yellow Peril' sculpture in Melbourne's new City Square.

*

You'll note the word 'pictorial' in the title *Sun News-Pictorial*, and I worked with expert photographers. The use of their compelling images made our paper stand out from other grey offerings on newsstands. There was no better assignment than accompanying a 'snapper' on a job and supplying a few paragraphs to go with a middle-page spread of their fabulous images. A record wheat harvest in Victoria's north-western Mallee district demanded the full editorial treatment and I was up for the gig, but there was no precedent for a young woman reporter to be sent overnight with a young male photographer. After much consternation and fretting from management, we set out from Melbourne in the company's trusty Datsun Bluebird.

Of course, we got up to no good! At the end of one day, driving through newly harvested wheatfields, we noticed smoke rising from the back of our car. Jumping out, we saw stubble had bunched around the exhaust and caught fire. No problem. We opened the boot, grabbed the cans of beer we'd bought, shook them to make foamy fire extinguishers and extinguished the blaze.

That night, downing what was left of our beer in our crappy motel room, we reflected that we'd almost burned down Victoria's record wheat harvest. Mind you, if there *had* been a conflagration, we would have been there to record the whole event and return to the office as conquering heroes!

*

The Phoenix hotel (aka 'the branch office') was within staggering distance across the road; it has mythical status among journos of the era. I soon figured out that, if I didn't go to the pub, I'd miss out on the office intrigue. So I braved the rowdy upstairs bar and pushed my way in to stand toe-to-stiletto in the boys' club. Learned how to hold court with an outrageous anecdote with the best of them.

I'd witnessed young players and old stagers tumble down the Phoenix's steep stairs, roll out through the front door and fall *SPLAT!* onto Flinders Street and resolved to keep myself 'nice'. But one evening I phoned the night COS and slurred that I was too drunk to return to finish my story. I've forgotten the exact wording of the reply, but the gist was: 'Hooray! We were wondering when that would happen. Now you're one of us!'

The *HWT* employed an Anglican chaplain, who did the rounds of the office, stopping at every desk and asking after our welfare. Don Baker furnishes the name John Stockdale (aka 'Creeping Jesus'). We all attempted to appear 'fresh' and 'well adjusted' when the chaplain came by because there was a rumour that the *HWT* retained a flat in Frankston or a home in the country where drunks would be sent to 'dry out'.

Don reckons this was pure fiction, but that didn't stop the rumours of colleagues being sent on suspicious 'holidays'.

Like old dogs sent to a 'farm' and never seen again.

Aka 'on special assignment'.

*

For a while there I shared an old weatherboard cottage in the suburb of Brighton with two gun women journos from the ABC—Heather Ewart and Linda Fuller. Heather hailed from Murchison, on the banks of the Goulburn River, Linda from Burnie in Tassie and I from everywhere in between. We three country gals were making our way in the Big Smoke, all bright-eyed and bushy-tailed. Watching Heather and Linda's enduring, stellar careers in journalism, I reflect that there was something to be said for the 'country' mindset we had. Isolated from the bigger world, we were naive enough to think our talent could take us anywhere. I auditioned for a reporting role on ABC TV but was rejected. I suspected this was because of my facial scarring. I nursed that hurt for a long time. More than once I would be told 'a woman who looks like you won't ever be on television'.

With Heather reporting from state parliament, Linda producing for TV and me at the *Sun*, our haphazard shifts rarely saw us home at the same time. When we were, it was mostly bargaining for time in front of the bathroom mirror or scrounging in the fridge for something to eat . . . or, more accurately, drink. I don't recall anyone cooking anything as exotic as an actual edible 'meal'.

From there, in possession of a steady wage and a bank loan for a car, I rented a tiny two-bedroom terrace in North Fitzroy, the first place of my own. My brother Phil moved in and it was a great comfort for us to be together again. He remembers that house as 'party central' with 'you and your hard-drinking journo mates'.

He'd get the guitar out and I'd sing—Neil Young's 'After the Gold Rush' was one of our star turns. We scored a couple of gigs at weddings, but our efforts were dismal. Terrible. We gave up on being the next Donny and Marie Osmond.

(At the time, I'd also formed a spectacularly forgettable musical duo with star Melbourne newspaper columnist Lawrence Money playing guitar. Except, he didn't forget. Writing in the *Herald* in '89, when I was fronting *The Big Gig*, he recalled our pitiful outings: 'After three hours of unapplauded minstrelling the team limped off into the night. Divided the modest spoils: $15 apiece for the night. Back then she was a mere newspaper hackette with vague ambitions towards the stage. The last time she did a night at the Hobart Casino, she charged $5000.')

After a few false starts, Phil was working in retail and sales, and had found his niche. He was on the first bend of a winding road that would eventually lead to the echelons of international IT company management, taking him to New York City, where he's lived with his wife and two daughters for the past seventeen years.

My path at the *Sun* seemed to be more clearly laid out—if I was talented and determined enough to take it. I'd been at Town Hall, done a stint on state rounds in Spring Street . . . next, surely, was a seat in the Canberra press gallery. From there, hopefully, to a posting overseas.

Perhaps I'd follow in the very large footsteps of Bruce Wilson, the legendary foreign correspondent. He'd become a friend, and I sat for hours, enthralled with his tales of working in Vietnam, Singapore, El Salvador and the United States. He was a brave, intrepid journalist and wrote like a dream.

If you'd told me then that in a few years time, I'd chuck it all to be a stand-up comedian?

Not a chance.

I'd never been to a live comedy or cabaret venue.

Never seen an Australian woman attempt any such thing as 'stand-up'.

What an absurd idea!

*

When the *Sun*'s features editor, Beryl Town, sent me to an 'alternative comedy' night to observe and report back, I was late to the party. Very late.

In the 1970s our appetite for home-grown sketch comedy on television had been well-served with *The Naked Vicar Show, The Aunty Jack Show* and its spin-off *The Norman Gunston Show. The Paul Hogan Show* was still on air in the early eighties. What was next? There were comedy spots on *The Mike Walsh Show* or *Hey Hey It's Saturday*—but they were mostly for beloved old-timers or talent quest hopefuls. Playing the banjo, acrobatics or juggling were a plus. There were few opportunities for new comedic voices to enter the mainstream, especially for those with even the mildest of satirical takes.

Meanwhile, in the Melbourne enclave of Fitzroy, Collingwood and Carlton, the live comedy/cabaret scene was in very rude health. Punters were travelling from the outer 'burbs on Friday and Saturday nights to visit Foibles, the Last Laugh, the Comedy Cafe and the Flying Trapeze to watch magic, circus, music and comedy acts reimagined in this 'new wave' of cabaret.

A few seemingly random events conspired to create this cultural revolution and the impetus for the development of our unique Australian comedy voice. The most important was the advent of free university. Rod Quantock, a pioneer in the days of Melbourne University's *Archi Revue* (staged by students in the architecture faculty), remembers his peers as the first generation with working-class parents who could attend tertiary education. They were bold and had plenty to say.

'There were all these people who—a generation earlier—would never have got into uni or thought about it,' he said. 'They chose architecture because it was the only creative subject.'

Former TV talk show host, comedy producer and performer Steve Vizard appeared in a few *Archi Revues* before striking out with an equally popular offering from the law faculty. He remembers those times as being an 'incredible melting pot of viewpoints'. There were working-class kids from Reservoir and Preston; upper-class kids from South Yarra and Toorak. Middle-class kids from anywhere and everywhere, who'd been to both private and public schools: 'Because there were no fees, and no narrow focus on a future vocation, students chose any old course—law, arts, medicine. It didn't matter. If there had been a degree in polar exploration, they probably would have signed up for that too.'

It was allegedly two or three years of 'study' but was actually about social experimentation with sexuality, relationships, politics . . . and drugs. Compulsory student union fees underwrote their creative endeavours.

Many male students had come from single-sex schools.

'I remember one bloke who always wrote these set-ups where he would be, literally, on stage, in bed with a female, just so he could crack onto the women,' Steve recalls.

There were also lots of skits designed purely to shock middle-class parents with 'half-baked' political views, partial nudity and lots of swearing.

Cheap rents—in what had once been factory workers' inner-city dormitory suburbs—helped too. These are expensive, sought-after postcodes now, but back then they housed immigrant families and broke students.

Carlton's Pram Factory (a theatre venue in a repurposed perambulator factory) was home to the Australian Performing Group (APG), fostering left-wing theatre. A cohort of feminist women, including Helen Garner, Sue Ingleton and Evelyn Krape, experimented with productions that went for the jugular . . . and the laughs.

The night my life was upended, I was at a Melbourne University venue, sitting up the front with my trusty notebook. On stage, from memory: Steve Vizard (aka Buddy Chuck), sending up old-fashioned cabaret crooners, with Paul Grabowsky on piano; the lunatic antics of David Argue on rollerskates miming the Peter Allen hit 'I Go To Rio' on a foam piano; Gina Riley in an all-girl trio singing wonderful, silly ditties; the surreal 'anti-tainment' slapstick stylings of the dinner-suited duo Los Trios Ringbarkus; and the amiable Richard Stubbs standing up with a routine so acutely observed and relatable that the audience cried with laughter.

Over that hour or so I was transported. Just as when small children first go to the circus and, on leaving the magical realm of the Big Top in a starry daze, start practising juggling in their bedrooms. I returned to the office, wrote my article and later informed my colleagues that I intended to give up journalism for a crack at comedy.

No one believed me.

It was so improbable I hardly believed it myself.

I had no idea how I'd do it; just knew it was where I wanted to be. In that place where you laughed so much your sides hurt, and nothing else mattered.

I'm told there was talk in the newsroom of some kind of 'group intervention' to stop me from making the biggest mistake of my life.

10

Faking it

Bedroom mirror
Scotchmer Street
North Fitzroy

Aaaargh!

What are you going to wear?

The suede jacket with the fringes? Cowboy boots? Kinda swamp rockabilly.

Something leather with studs? Vaguely punk-ish.

Sixties polka-dot miniskirt with ripped fishnets and suspenders? Ironic.

Definitely no Jane Fonda pastel lycra or Princess Di puffy sleeves. No, like, Valley Girl denim and leg warmers! Yikes!

C'mon, you know the rule: *Whatever you wear, look like you mean it.*

Anyway, there's no point. Helen just walked in. That girl could look good if she was wearing a see-through string-bag top and camo shorts.

Oh, that's right. She already did.

*

My sister, Helen, is drop-dead gorgeous.

Once, on a trip together to Paris, a group of men called after her: 'Sophia! Sophia!' She'd drawn attention as a young Sophia Loren look-alike. When we ate at Melbourne restaurants she was plagued by suggestive notes and bottles of champagne delivered by waiters from adoring men at adjoining tables.

With her mane of dark wild hair, her big hazel eyes, her wide dazzling smile and athletic, toned body, she was the antithesis of the permed, blonde eighties 'dolly bird'. An exotic, sexy creature. When men encountered her quick wit and outrageously loud laugh, she sent them over the edge without even trying.

Dad was teaching at Lucknow Primary School No. 1231 near Bairnsdale and Helen was the last to be living under the same roof as Alison when I implored her to come live with me. She moved first into Phil's bedroom, after he left the old terrace house in North Fitzroy, then to more salubrious digs around the corner with my boyfriend, Stephen Mepham, an aspiring filmmaker I'd met at an arty event called Collabaret. Steve had a certain stylish swagger and an arch, funny take on life that I found irresistible. At the time he managed the Flying Trapeze, and, after a day working at the *Sun*, that's where I was most nights, taking in mad shows staged by an inspired bunch of lunatics. Then we'd hit the nightclubs.

Figuring out what to wear was no small problem. There I'd be in front of the mirror, endlessly primping and fluffing. Helen would walk up behind me and say, 'You look great, Wen.' I'd chuck in the make-up brush. There really was no point. She was effortlessly stunning.

In 1981 Helen Brown was Australian *Penthouse*'s 'Pet of the Month' and later became its 'Pet of the Year'.

I supported anything my sister did and this was no different. I was more concerned that the bastards at *Penthouse* hadn't coughed up all the prizes she was promised. But she did get a snazzy gold Lancia sports car with personalised number plates: PET 81. A notorious leadfoot, Helen was once stopped for speeding by a motorcycle cop. She opened the boot full of magazines, personally signed copies of her centrefold and was cheerily sent on her way. That girl could talk her way out of, and into, anything.

As for what our father thought? 'People said to me, "What did you think of your daughter appearing in *Penthouse*?" And my answer was: "Well, if I had a Best In Show in the Melbourne show, I'd be rapt. But I'm more rapt that she's my daughter. Best in the country!"'

So, better than one of his pedigree whippets—a fine accolade!

He was more disappointed that Helen hadn't pursued an athletic career.

'She was a great athlete. She'd only ever been beaten once in flat running. She was a good hurdler. She entered the long jump and she broke the open record by three feet! And then she did three "no jumps" on purpose, so she wouldn't have to do it anymore.'

One day Helen came to visit me at the *Sun* in a see-through top that almost caused a riot on the editorial floor. I bundled her out the door as fast as I possibly could, remembering the days back in Warncoort when she used to toddle into the schoolroom in the nude in front of the grade six boys.

She was a 'door bitch' at Melbourne's Inflation nightclub and was known for her daring, barely-there outfits and flirty banter. I once saw her walk out the door in a get-up fashioned out of leather belts and not much else. When she worked the door on comedy clubs I performed at, I was often asked: 'Is she *really* your sister?' All the boys were in love with Helen.

In that *Australian Story* of 2005, Helen said: 'People say, "Look, Wendy's the clever one and her sister is the beautiful one." I'd say to Wendy: "Oh, God, I wish you weren't so damn clever," and she'd say: "I wish you weren't so gorgeous," and we'd just go, "Grrr".'

*

The same year the *Vault* sculpture (aka the Yellow Peril) was unceremoniously banished from Melbourne's City Square, I wrote a feature article for the *Sun* on 'the group of clever comics in Hieronymus Bosch', who were staging a show in the Banana Lounge, a tiny upstairs performance space in the Comedy Cafe shopfront in Brunswick Street, Fitzroy. Their sketch show,

Carnival Knowledge, featured Ian McFadyen, Peter Moon, Mary-Anne Fahey and the enigmatic Eddie Zandberg.

'If you think the Oedipus complex is a Greek shopping centre, this show isn't for you,' I wrote, quoting Ian's clever one-liner. 'A roller-coaster ride of sexuality in the '80s, the show is full-frontal, fast-paced and packed with incisive observations and wit.'

The show sent up the hardliners in the radical separatist feminist movement with portrayals of 'male libbers' in 'consciousness-raising' groups: 'I know I used to be sexist, but now I find I can only become interested in women I'm not attracted to . . . the ones with nice personalities,' Peter Moon quipped.

It was a backlash against the extremes of the feminist old guard, which was challenging gender stereotypes: 'pink' for girls and 'blue' for boys; 'sexual objectification' and the 'male gaze'. This was an overdue conversation, for sure, but was leaving behind many young women, disillusioned when they were scolded for wearing lipstick and high heels by the uncompromising brigade in their overalls and sensible footwear. It was all fodder for edgy comedy. If you dared.

Mary-Anne strutted the stage as Madam Lash, the 'loin tamer', taking a whip to wimpy men who felt emasculated and confused about gender roles. Pregnant, and becoming visibly more so by the day, it was just plain weird for Mary-Anne to be up there dissecting pathetic pick-up lines when, by the looks of it, she'd picked up someone eight months earlier.

She bowed out. There were auditions. I put my name down.

'You were super-enthusiastic,' writer and director Ian McFadyen recalls. 'You could sing. And we figured it couldn't hurt to have someone in the show with such good media connections.' Ouch! He quickly adds: 'You knew your pop culture and were ready to stop reporting on it and make fun of it instead. We also knew you'd take no shit from anyone.'

I wasn't quite as brave as Ian remembers, but I believed in myself enough to give it a red-hot go.

I got the gig.

*

It was time to leave the *Sun*, but I didn't give up journalism. I took a job with the independent, free community newspaper the *Melbourne Times*, working out of a terrace in Carlton. We were a few part-time journos and a couple of subeditors. I grabbed the local government and urban planning beat, and loved nothing better than scooping the metro papers with the odd yarn. I also moonlighted, contributing to *The National Times*, a Fairfax weekly newspaper.

My purview also included writing theatre reviews and I was shit at it. If the performers or the scripts were awful, I instead complimented the set design, or even the lighting. By now I was socialising with all the performers backstage or in bars and cafes, and couldn't have looked them in the eye if I'd written something scathing.

Even my carefully worded sympathetic reviews didn't always meet with a warm reception. One night I arrived at the Last

Laugh theatre restaurant to review a show and was kicked out by the co-owner, comedy impresario John Pinder: 'HARMER! You're not welcome here! LEAVE!' he bellowed in front of a crowd at the box office. Cringe.

He was renowned for his hatred of critics and relished telling the story of how he'd once sent *The Age* cabaret and comedy critic Peter Weiniger a bucket full of cow shit. *Real* cow shit, he emphasised. When Weiniger got back to his desk he was greeted by a swarm of flies, said John.

One thing, above all, strikes me about this story . . . It's that *The Age* had a critic dedicated to comedy and cabaret. A rarity. Too often it's left to whichever journo scores a free ticket and rocks up. At festival time, when there are hundreds of shows to catch, you're just as likely to find your review has been penned by the motoring writer.

My favourite 'review' ever was of a Melbourne stand-up comedian: 'The trouble is that he makes things seem funnier than they really are.'

Er . . . isn't that the job description of a comic?

*

In *Carnival Knowledge,* I took over the roles played by Mary-Anne and invented a character of my own. The cranky cleaning lady and kitchen hand Val Cronk channelled the attitudes of the no-nonsense country women I'd grown up with. She berated the inner-city trendies for the range of bread and milk on offer in the shops: 'High-fibre, low-fat, extra-dollop, full-protein? When I was a kid, we had Tip Top white bread. Milk was milk. We ate Arnott's Tic Toc bikkies—and we didn't get to choose what time it was!'

Gawd! Can you see Val now, catering for vegans? It doesn't bear thinking about.

Stepping out as Val in a blue apron, headscarf and wielding an accusatory Chux, I had a rudimentary script, but I liked to pick up what was happening in the audience for ad-lib fun. (She was a character I played for years. As a regular on Ray Martin's *The Midday Show* in the 1990s, I recall scrubbing away at Johnny Depp's arm, trying to erase his 'Winona Forever' tattoo. Often *The Midday Show* audience was made up of uncomprehending elderly folk bussed in from local aged-care facilities in North Sydney to make up the numbers. When you were tanking, live on air, nationally, no one laughed harder than Ray. He knew the whole set-up was beyond ridiculous. After the show he'd laugh some more . . . then we'd both laugh at the absurdity of it all. He was always my great supporter and I've always admired him. I should have a tattoo that reads 'Ray Forever'.)

After *Carnival Knowledge* wrapped, there were new avenues to explore.

An all-woman sketch show seemed the logical step.

*

I was instantly drawn to Mary-Anne Fahey, with her softly spoken demeanour and cherubic face. Her unruly, curly brown hair was half caught up in a floral scrunchie; men's braces held up skinny jeans ending in ankle boots.

You'll remember her as schoolgirl Kylie Mole, one of Australia's most celebrated comic characters. Everyone from that era can chant the catchphrase: 'She goes, she goes . . . she just goes . . .' from the wildly successful show *The Comedy Company*. 'So excellent.'

I would soon learn that sweet Mary-Anne was an eccentric lateral thinker and scriptwriter. She was also a talented ventriloquist. I was a good foil for her off-the-wall nuttiness. With her then partner, Ian McFadyen, we collaborated to present *Faking It*. Some of the sketches had already been tested in front of a live audience at the Catch a Rising Star venue in Richmond on Catch Tuesday, a night hosted by Ian for comics trying new material. In various iterations, *Faking It* would run and run in live comedy venues, finishing up at the Edinburgh Festival in 1988, when I teamed up with Magda Szubanski and Gina Riley.

The poster for the very first *Faking It* at the Banana Lounge in 1983 pictured a Glomesh handbag spilling its contents—a condom, a contraceptive pill packet, lipstick, a cigarette butt and a jar of Vaseline. Peeking out are Polaroids of the cast: me, Mary-Anne, Jane Turner, Jo Campbell and the 'token male' in the show, Rob Meadows.

Mary-Anne's program bio reads: 'She's 27 and a product of the Flinders University drama department. Most memorable stage experience: being chased off Monash University campus by angry lesbians intent on murder.'

Jane: 'At 22 already a veteran of five fabulous shows at St. Martin's Theatre. Watch for her coming up on "Prisoner" as a blind ex-prostitute.'

Jo and Rob, both seasoned cabaret performers, joined us from the Rusden drama department at Victoria College. Rob was our musical arranger and, as pianist in residence at the Comedy Cafe, performed regularly on the bigger downstairs stage with the cast of *Australia You're Standing In It*.

Rod Quantock, Mary Kenneally, Steve Blackburn, Geoff Brooks and Sue Ingleton had broken the ABC TV's Aussie sketch comedy drought. You couldn't go anywhere without hearing someone impersonating those iconic characters, the Dodgy Brothers, or Tim and Debbie, whose 'Brain Space' skit took aim at the pretensions of the earnest, boiler-suited 'left'—'*Amaaazing*' (complete with air quotes).

Faking It was a family enterprise. Ian directed, wrote all our songs, some of the scripts, and edited the rest. Mary-Anne brought their baby, James, along in his stroller to rehearsals. My boyfriend, Steve, did the set design and lighting. Brother Phil recorded everything on his Sony Beta camera. Sister Helen was dating the venue's mercurial chef, Roscoe.

We jammed everything into that show. It ran for two hours!

Looking at Phil's grainy recording now, I give full marks to the sixty or so punters crammed into the room who stayed the course for what were often patchy sketches. Some of the jokes were real 'groaners'. A savage cut would have helped in places. But the performances are surprisingly good and the musical numbers all excellent, featuring some fabulous four-part harmony work. Top marks for sheer chutzpah. And how we managed all the costume changes in those tiny nooks either side of the tiny stage is a mystery.

Our satirical targets were a roll call of eighties pop culture, fashion and fads. I did a pre-show turn as Val, and then the four of us, wearing Lycra, hit out with a song and a skit sending up Jane Fonda's workout videos, which had sold 17 million copies the year before. Jane was unmissable as a bitchy, chain-smoking, radio talkback host on the *Morning Coffee Crisis Show*, dispensing callous advice. Jo was a cynical women's magazine editor inventing new diets for gullible readers. I was an obnoxious Fitzroy copper on the subject of deaths in custody, 'Good evening male and female Caucasians . . .'

In capes and tights as Super Girl, Wonder Woman, Batgirl and The Bionic Woman we dished the dirt on the male superheroes we were dating and sang: 'What good is being superwomen when . . . there are no supermen?'

Mary-Anne appeared with 'Cheryl', her life-sized ventriloquist doll, ogling the blokes at a nightclub in an X-rated conversation about 'sucking off' and 'swallowing', including an extraordinary display of her acrobatic tongue. The routine ended with the incendiary line, 'God that shits me! Why do men always have to view women sexually?'

We finished with our theme tune: 'We'll keep fakin' it . . . and if you keep takin' it . . . we'll keep fakin' it until somethin' else comes along.'

Phew!

*

We garnered a lot of attention and column inches for that first show. We were doing something fresh and funny, *but were we feminists*? It was the question that preoccupied the mind of every journalist who wrote about us. Apparently it was all very puzzling.

In a lengthy article in *The Age*, Karen Cooke (aka Kaz Cooke, the soon-to be-famous cartoonist and prolific author) wrote that the local radical feminists were warning people not to come and see us because we were 'anti-women'. Baffling, because at the same time we were dealing with men in the audience shouting: 'Show us ya tits!'

Kaz identified the 'strange expectations' of an all-women production: 'Some people think it's serious consciousness raising and others expect a strip show.' She added, 'The women in *Faking It* do not fit the stereotype of women in comedy: they are nobody's foils. They swear, they are funny in their own right.'

A review in my own paper, the *Melbourne Times*, was complimentary: '. . . simply good comedy free of ideological tightropes, four comedians who happen to be comediennes, having a go at what they know best—the collusion of women with men in their own suppression. If you're a feminist seeking a pound of retributive flesh, however, I suggest you stay away.'

We were consistently sold out and the show ran for months. It was huge fun to perform, especially when our aim—to break new ground—had been acknowledged. It sure *felt like* we were doing feminism.

Of course, the Last Laugh owner, John Pinder, couldn't help coming to see what the fuss was about, and afterwards declared in his booming voice to anyone within earshot: 'Harmer will *never* make it as a comedian! SHE JUST DOESN'T HAVE WHAT IT TAKES!' So happened that my sister Helen was standing next to him; she gave him a blistering bollocking and kicked him out.

Last laugh, anyone? It wasn't long before Mary-Anne and I were together on stage at Le Joke, the intimate room above the Last Laugh, in *Faking It 2* and packing the crowds in there too. It was a three-ring circus. We had to deal with both drunken bucks' and hens' nights, and the occasional very sober brigade, who'd dropped by after an evening of serious-minded feminist works at the nearby Universal Theatre for a drink or two.

It was always going to be dangerous working with Mary-Anne, who loved to push the boundaries and found in me a willing accomplice. She introduced Rob Meadows, on sound, with: 'Sorry for having a man in the show, but he's the only one who could operate the tape deck.'

It got worse. As Val, I approached one table of sour women, who'd been giving us a hard time. I whispered: 'C'mon, girls, there's a table of blokes over there. You could get boyfriends; you're not *that* unattractive.'

This time there were two of us chased offstage, down the back stairs and into the staff car park by angry hardliners in Doc Martens boots.

It was infuriating to be always judged on our 'feminist' credentials when the same forensic lens was never applied to our male colleagues. We had to repeatedly deny we were 'anti-men'.

We graduated to the main stage at the Laugh in *Faking It 2½*.

In our new show, the consistent theme seemed to be that we didn't have one. If you didn't like that bit, you might like the next. Mary-Anne playing Nancy Reagan and me as Raisa Gorbacheva, commenting on the Strategic Arms Limitation Talks, sat alongside a satirical take on the TV soap opera *Dynasty*. Again, Ian directed, script-edited and composed our songs, accompanied on piano by new team member Kristin Keam.

Mary-Anne wrote the sketch we became most famous for— a classic role-reversal with us in overalls at lunch on a building site sizing up the men passing by. 'Phwoaaar! Look at you in your sexy suit and tie, swingin' your little briefcase, walkin' in the street in broad daylight. Whaddya expect? You're *askin'* for it!'

I told a journalist from the *Sun*: 'It's really gone past the point where we want to preach to any particular group. We just kick heads all round, and that way you can't lose.'

'While Harmer and Fahey are feminists, they are not chronically so, and as a result their humour makes a point without alienating most of the audience', wrote a male reviewer in *The Age*. Good thing, too. Only one thing worse than a chronic feminist on stage and that's an incurable misogynist in the audience.

Right, *laydeez*?

A run-in with critic Peter Goers, writing for Adelaide's *The Advertiser*, made national—yes, *national*—headlines when Mary-Anne and I took a show there to the Fringe Festival of '86.

There was I, doing my usual Val routine with my trusty cleaning cloth, when I saw a bloke busily jotting in his notebook and realised he was there to review the night. Here was fun to be had!

After a bit of banter, I cheekily whipped off his specs, cleaned them with a bit of a spit and a polish, and popped them back on his head. Nothing I hadn't done a hundred times before.

I woke up to a scandal.

COMEDIENNE SPAT, BROKE MY GLASSES, CRITIC CLAIMS.

So ran a headline in *The Advertiser* that was picked up all across Australia. For effect, Mr Goers had posed for an accompanying photo with his glasses skew-whiff. She 'took my glasses off and bent them round. Spat in my face and wiped my eyes with her dirty rag,' he accused.

That was bad enough, but Goers' accompanying review was truly vile:

> Ms Harmer's woeful act consists mainly of tasteless racist jokes and the most tedious kind of dreary feminist subversion. This sort of ball-tearing, hateful penis envy comedy is sick unto death . . . It's just as well this obscene harpy lacks both microphone technique and comic timing so that a lot of the garbage she inflicts on the audience is lost.

For good measure, he called me a 'female Idi Amin' and ended with: 'I've been to funnier car accidents.'

Racism, obscenity and common assault—it was an arresting trifecta.

My comedy comrades were outraged on my behalf and began wearing handmade 'I Hate Peter Goers' badges. There was talk of a street protest too. 'Heavy stuff, Pete!' wrote my friend, the playwright Hannie Rayson, in the *Melbourne Times*. 'Such vitriol would appear to reveal more about the reviewer than the performer.' My mates at the paper also helpfully pointed out that, while I had been known for the odd 'chuck' at an office party, spitting on people was definitely not my style. Jeez. Thanks, guys!

Boyfriend Steve, who'd also been watching this unfold from Melbourne, arrived to keep me company in his home town and was furiously plotting ways to avenge my honour. Thankfully, my rescue came not long after with a letter to the editor in the pages of *The Advertiser*.

Sir—So your theatre 'critic' Mr Goers got his nose pushed out of joint (not to mention his glasses!). I was in that audience and sitting directly behind Mr Goers. I distinctly remember thinking to myself, once I realised he was a critic, how much he was enjoying the show, and I waited all week to read his critique, anticipating his favourable comments. How naïve can we be!

The next paragraph delivered the delicious coup de grâce:

I work for an optometrist. At the end of the show Mr Goer's face and the glasses thereon certainly did not look like the caricature that the photograph of him *The Advertiser* portrays. So far as I could see, no structural damage was done to his glasses only, obviously, to his ego—or is it just that it made a better story that way? After all, he did make page 2 of the Saturday paper, didn't he?

—Penny Baker, Glenelg

For the record, I have never met 'Penny from Glenelg', and I belatedly thank her for putting pen to paper.

Ticket sales went through the roof.

11

Swimming with sharks

Small wall mirror
Dingy backstage at Le Joke
Upstairs, Last Laugh
Smith Street, Collingwood

You don't have to do this for a living.

No one is forcing you to go out there.

You could turn around, walk down the back stairs and no one would ever know you'd been here.

So, you'd better love it. Enjoy yourself.

Or do something else.

You can stay in journalism. You can be anything you want.

This is the last thing you *need* to do.

But you *chose* to do it.

So . . . *prove* that you can do it.

Go get 'em!

*

For all the years I spent performing stand-up comedy, my mantra was: 'You don't have to do this for a living.'

I'd say it to myself, or say it aloud; but, after fiddling with my hair, adjusting my bra straps, peeping through the curtains to check out the crowd or to see whether the microphone had been left up or down, it was my very last thought before I stepped into the light.

As pre-performance self-talk goes, I admit it's banal. But better than throwing up in a sink, doing a last-minute nervous wee or curling up in the foetal position in a corner, muttering self-help mantras.

I've witnessed all these backstage 'preparations', but it's never been me. I'm not an anxious person. I just don't seem to be wired that way. Apart from the occasional panicky meltdown when things really go pear-shaped, an uncanny sense of calm washes over me. Time slows as I consider options to get me out of my predicament. If none immediately present, then a sense of fatalism kicks in—or even amusement at my puny human efforts to stop the inevitable. It's my way of preparing for the painful aftermath of failure.

I suspect that the way I go about things is partly 'nature'— the personality type I was born with—but it is also 'nurture', and comes from long years of learning to cope with uncertainty through my father's often painful lessons in 'self-regulation'.

This is not to say I don't have my fair share of self-doubt and sometimes give in to it; I can furnish you with a *very* long list of faults in my character and appearance. But mostly I'm able to name and tame any rising tide of fear and apprehension. After all, I've been practising since I was very young.

I've never believed in the so-called 'imposter syndrome'. I figure that every time we do something we've never done before, it's entirely natural to feel like we're faking it—until we understand what's expected of us and rise to the occasion . . . or, perhaps, fall short.

And if you're not recognising and admitting mistakes, working on doing things better, you're usually a man with a severe case of 'entitlement syndrome'. There's a plague of it in the male-dominated workplaces I've been in.

'Life is short, make every mistake possible' is one of my favourite maxims.

Working on it.

My modest mantra was a reflection of the fact that I'd grown up with little ambition to be on stage—apart from singing into my hairbrush and imagining starring in *Guys and Dolls* on Broadway. I'd taken a role in a student revue, sung a bit here and there, but hadn't attended a performing arts college, knew zilch about the theatre, and only stumbled by accident into the world of 'alternative' comedy at a later age than most of my stage pals.

Also, I'd spent my young life with little to no money, and I knew that wasn't any fun. So if this new thing failed? There was no way I would be starving in a garret, making sacrifices to the gods of arts and culture. Financial security was important.

The childhood experience of seeing our furniture being repossessed has never left me. All my life I've had nightmares in which the house is empty and the car gone; I wake up in a panic before I take inventory of the bedroom. Yes, I actually own the bed I sleep in. There's a kitchen with a fridge and television, and I own them too.

If comedy didn't pay the rent? That was the end of it. A momentary brain-lapse. A folly. Life would return to 'normal'. I didn't have to do it to earn a living.

So the question, I guess, is *why*? Why did I choose the bruising arena of live stand-up comedy?

Two motivations I can readily identify.

On the night I was sent to cover that comedy gig at Melbourne Uni, I was entranced by the sheer skill of the performers. But one aspect of what I'd seen had nagged at me. The men on stage were the ones doing the talking. Where was the women's perspective? The more I saw this at comedy gigs, the more it struck me as an injustice—and a huge opportunity going begging.

The male stand-up comics played the antics of their kids and pets, their schooldays and familiar, daily frustrations for laughs. They seemed to own the space. Why? Half the audience was female and surely they'd relate to hearing the same observations from a woman? Our lives were funny too.

To say that 'women aren't funny', as a march of male mis-ogynists have done over many years, denies us a fundamental part of our humanity. A pet budgie in a cage can make you laugh, the family dog, but not a woman?

I wasn't having it.

I could see how the jokes worked; I could write that stuff. I just needed to find a woman who could perform them. Turned out it would be me.

The other motivation was as plain as the very plain nose on my face. As long as I could remember, my cleft lip and palate had made me the object of unwanted attention. I'd been stared at for so long that I decided: 'Take a good look. Look as long as you like. I'll give you something to stare at!'

For my whole life I'd pushed myself to do the hardest thing I could think of to slay my inner demons. Stand-up comedy seemed the hardest of all. Especially for a chick.

I was in.

*

I can't remember exactly when I first gave stand-up a go, but I'd been watching the greats at Le Joke—among them, Richard Stubbs, Glenn Robbins, Shane Bourne and Pete Rowsthorn. They were in total command and reduced the place to helpless laughter. How could you not want to make people laugh? It was such a life-affirming, embracing, thing to do.

I was in awe; I took notes. I'd been having fun on stage at the Banana Lounge in sketch comedy, but more and more I felt that being 'in character' was limiting. There was so much more I wanted to say.

My then-boyfriend, Steve, remembers our endless discussions when I first decided to attempt stand-up. I'd never seen an Australian woman do it. How would *I* do it? What would I sound like? How much would I have to reveal about myself? What kind of persona would resonate with an audience? Where did the set-up and the punchline go? How long between each gag? How did you segue between one topic and another?

I became a student of the craft and bought the comedy albums of Joan Rivers, Steve Martin, George Carlin, Whoopie Goldberg and Woody Allen, and listened to them over and over. I drove Steve mad, but he never once tried to talk me out of it. He was always supportive. 'I thought you were being very brave,' he says.

The night I put my name down for a late-night try-out, I'd come up with a scrappy five-minute routine on school lunches. All familiar, 'relatable' stuff. Comedy staples back then. Sandwiches in rainbow waxed paper; pushing butter and Vegemite 'worms' through Vita-Weat biscuits; the proper way to consume a Chocolate Royal—by first smashing it on your forehead. I ended with a few observations about the daggy kids in hand-knitted jumpers who *went home* for lunch. They'd certainly looked like jokes . . . on paper.

Backstage, the staff and other acts were more nervous for me than I was for myself. They kept saying, 'Are you okay?' and, 'Don't worry if this first time is frightening,' as if I was preparing to jump out of a plane or go swimming with sharks. (Both good analogies, as I would later learn.) I could feel the anxiety ratcheting up. That's when my 'I don't have to do this for a living' mantra kicked in.

When I took to the stage, the familiar calm descended. I took a moment to look about and it hit me with a startling clarity. You mean, I have the microphone *all to myself*, I can say *anything I like* and people will *pay* to listen? Excellent!

I enjoyed being out there. It wasn't that much different to the nights I'd spent in bars telling yarns with my journo mates.

The first routine got a smattering of laughs. I was encouraged enough to stay with it. I rewrote what didn't work and added more gags until I had fifteen minutes that did work. The boys were endlessly kind and loved having me on the bill. With half the audience being women, they were aware that the female point of view in stand-up was sorely lacking.

I'd noticed that when the blokes were on stage the women sometimes looked to their boyfriends or husbands to check if something was funny. When I was on, it was the opposite. The men looked to their partners to check if they should laugh at the jokes about playing with dolls and going shopping with your mum.

The best compliment came from one of my fellow male performers: 'When you're on stage I hear something I've never heard before. The pitch of laughter changes from a low *ho-ho-ho* to a high *tee-hee-hee*.'

I developed a comeback to the constant refrain of: 'Show us ya tits!'

'You can always tell the bottle-fed boys. Never mind, sweetheart—you might get a girlfriend one day and she might show you hers.'

*

At Le Joke I'd found a kindred spirit in Richard Stubbs. By day he was a finance guy in sales at Conzinc Riotinto of Australia

(CRA) flogging—what else?—zinc. At night he was behind the bar downstairs, where it was expected that the staff would all dress 'zany, madcap'.

Worlds collided for him when his unsuspecting CRA office colleagues booked an end-of-financial-year knees-up at the Last Laugh and encountered Richard (imagine a big bloke, buff, six-one) in a tutu, leopard-print tights and tiger ears. Much explaining to do on Monday morning. Like me, he was running away to join the circus.

Richard made me laugh more than anyone had ever done before. His perfect timing, his inspired ad-libs, his uber-confident ownership of the stage and the audience—these were everything I aspired to. In turn, he watched my gigs and gave excellent advice I was most grateful for: 'That topic was great. Your set-up was too long. You could add some extra jokes there. Run with it.'

In the summer of '84, with me at a loose end after finishing *Faking It* and him winding up his stand-up run at Le Joke (*I'm Dreaming of a Beige Christmas*), we decided to collaborate on a new show.

We had six days to pull it together and it ended up being my ticket to fame and fortune.

The premise of the thing was as genius as it was obvious.

Sunburn Bloody Sunburn was for the hoi polloi stuck in the dreary, sweltering suburbs of inner-city Melbourne when the rest of town had escaped to the coast for the summer. This was your substitute cheap and nasty 'holiday', and you paid extra for cheap and nasty drinks at Le Joke.

Steve made us a poster, using the famous image of Marines erecting an American flag on Iwo Jima, only this time it was a striped beach umbrella.

Jane Turner and Mark Neal, a cheeky, ridiculously good-looking and talented stand-up, completed our foursome as we took on every tired cliché of the season—B-grade surf movies; hapless overseas tourists; absurd warnings on water safety and the road toll from my insufferable policewoman; Jane and Mark as two obnoxious FM radio hosts in their ludicrous 'fun bus', with Richard supplying frequent, increasingly gruesome and hilarious shark and cyclone warnings from the sound booth.

It was mayhem and, as they say, 'a hit'.

On the last night of the show, the queue stretched right down Smith Street, Collingwood. John Pinder reckoned that 1000 punters were turned away and immediately booked us for the bigger venue downstairs. (After our rocky start, John was to become one of my greatest promoters and closest friends. We lost him to cancer in 2015, aged just seventy. His influence on the Australian comedy/cabaret scene is immeasurable.)

As *Sunburn The Day After*, now at the Last Laugh, we played the show right through April, May and June, long after the last mozzie had vacated town. We added a few new bits and pieces. Bad pick-up lines in a bar were delivered in a shark costume. Mark was a confused Japanese tourist. Jane and I were Razor and Blade, two leather-wearing punks sweating it out at the Fitzroy pool. Richard and I were back at Rosebud caravan park (a sketch re-written from *Faking It*), this time as Len and Joyce with our offspring—Mark as a teenaged partying drug fiend and Jane in bathers, a blow-up swim ring and beach towel turban with a handful of blue-ringed octopus. She was fabulous. Stole every scene.

The forthcoming 1984 Los Angeles Olympics was a gift, and we ran a mock fundraiser for the Aussie team. I took a turn as Willy, the Olympic koala mascot, in a giant, furry suit. Earlier in the show I'd keep an eye out for any pissed patrons who were heckling and giving us shit then, incognito as Willy, later exact our revenge: as I danced through the auditorium to the stage in costume, I made sure to detour via the loudmouths and deliver a mighty WHACK! across the head with my paw.

Later, Richard would hear at the bar: 'That fucken bear hit me. Really hard!'

His mates would reply: 'Robbo, ya big girl! It's a fucken KOALA!'

As long as I live, I will never not find this funny.

'Neal, Harmer, Stubbs and Turner are among the brightest new talents to emerge on the Melbourne comedy scene. *Sunburn The Day After* will be the springboard to success for the young performers,' wrote one reviewer.

It was for me, because one night some bloke I'd never met before asked: 'Who wrote this show?'

I replied that I'd written most of the sketches.

Turned out his name was John Clarke and his enquiry was to pay off in ways I couldn't have imagined.

*

The year 1984 was a huge one of back-to-back gigs.

I hadn't ever performed in Sydney and so jumped at an invitation to join a show called *Characters* at the Trade Union Club, a grungy venue in Surry Hills. The line-up of women comics was put together by producers Larry Buttrose and Judy Barnsley for that summer's Sydney Festival and included Gretel Killeen, Mandy Salomon and her sister Melanie, Julie McCrossin, Victoria Roberts and Sue Ingleton—all 'in character'.

I was the only one performing stand-up as 'me' and I got a great reception, even calls for an encore. The word spread that here was a novelty—women comedians! The show was sold out every night.

I adored Sydney and spent lazy days at the Boy Charlton swimming pool on the edge of the Domain overlooking the sparkling waters of Woolloomooloo Bay or walking along the harbour, watching the green-and-yellow ferries chug by. The fragrance of gardenias and frangipani was intoxicating. It was a magical few weeks.

In the audience of *Characters* was the woman who would change everything for me: the talent agent Hilary Linstead. She approached me after a show and said in her posh English accent: 'Darling, I'd like to represent you.'

I skipped back to Melbourne with something unheard of in comedy circles . . . a big-deal Sydney agent! For the almost four decades Hilary would be my most tireless supporter and confidante. Like a mother to me. After my rural upbringing where there was a deep suspicion of 'arty' types, Hilary convinced me that I belonged in the milieu of the creative people I'd so long admired. More than that, she worked tirelessly to ensure my financial stability, even though I was a terrible spendthrift with no 'money-sense' at all. 'Dear girl! I trust you are putting something away!' she would scold after any new extravagance. It wasn't until I was in my forties that I finally took her advice, and it's because of Hilary that I've been able to provide for my family. I cannot imagine how life would have gone without her.

Somewhere there in '84 I also fitted in a stint in Perth with the *Sunburn* crew at the Pink Galah cabaret room at the Melbourne Hotel. We were impressed when we rocked up to the lovely old building, only to walk straight into the bar and a lunchtime 'skimpy' show with young women in their lingerie. The sleazy compere was ordering the girls to parade up and down, yelling: 'Check 'em out, gents! They remind you of crayfish, don't they? Ya know what I mean . . . A lot of meat on the body and shit in the head.'

The season went well, even though we had to cope with the thumping of the disco directly below our rooms that wound up at about 3 a.m., when the patrons fell out the door to punch on in the street.

I really needed a proper job.

*

I'd auditioned and been cast in a new ABC TV kids show, *Trapp, Winkle and Box*. The set-up was that we were three buskers who dreamed of stardom and lived on a houseboat on the Maribyrnong River—Hugo the guitarist (Robert Forza), Max the mime artist

(Paul Voermans) and me, the all-singing, all-dancing Anita Winkle, in a hideous pink sailor suit.

I threw a massive tantrum over that suit and, in a pathetic 'diva' display, threw it on the floor of the dressing room and jumped on it, to the horror of the wardrobe mistress. (I did apologise profusely.)

It was a bonkers series, most enjoyable to make, although completely exhausting. It featured huge puppets and animation, and there were weird dream sequences, with us dressed as bushrangers, underwater creatures or fairy folk. There were even send-ups of TV quiz shows and ads. Many future household comedy names appeared in cameos—Mark Mitchell, Peter Moon and Richard Stubbs among them. I still have some of the episodes on VHS and my kids loved watching them when they were small: 'Put on the Mum show!'

The series was shot half on location and half on elaborate sets at the famous ABC studios in Gordon Street, Elsternwick. It was here that I had a chance encounter in a hallway with the noted producer Ted Robinson. 'We're making a pilot for a new political comedy TV show,' said Ted. 'John Clarke tells me you can write. We're getting together for a workshop if you can make it.'

A few weeks later I was at a church hall in Elwood with Max Gillies, reading scripts from his team of genius writers—John, Patrick Cook, Phil Scott and Don Watson. I knew in an instant that I was utterly out of my depth. These were master satirists. The most I had to offer were a few half-arsed sketches from live stage shows, but I willed myself not to be daunted and stayed when I would much rather have bolted out the door and down the street. Happily, my policewoman scripts seemed to find favour and I scored a gig as a writer.

Ted tells me that I ended up being cast in the on-screen ensemble because he was concerned the cast needed more women. John said, 'Well, Wendy can be a performer too. And she sings.'

It was only weeks later, with my head still spinning, that I was on national television in the magnificent *The Gillies Report* with Max, John, Patrick, Phil, Geoff Kelso and the wonderfully daft, charismatic comic actress Tracy Harvey.

I liked to hang out in the make-up department to watch Max undergo extraordinary transformations into Australian politicians of the day—Bob Hawke, Andrew Peacock, Malcolm Fraser, Ian Sinclair, Russ Hinze, Don Chipp, Joh Bjelke-Petersen and Neville Wran. Max also did fine turns as Margaret Thatcher, Ronald Reagan and Mikhail Gorbachev. Not to mention the Pope: 'STOP IT . . .' he'd shout, and the studio audience would chorus: 'OR YOU'LL GO BLIND!'

In those days, the Gordon Street studios were home to incredibly skilled wigmakers and costume designers; some were refugees from the Hungarian State Opera, who'd fled to Australia after the 1956 uprising. The wardrobe department was an astonishing treasure trove of bespoke costumes from ABC TV-staged operettas and historical drama series like *Rush*. If required, the team of seamstresses could whip up anything overnight—from a lavish, velvet Louis XIV costume to a crinoline with matching, be-ribboned bonnet.

Director Ted Robinson used every resource at his disposal. (This was back in the days when the ABC had a healthy budget.) He brought in dancers and singers to mount huge, extravagant musical numbers that saw *Casablanca* reimagined as *Casanoosa. NSW: The Musical*, which targeted drug and gambling corruption. The royal commission into British nuclear testing at Maralinga and the Whitlam dismissal got the same lavish treatment. The operatic *Il Dismissale*, featuring Max as all the main players—Gough, Malcolm, the Queen and a drunken, dishevelled Sir John Kerr—remains a satirical masterpiece, the likes of which we'll never see again.

It was a weekly fancy dress show for Tracy and me. I was Susan Renouf, Michelle Grattan, Flo Bjelke-Petersen, Tammy Fraser, the Queen of Hearts, a royal chambermaid, a geisha and a Russian folk dancer.

And who could forget John Clarke's arcane invented sport of 'Farnarkeling', with us as cheerleaders in pastel Lycra?

My copper was scripted as a pugnacious apologist for police brutality: 'ALL RIGHT, SETTLE DOWN. Now, there are a number of circumstantial photographs appearing of a criminal who had a heart attack while chained to our filing cabinet. Well, what could we have done? I mean, if he had any sense, he would have had himself arrested by the St John's Ambulance people.'

Soon it seemed that everyone in the nation could do an impersonation of Max Gillies impersonating Bob Hawke. For his part, Hawke claimed: 'I don't think he's cracked me.' Australia . . . aaarrr . . . errr . . . gurgle . . . disagreed.

Queensland premier Joh Bjelke-Petersen never watched the show, judging by this priceless exchange on Brisbane radio, as reported by *The Sydney Morning Herald*:

Talk-back caller: 'Can I ask Sir Joh what he thinks of *The Gillies Report?*'

Joh: 'What angle are you thinking of?'

Caller: 'The whole of it, I think, is brilliant.'

Joh: 'Yes, there are many, many, many, many good things in that report, I . . . it's a long report, and very . . . well, I suppose difficult to sum up in a few short words like we have today.'

The acerbic political commentary cut close to the bone, and many pollies loathed the show, but I have a copy of *The Gillies Report* almanac, kindly signed by Andrew Peacock, urging me to 'keep up the good work'. Very gracious of him, considering that, as the then Leader of the Opposition, he was pilloried mercilessly.

It was our infamous 'Goanna' sketch that landed me on *The Mike Walsh Show* in prime time in May 1985 and drew the ire of Mattel, makers of the Barbie doll.

It's a strange story.

The Costigan royal commission into organised crime had been running since 1980; in 1984 *The National Times* leaked extracts of its draft report. A prominent Australian business-man was alleged to be involved in large-scale tax evasion, drug-running, pornography and even a murder. The report code-named the businessman 'Squirrel', but the newspaper's editor, Brian Toohey, renamed him 'Goanna'. Kerry Packer, a colossus in Australian media, immediately outed himself as the 'Goanna' and, incandescent with rage, denied everything.

Enter the fearless satirical team at *The Gillies Report*. In an eight-minute-long sketch, Max played Packer as a chain-smoking bully in an outsized suit, who bragged that he'd bought the cricket and the snow, and ranted about his rival, Rupert Murdoch. In a musical parody of the movies *King Kong* and *Godzilla*, Goanna, with a huge reptilian tail, scales Sydney's Channel Nine tower and swats away, then crushes, a buzzing helicopter from rival TV network Channel Seven.

By coincidence, Max had been booked to appear on Mike Walsh's evening talk and variety show on Channel Nine but, when the furore blew up, a furious Packer ensured that didn't happen. Oddly, it was agreed that I could appear instead. The sketch had caused such a ruckus that everyone pressured me either to pull out in protest, or to appear and make a political statement.

I was torn. This was a great opportunity to go 'commercial', 'nationwide' and 'prime time'. I knew I had to say something, but I wasn't about to sign the media death warrant that others had drafted for me. I flew to Sydney, unsure of what I could possibly say and dreading the thought of letting down my colleagues.

In the end, I prefaced my stand-up act with: 'Good evening. I'm *not* Wendy Harmer. I'm *actually* Max Gillies *playing* Wendy Harmer.' No one in the live audience had a clue what that was about; they didn't watch the ABC.

I did the Barbie doll routine that worked well on stage in the comedy clubs and got huge laughs from the audience. In it, I noted that, with her disproportionate measurements—her big boobs and little feet—she would struggle to stay upright. Also, she had no genitals. Just as well, or she would come with these *teeny, tiny* tampons. That was as far as the joke went; it was no more graphic than that. Pretty tame stuff, but that was almost forty years ago. Had I *really* said the word 'tampons' on TV?

After the show, I headed to a late-night bar in Kings Cross and people in the street yelled: 'We just saw you on TV! That Barbie doll thing was funny!' But one thing I hadn't expected was a two-page letter from the general manager of Mattel Pty Ltd. The heart of his complaint was:

> In your act you discuss the lack of physical attributes of the doll, that you understand as an adult, a woman will have in real life, why is it necessary to tarnish the product in this way? After all, the doll has been designed in the way little girls have wished them to be.
>
> Therefore, on behalf of small girls, their mothers and we at Mattel, who all look to Barbie with great affection, I ask you to refrain from using our products in your act.

I passed on the letter to the satirical magazine *Matilda*, which published it in full, alongside a reply penned by Barbie herself (i.e., me) and addressed to 'Dear Wendy'. The letter goes on for a bit with 'Barbie' longing for a day with Ken, eating pizza, drinking beer and getting out to see a heavy-metal band.

There's a final 'thank you' for taking her to the cabaret venues—'it's been a real eye opener'—and is signed: 'Yours in sisterhood, Barbie. PS: Amnesty look after political prisoners, don't they? Do you think you could contact them for us?'

Kerry Packer subsequently won damages from Fairfax and was formally exonerated by Attorney-General Lionel Bowen.

(He and Mike Walsh would later turn up in my life in the most peculiar of circumstances.)

My face was starting to pop up in the media more and more. The comedian David Argue stuck posters for his show on light poles in Fitzroy guaranteeing the night would be a 'Wendy Harmer-free zone'.

Honestly, I couldn't blame him.

*

I was now single and 'looking'. Steve and I had parted ways after a few hectic years in which he'd been pursuing his dream of film-making and I was focused on comedy.

We'd given our relationship a good go. At one point we'd lived together in a converted warehouse on Rankins Lane, near the GPO, right in the heart of Melbourne. The artist Mirka Mora lived a few doors up, and I'd sometimes drop into her studio for a chat and a cup of tea. The space was packed to the ceiling with all manner of curiosities and her wonderful, whimsical works. It was a marvel to behold. I count myself very fortunate to have spent time with such a beloved and important figure in Melbourne's cultural life.

Our living space at the front of the lane, facing the street, was so vast that Steve and I would rollerskate on the concrete floor. We once hosted an album launch for the experimental avant-garde band and multimedia ensemble Tsk Tsk Tsk. So many people turned up that I met a German tourist at the top of our stairs asking: 'Excuse me, is this a disco?'

We were hanging with the coolest kids in town. But the reality of living in a warehouse was not 'cool' at all. It was bitterly cold. The incessant *Bong! Bong!* from the GPO clock tower and the *Beep! Beep!* of garbage and delivery trucks running day and night meant I couldn't sleep. My nerves were totally shot. I'd burst into tears over any small thing.

Add to that Steve's womanising ways, and we had our fair share of amateur theatrics. We both recall the night when he walked through the door at the warehouse to find I'd lined up on a bench every piece of crockery we owned, and I began hurling the plates, bowls and cups at his head one by one. They all missed and smashed on the concrete floor.

When I was with Steve, I'd followed his passion for Formula 1 racing, and in 1985 we were VIP guests at the first-ever Adelaide Grand Prix. Inhaled the fumes of racing fuel on the grid and got to visit the pits. Thrilling!

I was booked for a stand-up gig at the Hilton Hotel at an after-race event with the superstar drivers. There could not have been a single, young, beautiful woman in the whole of Adelaide who didn't walk through the door that night, invited for the delectation of the visitors. I met Ayrton Senna and after my spot, which went well, was invited by the boss of McLaren to accompany them on next year's tour as some kind of comedy mascot. We'd go to Brazil, San Marino, Belgium, Monaco, Detroit . . . I turned down the offer and I don't think Steve ever recovered.

(Steve and I remain on exceedingly good terms, and he was my 'bridesman' when I got married, years later.)

After our split, I moved into a shared household with two single friends, Molly Hanrahan and Amanda Smith, who were

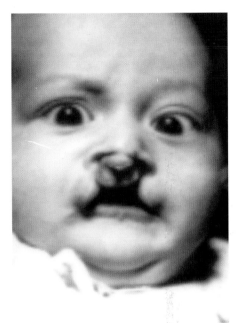

Me. Born at Yarram Hospital with a bilateral cleft lip and palate, 10 October 1955. 'Disastrous-looking thing.'

My father Graham's amateur arty photography: Margaret ('Margie'), my mother, with gun.

Dad was handy with a gun, too. Kangaroo shooting at Woodend, 1953.

Wedding day in Woodend, January 1955. Uncle Ron, Dad, Mum and Auntie Pat.

My mother Margaret, still in her school jumper, with baby me.

With one of Dad's prized whippets, 'Bernadette'. Brother Phil and me make a dirt-encrusted three.

School's in at Warncoort with The Headmaster. That's me, front row, third bandicoot from the right.

One of many shots Dad took of me when I was small. This one from when I was five years old.

Me, eight years old, unimpressed with my present from Santa. A comb and brush set . . . including a stupid mirror.

A move up in the world to Sandhurst Road, California Gully, Bendigo. A proper suburban house with neighbours either side. In 1963 this was really living!

Dad in footy kit playing for North Bendigo in 1965. Football . . . always the bloody football!

Dad. A good-looking rooster. Wouldn't be out of place now as a hipster barista.

Mum, from the swingin' sixties. A big-eyed beauty.

Grandfather Frederick Selwyn Brown delivering his peas and potatoes from Ballarat in the 1950s.

Nanna and Pop Brown in the garden at Trevor Street, East Ballarat. You can't quite see the fairies in this photograph, but I'm sure they are there.

Final year at Upwey High, Form 4, 1970, and the last of my old face. Photographs of teenage me are rare.

The old schoolhouse and residence from Freshwater Creek. (House to the left, classroom to the right.) Dad and I visiting it as a museum piece, then at Deakin University campus.

With my girl posse from Oberon High (clockwise from left: Debbie, Chris, Julie, Karen and Krys), with my new face. Still waiting for another operation on my nose and some presentable front teeth, thank you.

Mum as a nurse and Dad as a teacher—direct from central casting.

Little sister Helen and me in the early eighties.

With boyfriend, Michael, soon to be my husband. Still not opening my mouth to smile!

Me and Maryanne in our infamous building site sketch. 'Aww, c'mon, you're askin' for it!'
Photo: John Webber

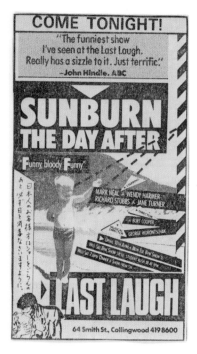

Hitting the big time, downstairs at the Last Laugh.

With Richard Stubbs, off to the 1985 Edinburgh Festival. Photo: Michel Lawrence

A portrait of me my daughter keeps on her bedside table, at the Last Laugh 1985. Photo: Michael Rayner

'Oh really? Tell your story walkin', pal.' Policewoman Wendy. Photo: Courtesy Australian Broadcasting Corporation Library Sales

In rehearsal for *The Gillies Report*. From left: Patrick Cook, Tracy Harvey, Max Gillies, John Clarke, me and Geoff Kelso. (Phil Scott is missing, but that's his piano.)

In the famous Gordon Street studio, Elsternwick, Melbourne. Cast and crew of *The Big Gig*, 1989. Director Ted Robinson is in the back row, right. Photo: Greg Noakes

Two spunky chicks. Sheree (me) and Miranda (Jean Kittson). Photo: Courtesy Australian Broadcasting Corporation Library Sales

The 2DAY FM
Morning Crew

The birth of the Morning Crew. From left: Newsreader Michelle Aleksandrovics, Paul Holmes, Agro, me and Jamie Dunn.

With Andrew Denton for *World Series Debating*, 1993–94. Cuddles here, but on stage the rivalry was fierce. Photo: Greg Noakes

Peter Moon joins the *Crew* in 1994. Photo: Monique March

'Two Strangers and a Wedding', 1998. Peter, me, Glenn Emerton, Leif Bunyan and Paul in the bridal party. Photo: Rose Repic

Escaping the Oscars in 1998. Most drab outfit, ever. Making the best of tiny moth holes, too-short fringe and—'uh oh'—let-down.

Broadcasting from home with baby Maeve, January 2000. Marley is in the next room shouting, 'Thomas . . . toast'.

Should have asked Billy Crystal for some tips on hosting the Logies!
Photo: Monique March

We are wed! Rushcutters Bay, Sydney,
December 1994.

Backstage at the 2002 Logies.
Doing those old curtains proud!

Women on the highwire—
The Hoopla calling card.

Me and husband Brendan in our backyard on the side of the hill. Collaroy Gothic.

Maeve and Marley. Then.

And now.

Mum at Warncoort, with Helen, Noel, me and Phillip. Twenty-two years old and four children. 'The early breeding is a feature.'

Beautifully turned out and off to Sunday School, California Gully, 1965.

A visit with Mum in our teenage years.

All grown up.

Just a few minutes before going live. With my clipboard, memorising that opening monologue. Courtesy Australian Broadcasting Corporation Library Sales

waitresses at the Last Laugh at the time. Molly was a seamstress and costume designer. Amanda an aspiring arts writer. Our place was a classic Fitzroy terrace directly across the street from the hipster hangout The Black Cat cafe.

We were all single, enduring a man drought. (We stuck a banner above the doorway that read: ABANDON YE HOPE ALL WHO ENTER HERE.)

Didn't we have good times in that house! It was the ultimate single girl's venue. Amanda staged elaborate games nights and a dozen women would turn up with cheese platters and wine. We'd gossip and drink, play cards, Scrabble or Twister. Laugh ourselves sick.

For a while the front bedroom was occupied by Paul McDermott from the Doug Anthony All Stars (DAAS), who turned it into a gothic dungeon. By night he was a raucous bad boy of the comedy scene; by day he was a domestic angel who fixed the washing machine and cleared the guttering. Lovely Gina Riley moved into that room after he left.

None of what happened at Greeves Street would make for a grungy novel of rampant drug use, abusive relationships or existential despair. A decade on from Helen Garner's *Monkey Grip*, we too frequented the Fitzroy pool, but we could always touch the bottom of the 'aqua profonda'.

Living in that house in the midst of bohemian Fitzroy, gainfully employed as a comedian and freelance writer, with a huge circle of like-minded friends, haunting band rooms and clubbing until dawn . . . It was a golden time.

Beyond anything I could have dreamed of when I walked the desolate road as a sad teenager back in Freshwater Creek.

12

Scotland the brave

Toilet cubicle mirror
Boeing 747
35,000 feet up, somewhere over the Indian Ocean

Bleargh!

There's a dead person wearing your clothes.

You look like hell.

But you're going to the Edinburgh Festival! Then Paris and New York!

First time overseas. No sleep for you. It's all too exciting.

Still hours to go before you land in London.

How do people do this?

*

I went to the Edinburgh Festival Fringe four times in all, but no outing was more shambolic than the first time, in 1985, with Richard Stubbs.

It had been a hectic year, with a return season of *Characters* at the Trade Union Club in January: 'Gretel Killeen is the housewife. Maggie Lynch is Sarah Daytripper. Julie McCrossin is the doctor. Mandy Salomon is Fiona Smout. Sue Ingleton is Shelia Shit. Wendy Harmer is Wendy Harmer.'

A *Sydney Morning Herald* review from Prue Charlton notes that our first outing in an obscure venue had taken 'everyone by surprise' and been the hit of the previous year's Sydney Festival. 'Female comics, at that time, were so few in number and located in such far peripheries of the entertainment scene that it was hard to know where they'd come from. Unlike most women comics, Harmer does not adopt a character: hers is simply the style of the traditional stand-up comic, a style which requires a degree of self-assurance that most women would regard as unattainable.' It also proved, said the writer, that 'feminists could be funny'.

Who knew?

In April, due to demand, we transferred to the prestigious Sydney Theatre Company's Wharf Theatre, where, on opening night, cleaning lady Val gaily mistook Premier Neville Wran and his wife Jill for Max Gillies and Susan Renouf.

The aroma of sheep lanolin embedded in the old floorboards took me back to the days of the shearing sheds I'd known as a kid. I could barely tear myself away from the floor-to-ceiling windows, which afforded an enchanting view of the harbour by night. A spellbinding setting for a theatre.

I returned to Melbourne on a high, with critical acclaim in my swag, to appear in the second TV series of *Gillies*, but I bowed out of the third series to work live on stage with Richard. My heart was in stand-up.

We'd performed as a duo at St Kilda's Dick Whittington Tavern in a show we called *Do You Come Here Often*. I do not know how we managed it, because 'Stubbsy' was hosting the breakfast show on radio 3XY, going to air at 5.30 a.m., and was getting by on only a few hours sleep. I was in the ABC's TV studios during daylight hours.

For me, cocaine helped.

I've never been much of drug taker. Enthusiastic, but an amateur. Can't do marijuana. My first two puffs on a joint made me vomit, and I've never been back. Ever. Tried magic mushrooms just the once; hallucinated for two days. Never again. No 'trips' for me, either. Took ecstasy; slept for eighteen hours straight. I reckon it was horse tranquilliser. No!

One night, after a million vodkas, I snorted Amyl on the dance floor at a Sydney nightclub and was so hungover and dehydrated in my hotel room the next morning, thought I was having a brain haemorrhage. I couldn't stand upright to get a glass of water and was reduced to drinking the greenish dregs out of a vase of flowers on the bedside table. Nope. Nope. Nope!

But cocaine? Yes, ma'am. That suited me just fine. Coke never became habitual and, in the days when it came in a tiny paper envelope, I sometimes found half a gram in my purse that I'd long forgotten. By then, the powder was mushy and useless for snorting, but later, out clubbing, I'd chew on the paper and blow my head off.

I was always very careful to measure when I indulged—a modest line a few hours before a performance, dancing in my bedroom? Fine. Any more than that and I couldn't trust myself not to gabble on like an idiot. It seemed to me that in comedy you needed to be sharp. On your wits. The one time I took to a stage drug affected was a total disaster (read on).

My drug of choice has always been alcohol. Preferably champagne. I've always had a drink to steady my nerves before a show . . . and then, often, one too many after.

Wish I could take back some of the idiotic things I've said and done when I've been drunk and disorderly.

Sincere apologies to all.

You know who you are.

*

'JUST A COUPLE OF JOKERS' read a headline from my alma mater, the *Sun*, in May 1985.

Richard and I were billed at the Laugh in our show *Two Up*, as 'Our Top Two Live Comedy Stars'. 'She's hilarious'—*Sydney Morning Herald*. 'He's sideclutchingly funny'—*The Age*. 'Together Sensational!'

The concept was totally mad. We performed our individual stand-up, and then combined in a line-for-line duelling routine in which Richard was at the dentist and I was at the hairdresser.

We were a good double act in press interviews. According to Gary Hughes in the *Sun*: 'The mistake was arranging an interview in a public place. Apart they have the ability to raise eyebrows and turn heads . . . Bring them together and you have an event about as unobtrusive as a six-car pile-up in Bourke Street, or a football match at the MCG. Only it's noisier. Interviewing Harmer and Stubbs is like umpiring a Wimbledon tennis final.'

In the *Melbourne Times*: 'In fact, how many teams like this can you remember since Bobby Limb and Dawn Lake in the 60s? Except . . . the girl is the macho type and the boy is the wimp. The quintessential 80s twist.'

'I think it's going to be a bit like the comedy partnership of Mike Nichols and Elaine May back in the 1950s,' said John Pinder. But it wasn't.

No wonder I've never seen a male and female stand-up attempt it since. Not so much a pas de deux, as a pas de don't-ever-try-this-again.

It was really hard work judging your timing with another comic, live, in the way we did. I loved performing with Richard— it was like having a rowdy big brother next to me, in charge of any situation and never without a sensational punchline—but when we got back to performing stand-up solo, we were both mightily relieved.

*

I estimate that it cost us about forty bucks a head for every person who came to see our show *Harmer and Stubbs* at the Edinburgh Festival of 1985.

We paid for everything, and our inexperience showed. The venue we'd booked was in a small bar, way off the beaten track, and our fabulous poster had a phone number for bookings that none of the staff there could identify. With almost a thousand acts at the Fringe, all vying to get bums on seats, it averaged out that each performance attracted an audience of three. Publicity was a matter of breaking even or going home broke. We were royally stuffed.

We spent nights handing out flyers on the cobblestone streets with our trusty stage manager and cheerleader, the indispensable Rick McKenna. (Who would go on to be the Executive Producer of Australian TV icons 'Kath & Kim'.)

Coming across a bagpiper in Black Watch tartan sobbing, 'Feck, ah hate the bloody Tattoo,' a random bloke, equally bladdered, took hold of his crumpled pipes and blasted 'Scotland the Brave'. Richard and I passed around a Glengarry bonnet, got seven quid and poured the sad piper into a cab.

At one rough pub we hit, we were warned to take good care of our pint glasses. 'We've had a wee problem with lads breakin' 'em and stickin' 'em into other lads' necks.' Goodo!

Los Trios Ringbarkus, who'd won the Perrier Award for best new talent in '83, were doing good business, and Sue Ingleton was the talk of the town with her one-woman show, selling out at the famous Assembly Rooms. Despite our obscure venue, we garnered a good review in the *Festival Times*: 'Hilarious. Individually they're funny—together they're inspired. Look set to be one of this year's Fringe hits.' Not so much. Mind you, we were probably doing better than a university revue from Adelaide titled *The Wagga Wagga High High Show*.

We performed two shows a night. Richard described the audience as 'small, but beautifully marked'. We always gave it our all, but the paltry turnout was dispiriting.

We did better at the late-night Fringe Festival bar where Richard killed it, even overcoming his opening line on the first night: 'It's good to be here in England.' To be greeted with: 'Feck off, yer Sassenach basterd!'

One evening, between shows, Mike Walsh rocked up. *The* Mike Walsh. *The Australian TV legend, Mike Walsh!* Said he was in town, thought he'd catch our show. I had no idea how he'd found us. Barely anyone else had.

What I hadn't known was that Mike Walsh had been mentoring Richard. After his appearance on Mike's talk show, Richard had been ringing for advice: 'Is this the right career move?' Mike had been endlessly encouraging, and that's why he'd come to see us.

Mike invited us for drinks at the Caledonian, a luxury hotel up the road with stunning views of Edinburgh Castle, and bought hideously expensive champagne cocktails, which I downed one after the other. He was lovely, and regaled us with showbiz stories, none of which I can remember. Too drunk.

Richard left the hotel ahead of me to get back to the venue for our second show and, with barely a few minutes before 'curtain up', I fell through the door. No wonder he was unimpressed with the state of me. I have never sobered up so fast in my life.

We did that show to about five people, with Mike Walsh laughing like a drain all the way through. Perhaps fitting because, the last time I ever saw him, Mike was weaving his way along a gutter in Princes Street.

*

With so many Aussie acts in Edinburgh forming a huge entourage, I'd barely met anyone who didn't hail from Fitzroy, Collingwood or Carlton. Two weeks of sharing a flat with five others from home had been bedlam.

A surging tide of tourists crammed into every pub, sandwich shop, restaurant and bakery. Jigging out of the doors along the Royal Mile were Loch Ness Monster fridge magnets, whisky glasses and anything in tartan that had been in the vicinity of a sheep. A New York tourist I overheard: 'Oh, Harry, look that castle. It's so gorgeous. It's so old. But why would anyone build it so close to a railway station?'

But with summer over and the crowds dispersed, the city resumed its character as dour, foggy, ancient Auld Reekie, dominated by the glowering pile of its famous castle. I rented a car and headed off alone to the Isle of Skye to see the last of the purple heather on the moors and explore the craggy mountains, lochs and weathered stone castles that had so captured my imagination in the fantastical tales I'd read as a child.

Exploring Scotland for those two weeks, solo, was a rite of passage. I hadn't booked anywhere to stay, just drove in my little car, stopped, rambled and rolled up to wherever I fancied for the night.

On the shores of Loch Lomond, the dotty owner of an historic pile showed me to an immense room with a bathroom as big as our entire lounge room back home in Fitzroy. At dusk, she and I set off to gather the last of the summer blackberries for a fresh-baked pie and then to harvest herbs and vegetables from her glorious kitchen garden to accompany a delicious lamb roast.

It was blissful after the stodge I'd lived on in Edinburgh. Deep-fried pizzas and Mars bars, baps and bridies from the bakery were local delicacies. Tagliatelle . . . with chips. And everything doused in Brown Sauce. So named, I reckon, because it has no other characteristic. It's nae hot. It's nae spicy. It's just broon.

In an old album, there are photographs of sweeping land-scapes under leaden skies with not a person in sight. Looking at them, I can recall both the exhilaration and the deep sense of peace I felt at being quite alone at what I imagined to be the very end of the world.

*

From there to Paris and New York. I wrote a fortnightly letter home in the *Sun*, chronicling my adventures as 'Australia's zaniest funny lady'. This was before the Internet, so I must have been either typing or writing long-hand, and then sending my words by fax. Please tell me I didn't bore a blameless copytaker to tears.

It's never a good idea to re-read your old novels, much less your ancient columns, but I've kept them from that time, record-ing, among other astounding revelations, that a soft drink cost an eye-watering $1.60 at street stalls in Paris but 'even the toasted sandwiches here are brilliant'. In New York, I marvel: 'In my mid-town hotel I get 13 different channels . . . there's even a channel that runs the weather 24 hours a day.'

As a country kid, getting to Melbourne, then Sydney, was an amazing achievement. Now I'd been around the world! I would board a plane to go anywhere, anytime.

In the hands of my industrious agents, Hilary Linstead and Associates, who were taking care of business, gigs were lined up at comedy clubs and festivals for the next few years. In 1986 I teamed up with Mary-Anne again for a stint at Le Joke, the Adelaide Festival and the final *Characters III* at the Wharf. I performed stand-up at Sydney's Hip Hop Club and Queensland Uni. Appeared in the Last Laugh's Christmas show and saw in the New Year at Salamanca in Hobart. Looking at my itinerary from that time, I must have rarely slept in my own bed.

I'd never expected to find my tribe in the shabby backstage rooms of comedy and music venues with a cast of funny, sweary, scandalous oddballs. Some were escapees from uneventful, middle-class lives. Others had backstories that almost defied belief, and for them, performing to an audience was confirmation they were 'normal-ish'. I was somewhere in the middle. Bit from column A, bit from column B.

(One of my comedy idols, Sue Ingleton, said I should do a show about my cleft lip and palate. It would be 'real' and break new ground. The idea of it was horrifying to me. I stuck with my observations on Aussie manners and rituals, where I felt safe and in command.)

By now there were lots of women performers and we'd swap war stories of surviving bucks' nights or taking an emergency wee in the sink because the women's toilets were up three flights of stairs and down the end of a corridor. Lifelong friendships were formed in those bunkers of adversity.

We were like 'carny folk', travelling from stage to stage in cities and country towns. No one ever asked, 'What school did you go to?' or judged you on your appearance. If you were in the dressing room, you had as much right to be there as anyone else. Comedy was the ultimate leveller. You either got the laughs or you didn't.

The audience may have been unforgiving, but there was great camaraderie as we stood in the wings or up the back and watched each other's acts, often laughing the loudest, especially if the jokes weren't landing. As the baton was passed, you'd be told: 'They're a great crowd, you'll have fun,' or, 'They're really tough tonight. Watch out for that table up the back on the right—they're pissed.'

Everyone was invested in us all doing well and making the night a success. There was no pleasure in watching someone do badly; they'd be beating themselves up, brutal in their self-assessment, and you could easily be next. When I hear accounts of the dog-eat-dog competitive scene at today's comedy venues and festivals, I thank my lucky stars that I started out in an easier time when there were far fewer on the circuit than there are now and well before the excoriating commentary in the Wild West of social media.

At the time I began performing, I garnered huge publicity as that rarity: an Aussie female stand-up. I've often said that if I hadn't turned up when I did, someone would have had to invent me.

*

Satirist, writer, poet and beloved comic performer the late, great John Clarke, once told me that the difference between tragedy and comedy is that, while we can all agree on what's sad, what's funny is never universal. If you promise to make people cry and you don't, an audience doesn't mind. But if you promise to make them laugh and you don't, they get angry.

It's true. 'I'm going to make you laugh!' What hubris, when you remember that what makes one person fall about in hysterics and the next sit stony-faced is informed by family, culture and life experience. Humour is both subjective and divisive. Only at its rare best, transformative.

On radio, I once interviewed Robin Williams, at the time the world's hottest comedy star, and I thought he sounded a little downbeat. I asked him if he was okay, and he replied that he'd performed comedy the night before and bombed. 'They just weren't my crowd,' he sighed.

Not Robin Williams' crowd? I was astonished. Who could these people be? *Everyone* loves Robin Williams.

Reality is, no comic is universally loved. All of us can name a comedian we really dislike. And often we can't even explain why, exactly.

When a joke falls flat it feels like a broken promise, a betrayal of trust.

Like John said, it's personal.

*

Australia's live comedy culture is unique. There's nothing to match it anywhere for sheer invention and variety. I know this as someone who played comedy clubs in the UK, Ireland and throughout America in the 1980s and 90s and watched a parade of stand-ups, many with similar routines. Same joke. Different accent. It became mundane. The Australian scene, and Melbourne in particular, was an intoxicating brew of stand-up, sketch, circus, cabaret, choir, magic and music. It bubbled, fizzed and popped wherever there was a stage, a few lights and a microphone or three.

We comedians had *chosen* life on the stage; but for musicians it was almost inevitable, ever since they strummed or tootled that first note. Musicians have always been the performers I admire most, funny musicians the best of the best, and they are adored. Ask any stand-up who looks at the running order and finds there's a musical comedy act slotted to go on before them.

Game over. Go home.

I first saw the Cabbage Brothers at the Prince Patrick hotel in Collingwood, and one 'brother' in particular became *mon petit chou* for the next few years.

They were part of an exuberant comedy-cabaret style that brought us the Castanet Club from Newcastle; the Doug Anthony All Stars from Canberra; the Hot Bagels from the Jewish bakeries in Acland Street, St Kilda and the Whittle Family from Tamworth, via tram from Pentridge Prison and North Coburg.

'Istanbul (Not Constantinople)' is a swingin' ditty originally recorded by Canadian quartet the Four Lads in 1953. In the hands of the Cabbage Brothers it got an hysterical do-over.

Richard Gray, Paul Winterbine, Louis Dingemans and Patrick Cronin, all in tuxedos, played ukulele and jazz trumpet with a heapin' helpin' of slapstick. It all looked silly and chaotic, but was slickly choreographed and musically accomplished.

I loved it to bits.

Patrick was the consummate showman. His comic timing was impeccable. He embraced any audience, won them over and blew the bejesus out of his trumpet. Offstage he was congenial company, unassuming, kind and softly spoken, but with a wicked wit that underscored any conversation. One of those people you look to and wonder: *What does Patrick make of all this?*

He was seven years younger than me. Sandy-haired, brown-eyed and . . . sigh . . . lovely.

I can recall the very instant the spark between Patrick and me ignited. It was in Mietta's late-night cocktail lounge in Alfred Place down a laneway in the heart of the City. I can still see the chairs we were sitting in, the drinks in our hands, when he told me he'd lost his mother to suicide when he was young and living in country Victoria. The match was struck.

We began dating and said 'I love you' at almost the same time.

Our break-up would be spectacular, involve a large pair of scissors, send me into long-overdue therapy, produce two books, a one-woman show and eventually see me flee from Melbourne to Sydney for good.

He blew out the candle first.

It could have just as easily been me.

13

Over oceans and in lakes

Handbag make-up mirror
The Tunnel comedy club
Mitre Arms pub
Greenwich, London

Holy shit. Oh. My. God.
　　Why are you here?
　　Where even is 'here'?
　　Why did you agree to do this?
　　No amount of money is worth it.
　　They are going to kill you.
　　You are going to die.

*

FUCK OFF! FUCK OFF! FUCK OFF! FUCK OFF!
　　FUCK! FUCK! FUCK!
　　OFF! OFF! OFF!

I watched in horror as, one by one, the acts on before me scarpered, subjected to a barrage of abuse. The drag queen opera singer had stomped off, calling the audience 'a pack of cunts'. A group singing a cappella only got halfway through 'Summertime' before being pelted with coins for a taxi fare home. The magician, just . . . disappeared, when the door to her magic cupboard jammed.

Welcome to 'Sunday Night at the Tunnel Palladium', a comedy club run by the anarchist comedian Malcolm Hardee. In the 1980s it was renowned as the wildest, most raucous, grizzly bear pit in London. A coliseum where comics were thrown to an audience and ritually torn apart by some 300 drunken punks in studded leather jackets and hooligans in football colours. Those bastards could detect the slightest whiff of fear, even through a noxious haze of ciggie smoke, belches and beer farts.

If you could survive The Tunnel, you could survive anything. Inexplicably, it had become a rite of passage for rising comedy stars to test themselves against the roughest audience anywhere. Hardee encouraged heckling, and it was a badge of honour to survive even ten minutes on stage before surrendering.

And yet, Hardee would later be lauded as the 'Father of Alternative Comedy', boosting the careers of Britain's biggest names, including Jo Brand, Jenny Eclair, Jeremy Hardy, Harry Enfield, Paul Merton, Alan Davies and Vic Reeves.

The avuncular elder statesman of the new-wave of British comedy Arthur Smith says: 'The audience were almost an act in themselves and the ringleader was Malcolm. Malcolm loved things to go wrong, and things often went wrong at The Tunnel, but that was part of the pleasure of it.'

Steve Coogan says he had his worst gig ever there—it was a 'baptism by fire'—and Rob Brydon, when the crowd clocked he was Welsh, was sent off to a chorus of 'baa . . . baa'.

Not sure how I got booked, but around this time I was playing the London comedy circuit and getting nice mentions in *Time Out* as 'someone to watch'. I realised something was up when other comics kept asking, 'Really? *The Tunnel*? Are you *sure*?'

On the night, I took the Tube to the end of the line and a cab for the rest of the way to a clapped-out industrial landscape. I found the grotty pub, peered inside, and through the gloom spied the shambolic figure of Malcolm by the pool table, puffing on a cigar. 'Forget it,' I said. 'I'm off.'

He wheedled and cajoled: 'Tell yer what. If you go on, I'll give yer an extra ten quid so yer can get a cab 'ome. They're just in 'igh spirits, that's all. They'll love yer.'

I was staying with a friend in Notting Hill and wasn't keen on braving the Tube so late on a Sunday night. My usual mantra of 'I don't have to do this for a living' was wearing thin. This time I needed the dosh. Done deal.

Malcolm introduced me on stage with: 'Here's a gel, then. Been on the telly in Australia. Doesn't make 'er any good.' At least it was better than his usual, 'This next act's probably a bit shit.'

The first word out of my mouth was 'G'day' and the heckling fired up. They were on their feet: 'Give us a suck on yer Fosters, cobber ... Hullo, Bruce ... Pineapples ... Kangaroos ... Wombats!'

What was a red-blooded Aussie girl to do? Remember Bay 13, remember The Hill, remember Gallipoli (perhaps not). Remember that outdoor gig at Moomba. Yell back!

I stood my ground and shouted, 'MCEWAN'S EIGHTY SHILLING! ... BADGERS! ... 'HEDGEHOGS!'

We were all blindsided by what had just happened, and there was an eerie lull before anyone could think of what to say or do next. No one there could pull off a kangaroo, wombat or pineapple impersonation, so the inevitable 'Show us yer tits' started—the standby insult in any comedy venue. But after handling pissed dickheads the length and breadth of Australia for so long, this was my bread and butter.

So we had what Malcolm might call 'a bit o' the ol' chat', and I left the stage when I'd had enough. On my own terms. Got my twenty-five quid and went home in a cab. Never again.

I'd always heard that the Doug Anthony All Stars had slayed at The Tunnel. But that's not how it was, Tim Ferguson tells me: 'The first night, when they started abusing us, Paul shouted: "WELL, THIS IS JUST A SAD INDICTMENT OF THE ENGLISH EDUCATION SYSTEM." They went berserk and we were eaten alive. We barely got away with our lives intact.'

DAAS went back. Played there six times. Legends!

'We survived and got our fifteen quid each. Every night they threw stuff at us.'

*

If The Tunnel audience was South London natives, the Comedy Store in Soho, West End, had more of an upmarket vibe. God knows, anywhere was 'upmarket' compared to the Mitre Arms.

The Store attracted tourists who knew it from the Los Angeles club of the same name. It was where the biggest stars of British comedy—Ben Elton, Alexei Sayle, Rik Mayall, Adrian Edmondson, Nigel Planer and the brilliant duo of Dawn French and Jennifer Saunders—cut their teeth.

I'm told I was the first woman ever to MC there (if not, certainly the first Australian one). On my first hit-out, a tide of Hooray Henrys—upper-class, entitled toffs from the City— piled in after leaving the office on a Friday night and downing a million pints each.

It was a bloody hard room to manage. I liken my efforts to those of a doughty Aussie bush firefighter with a wet hessian bag. I'd flog one blaze of obnoxious behaviour, only for another spot fire to flare up. First night, I ended up dousing the conflagration by pouring the contents of a pint glass over the head of some donkey who was seated in the front row.

Last I heard, my photo was still on the wall there.

*

The inaugural Melbourne International Comedy Festival (MICF) was held in 1987, with a $170,000 grant from John Cain's Labor government. There were just fifty-six acts then; today there are more than 600.

I was on the board, and it was thrilling to see the festival come together with short runs of solo acts and one-off special events. My favourite was *Humourists Read Humourists*, the brain-child of John Clarke, who was keen to give the festival some cultural depth by inviting performers to read the works of authors they admired. Staged at the Atheneum Theatre, it immediately sold out.

Some readers went for the self-referential, others delivered satirically. That first year, alongside Barry Humphries reading from the Sandy Stone monologues, Ernie Dingo read the real diaries of a colonial administrator and his comments on First Nations people at the time of Invasion.

I was mistress of ceremonies at a few of these afternoon events, and one year I chose Barry Dickins—the prolific playwright and author who'd been a columnist with the *Melbourne Times* when I'd worked there. As I read aloud his 'ode' to a Melbourne Tramways meat pie and watched the audience reduced to tears of helpless laughter, I recall thinking, I will never, ever write anything as funny as this.

It was a lesson in humility and, I think, just what John was hoping for. He was right to remind us of our proud tradition in written satire. Also, that eliciting laughs off the page is some-thing only the very gifted, rare few can do. He was one of them, of course. The US satirist Fran Lebowitz has always done it for me.

John Pinder was at the helm for the festival and his associ-ate producer at the Last Laugh, Tory McBride, transformed the upstairs venue Le Joke into La Joke, with an all-women line-up.

Tory championed women in comedy. The year before, she'd travelled to New York's Catch a Rising Star and signed up Adrianne Tolsch, Valery Pappas and Margaret Smith to stage *The Big Apple Comediennes*. For us local gals it was inspiring. We knew we were part of something bigger. A classic Adrianne line: 'I'm off marriage. I can't mate in captivity.'

During that inaugural MICF, Tory McBride was witness to one of the most cringeworthy moments of my entire career. And that's saying something. There are so many to choose from.

The special guest at that very first festival was Peter Cook. Trust I don't have to do much more than mention the name 'Peter Cook'. I'd grown up watching him and Dudley Moore in the 1960s on the BBC TV sketch show *Not Only . . . But Also*. My mum and dad loved him. I did too. Like everyone else drawn to edgy, anti-establishment satire, absurdity and silliness, I'd followed his every move since and was a huge fan.

At a swish celebratory lunch at Mietta's, I was seated next to him and couldn't believe I'd landed there. I never expected to get into a dispute about, of all things, the practice of clitoridectomy. His point was that as a feminist (particularly a Western one), I shouldn't condemn what we now call female genital mutilation as perpetrated by women on young girls. I couldn't just cherry-pick from the cultural and religious rituals I didn't care for, he argued.

He was being a boorish contrarian. A provocateur. I shouldn't have taken the bait, but 'Come in spinner'!

Tory remembers attempting to referee with, 'I think what you mean is . . .'

He rudely stubbed out his cigarettes into his fish entree—a delicate arrangement of plaited poached salmon—and ordered more drinks. I felt misunderstood and dismissed. Much later, I heard Mr Cook had been topping up his orange juice with vodka since 9 a.m. and was in a fragile state that year, in the grip of alcoholism. With hindsight, I could have been more compassionate, but I didn't know what I was dealing with then.

We would achieve a rapprochement, of sorts.

It was at the Last Laugh festival club. Tory, Peter Cook, Mel Smith (from the BBC TV comedy hit *Alas Smith and Jones*) and I were standing up the back in the shadows. Mel had accompanied Peter to the festival. He pops up in TV footage of that riotous opening morning media conference where Barry Humphries, as Sir Les Patterson, flops out the ol' fella into a tray of cement—the MICF answer to a star on Hollywood Boulevard. (The image was mercifully pixelated on Channel Nine's *Sunday* program.)

The venue was open late. A spot for festival-goers and performers to wind down, catch the odd act, have a last drink. Where we'd all been for the preceding hours, I don't recall. Reliable sources tell me Cook and Smith were well-supplied with drugs during their stay and had wreaked havoc in their hotel room. I'll admit that, thinking I'd finished duties for the day, I was coked to the eyeballs.

MC (on stage): 'Next up, ladies and gentlemen, is a Melbourne comedienne . . .'

Me (whispering in Peter Cook's ear): 'This will be great. We've got so many good women comics here . . . You watch.'

MC: 'She's been on TV and worked in London . . .'

Me: (whispering in Mel Smith's ear): 'Wonder who it is? Anyway, so many *great* women. This will be excellent . . . You'll *love* her!'

MC: 'Please welcome . . . WENDY HARMER!'

Me: 'What the . . .?!'

Unfortunately, I was at the perilous crossroads of knowing I was incapable of stringing together a coherent sentence and, simultaneously, thinking I was a totally-in-command comedy genius.

I lurched on stage and grabbed the microphone. At the time, my stand-up was a rant about the beauty and relationship advice columns in popular women's magazines. Yes, I am sorry to say, I had props. The routine required that I not only opened the magazines to the relevant page, but read from within. Neither of which I had any hope of doing. I fumbled and mumbled. Mangled every punchline.

As the minutes dragged by, to stony silence from the rest of the room, the only sound I could hear was Peter Cook and Mel Smith laughing so hard they almost died. It was me who was doing the dying.

'Funniest thing I ever saw in my life,' said Cook.

'Fuck off, Cook,' said I.

*

'There's been a lot of dirty talk about you,' said Patrick White, fixing me with a gimlet eye in a rehearsal room at the Adelaide State Theatre. 'People are telling me that because you're a comedian, you're stealing this role from a *proper* actor.' He was delighted with this mischief. 'I think you'll be terrific,' he added.

If he had said, 'You'll be terrified,' it would have been more accurate. Around the table sat Geoffrey Rush, John Gaden, Kerry Walker, Henri Szeps, Val Levkowicz, Carole Skinner and Catherine McClements. A cast of more distinguished actors from Australian theatre would have been difficult to assemble. I was to debut in White's play *Shepherd on the Rocks*, directed by wunderkind Neil Armfield. 'Wendy will bring in the "now" people,' Patrick assured Neil.

This was one of Hilary Linstead's set-ups. My amazing, hard-working agent was always looking for opportunities to expand my repertoire beyond live comedy. When she told me Neil had offered me the role, I was hesitant; I'd never seen myself as an actor. But then I thought, *Why not?*

With good reason, as it turned out.

The problem was, I had no idea whatsoever how to *act*. The whole thing was a mystery to me. I was cast as a serene, forbearing, middle-aged woman, wife of the Reverend Daniel Shepherd of Budgiwank, played by the consummate professional John Gaden. I got to sing a bit offstage, so that was fine. But there was a scene where I had to walk alone into the stark, moody set created by the award-winning designer Brian Thomson, fall to my knees and cry piteously.

Do you think I could do that? Cry on cue? No, I could fucking not. I asked Geoffrey Rush for advice on how to make the tears come. Should I recall a personal tragedy? Maybe hide a cut onion in a hanky?

He said, most gravely, 'Be very still. Turn your eyes to the heavens . . . Open them wide . . . do not blink . . . just stay that way . . . until the searing heat from the lighting rig makes your eyes water.'

Very funny.

All the cast were so kind. They were getting on with their roles, but I just couldn't nail mine. My usual sense of calm and logic deserted me. I could barely eat or sleep and eventually worried myself into emergency at Royal Adelaide Hospital.

To my huge embarrassment, it made *The Advertiser*: 'Melbourne actress and comedienne, Wendy Harmer . . . was admitted suffering an unconfirmed ailment. It is believed she complained of acute abdominal pain . . . no decision had been made whether she would undergo surgery.'

My only 'ailment' was a profound lack of confidence that had tied my stomach in agonising knots.

Neil Armfield came to visit me in hospital. Opening night was only a week away.

Me: 'I can't do this, Neil. I don't know how to play this character.'

Neil: 'Hmmm. Well, does she remind you of anyone you know?'

Me: 'Yes. Yes, she does. She's exactly like my auntie Pat.'

Neil: 'So, just do your auntie Pat then.'

Me: 'Are you allowed to do that? I mean, isn't that cheating?'

Neil: 'It's called acting.'

I did my 'auntie Pat' and, although I couldn't quite manage tears on opening night, howled in the wings when it was over.

Only then had it really struck me that I'd have to do it the next night . . . and the one after that.

The review in *The Australian* read: 'The comedian Wendy Harmer makes her debut as a straight actor in this play as Shepherd's saintly wife Elizabeth and she displays a fine sensitivity in this.'

Got away with it, but only just.

The rest of the season is a blur, but I do remember there was a moment at the beginning of the play where I was required to descend a staircase and deliver Patrick White's elegant words. All I wanted to do was to yell from the top step: 'HIYA! ANYONE HERE FROM GLENELG?'

I was not destined to be an actor.

Sent the script of the movie *Death in Brunswick*, I shoved it under my bed and forgot to read it. I auditioned for director Jane Campion for the lead role in *Sweetie*, her first feature film, and found her direction to visualise licking someone in a sexual swoon acutely embarrassing. So much so that Jane, very kindly, sent me a card, hoping I'd recovered.

I botched, bombed or self-sabotaged every audition for roles in plays, stage musicals, TV dramas and sit-coms Hilary sent me to. Even if I did get a call-back, the second audition was usually worse than the first.

Disastrous. But, then, I've never been one for sitting by the phone, waiting for someone to offer me a role that I couldn't write for myself.

*

In 1987, Patrick and I moved in together in St Kilda, not far from the busy cafes and bars on Acland Street. Our flat—with cream squashy linen-covered sofas, plush rugs and trailing house plants—was my creation of blissful domestication.

We'd taken shows to Sydney and Brisbane as 'Wendy and the Cabbage Brothers', then crisscrossed paths at various gigs. We were both often away from our little nest and, with our careers blossoming, the time wasn't right to think about marriage and children. Being a mother was definitely on my agenda, but I figured that at the age of thirty-two, and with Patrick still in his twenties, there was plenty of time for all that.

Dad had retired from teaching, and I hadn't visited him for the entire five years he'd taught at his last school, Carisbrook No. 1030 in Central Victoria. Typically, the hundred-year-old residence was plagued by rising damp. I'd felt horribly guilty about not dropping in, although Alison must have been pleased not to have any of us living under her roof or, indeed, see my face.

When, eventually, Patrick and I visited, they were farming in Katandra West, twenty-six kilometres outside Shepparton. (Just that *bit too far* out of town, you'll note.) Dad had two years of sick leave on full pay owing, but took early retirement at the age of fifty-five and bought a former dairy farm on seventeen hectares. He ran up to seventy-five head of Hereford, Murray Grey and Angus, and experimented with rare breeds in irrigation country where the grass grew fast and lush.

He applied his knowledge of dog breeding to broader animal husbandry, kept meticulous photo albums of every cow and bull, and especially loved the calving season. He'd been the secretary and treasurer of the gun club in Carisbrook and now took on the same positions at the bowling club in Katandra. Boasted he'd been honoured with a plaque. He was in his happy place.

Patrick and I drove the three hours from St Kilda to the farm to see Dad. We arrived late afternoon and, after a tour of the farm, ventured inside the house at dusk to a lukewarm reception.

Me: 'Oh, this overhead light in the lounge room is a bit bright. Why don't I just switch on these table lamps . . .'

Alison: 'You don't get to march in here and tell us which lights to turn on and off. If you don't like how we do things here, just go.'

Me: 'Okay. Bye.'

After a visit of less than an hour, we drove the three hours home.

*

I had no idea where my comedy career was taking me, but I was loving the ride. The gigs in stand-up and writing columns rolled in and kept me solvent. You could earn a good living from both back then.

In 1987 I was guest editor for an issue of *Cleo* magazine. For the occasion, I renamed it *Yobbo*: 'the only magazine poly-coated for reading in the gents!'

On the mocked-up front page:

• What's the difference between a tampon and a transistor battery . . . and why your girl won't send you shopping.

- Samantha Fox, Joan Collins, Britt Ekland. Do you reckon they'd be in it?
- The footy season's over: Can you still be mates?
- *Yobbo*'s guide to foreplay: 'Hey, you. Wake up!'
- Sealed section: Does size matter? An intimate guide to your beer gut and you.
- Fashion bonanza: Winning ways with thongs.
- Travel: Bali on two dozen cans a day.

That same year I was invited to the Montreal Comedy Festival, *Just for Laughs* (*Juste pour Rire*). I kept company with a band of English comics I'd come to know from around the traps in London—Harry Enfield, Paul Whitehouse, Ruby Wax and the Scottish comic Craig Ferguson, who was then performing as Bing Hitler.

At the entrance to the Hotel du Parc, I spied Rowan Atkinson and couldn't resist telling him how much I admired his work. 'Thank God someone knows who I am!' he said. Strange to think of it, but at the time he was largely unknown to a North American audience and was recovering from a disastrous one-man show on Broadway a year earlier. Reviewing the show in *The New York Times*, Frank Rich had written that Atkinson's performance 'is interminable proof that the melding of American and English cultures is not yet complete'.

Will it ever be?

The quest for humour that's universal is, literally, a fool's errand.

Graham Chapman was there too, wrestling himself as Colin 'Bomber' Harris, reviving his famous sketch from Monty Python days. From that same year, a few more names you'll recognise—John Candy, Chris Rock, Steven Wright and a guest appearance from octogenarian Henny 'Take my wife, please' Youngman, who received a standing ovation.

My schedule was bewildering. A few spots in almost-empty comedy clubs. An outing in an inflatable negotiating the Lachine Rapids on the St Lawrence River. (There's a metaphor for you.) Then to the vast stage at the Théâtre St-Denis, where we English-speaking comics stood at the back and tried to figure out what the Quebecois audience found so damn funny about the local acts. *On était complètement paumé!* (We didn't have a clue).

Just for Laughs was the premier showcase for North American talent scouts. Some of the gala events, filmed for TV, ran for *four* hours. God help you if you were on last. As noted in *Time Out*: 'The transatlantic comedy circuit is enormous, with at least one comedy club in every major town, a scene that has spawned hundreds of top-class comedians and many more second-raters. American kids don't want to be rock stars anymore, they want to be stand-up comics.'

This audience hadn't ever seen an Australian woman stand-up, but the massive success of *Crocodile Dundee* proved to be the perfect entree. A review (in French) declared me '*hilarante*' in my rant about Aussie blokes, saying that I'd made the audience '*rougir—et rugir*' (blush and roar). The *Time Out* notice was good too: 'The comediennes on show were, if anything, funnier than the men. Australian Wendy Harmer and American Rita Rudner showed the signs of greatness.'

Afterwards, like a scene from a B-grade movie, I was approached in a hotel corridor by an ageing gent wearing a white suit, pink-tinted aviator glasses and cradling a poodle. 'How'd ya like to come to New York, kiddo? Here's my card. I can make you a staaaar!'

Worth the price of admission alone.

I never did take up the offer.

Instead, I met up with Craig Ferguson in New York, where we hit the nefarious underground club scene and got totally trashed.

*

I went back to the Edinburgh Festival, solo, with no real plans. Fortuitously for me, and disastrously for the hugely popular UK comic Paul Merton, who'd broken his leg playing football on the Meadows, I picked up a few of his gigs. I was also hanging with the Brighton comedy crowd after performing at the Zap Club, housed in one of the infamous Kings Road arches on the seafront.

I counted the late, great Pete McCarthy from the local Cliffhanger theatre troupe as one of my best friends. He won the Perrier Award for his one-man *The Hangover Show* in 1990. I have never seen a funnier show.

Pete often visited Australia, and sometimes we worked as a duo.

Me: 'I had a great time at the Edinburgh Festival, although getting there was a long trip.'

Pete: 'Oh yeah. What route did you take?'

Me: 'You remember that fat German bloke I met at the beer festival?'

Boom Boom!

He died in 2004 from cancer at the age of fifty-two, just as his travel books hit *The New York Times* bestseller lists. I have the order of his memorial service pinned above my desk. The loss of him still seems outrageously unfair. In 2006, Brighton & Hove named a bus in his honour.

Pete would have loved that.

*

The next year 1988 was a big one for me professionally, and I had to think about what I wanted out of comedy and what comedy could offer me.

I'd already ruled out the grind of the US club circuit. The life of a comic there was precarious—shuttling from gig to gig across the country, grafting in front of drunk college kids, hoping for a spot on a late-night talk show. Then what? It sounded gruelling, lonely and soulless. It was the same on the UK circuit, where bookings were for serial one-night stands in clubs or, at best, in small theatres for a few consecutive nights. It was only at the annual Edinburgh Festival that you might have the luxury of a week or two to bed in a performance and get better at your craft.

I'd been thoroughly spoiled by the Melbourne theatre restaurant scene. There was nothing like it, anywhere. You could come up with a show—solo or in collaboration—and have a run of a month. Even more if it was a hit. It was almost like having a real job. And I wanted a 'real' job.

I've taken a few bold chances in my career, but I like to know where I'm heading, more or less. My upbringing has propelled me to seek stability.

When I was a young teenager, Dad had bowled in one day and told us he was on a shortlist of two for a teaching appointment in Nauru. Pardon? Where? What? I lay awake for weeks wondering what life would be like more than 4500 kilometres away on a remote island in the Pacific. No problem, my father said; I would be at boarding school in Far North Queensland.

Where is 'home' for me? When I'm asked, 'Where did you grow up?' I wave my arm in the vague direction of Victoria. Having a 'home town' has never been important to me. If I'm there? It's 'home'.

I've always had a back-up plan. Taken jobs, often doing a couple at once, not trusting they'd last. My list of options, if all else failed, has included some wacky stuff. For example: bring out a range of salsas, sauces and herbed vinegars. But I've been fortunate to be able to stay in my lane, more or less.

In April 1988 I flew to London to appear on Ben Elton's *Friday Night Live* for an Australian comedy 'special' with Barry Humphries and the Doug Anthony All Stars. This was a huge deal.

At the show rehearsal, the director asked me to cut down my routine and re-order a few of the jokes. I spent the afternoon in my hotel room, re-learning my routine, pacing up and down. Aaargh!

On the night, the BBC studio was jam-packed and the energy incredible. The viewing audience was national and enormous. From memory I pulled it off, got the laughs.

(As an aside, in the staff canteen I bumped into, of all people, that senior journalist from back in Geelong. The one who'd told me he'd always been 'a little bit in love' with me. No idea what he was doing there, but he greeted me with open arms and, you'll be happy to hear, I told him to go fuck himself.)

On arriving home, I rang Ted Robinson, director and mentor from *Gillies Report* days.

Me: 'We should do that kind of show here. Live, with comedy acts and great bands.'

Ted: 'I've been thinking the same thing.'

Me: 'I'd like to host it, Ted. I know I could do it.'

Ted: 'I'm sure you could. Leave it with me.'

And off he went to pitch the idea to all the networks in town.

Every month or so, I'd ring Ted to learn the answer had been the same: 'Love, love, LOVE it! But we don't want a woman compere. There are lots of good male comics around. Can't you get one of them?'

Ted told the male network executives that I was the deal-breaker. Either I hosted or no dice. They would not budge. Ted promised he wouldn't either.

I filed it away in my bottom drawer, put my head down and got on with life. It was probably a far-fetched fantasy anyway.

Me hosting a live comedy show on television?

As. If.

*

One thing I did not have on my bingo card was writing an opera with Baz Luhrmann.

In another of Hilary Linstead's schemes to expand my horizons and promote me, she'd hooked me up with Baz. She's credited with discovering him and launching his stratospheric career. Some eighteen months before, Hilary had dealt me in on his half-completed opera, *Lake Lost*. It was to be part of 'The Ra Project' for Australian Opera and to debut in 1988, Australia's bicentennial year, as a showcase for 'young people'.

I'd already co-written a couple of musical stage shows: *On a Clear Day You Can See Jane Clifton* and *I Only Wanna Be With You* for the all-girl group, The Fabulous Singlettes. Both shows had found success in Melbourne and Sydney. The process of working with a talented musical ensemble and a good director was immensely satisfying, and I loved writing more than anything.

An opera librettist? That was next level.

There's no one better than Baz himself to explain the thinking behind the enterprise: 'We were investigating ways of bringing a new audience to opera, so we created an opera workshop. It was the story of an emotionally disconnected property mogul, and how, after being kidnapped by a group of crazy old bohemians, he is convinced not to demolish the beautiful lake area that they inhabit.'

It was the age-old parable of Greed v. Good. Business big-shot Christopher Skase was slated to open the Sheraton Mirage resort in Port Douglas, Far North Queensland, in '88. That was top of mind. The extra 'witchy' element Baz wanted was right in my wheelhouse. I consulted my library of books on myths and witchcraft, passions of mine since childhood. Then, working with Baz and composer Felix Meagher, reworked the storyline, wrote dialogue and lyrics, and hummed tunes for what would become part of the musical score. Baz's vision for the project was clear-eyed—like everything Baz does—and he greeted my ideas with enthusiasm and was gentle if he disagreed. Felix, an accomplished composer, could have been underwhelmed about working with an amateur like me but was generous in collaboration.

The *Lake Lost* project remains a personal high-water mark, literally.

'We all truly loved doing this show,' said Baz some years later. 'I remember we built a lake of water in a film studio, had sports cars driving around in the water, and had to create special foot condoms for the opera singers so that they did not catch a cold as they acted all the scenes.'

It was performed over five nights at a sound stage in South Melbourne with the storied principals of the company sloshing around in the shallows and singing arias in boats.

In the program notes, artistic director Moffatt Oxenbould wrote: '*Lake Lost* may or may not be developed and performed again. Felix Meagher and Wendy Harmer may not write again for the lyric stage. Baz Luhrmann may or may not work in future with opera or with opera singers.'

The reviews were unanimous. It was 'innovative, imaginative, surprising and witty . . . *But is this opera?*'

The Age commended the production: 'It should probably be typified as music-theatre rather than opera, yet its vitality of production is of such a calibre that it ought to be seen by anyone who has found the current AO season lacking in stage interest.'

There was only one 'big problem' the reviewer added. And it did not lie with the cast, who were 'impossible to fault', but rather with me, the librettist. My emphasis on the 'supernatural' and mention of 'Mother Gaia' was unnecessary, he said. Honestly! Did he think I'd somehow managed to sneak in some subversive femmo-greenie message without Baz's imprimatur?

Another review lauded it as: '100 minutes of inspired creativity . . . See it!'

Sad to say, I didn't. A huge regret. It debuted when I was performing in Glasgow with the beloved late UK comic Paul O'Grady, in his divine drag-queen persona of Lily Savage, at the first outing in a showcase for comics called *So You Think You're Funny?* as part of the city's 'Mayfest' celebrations.

My mate from Brighton, Simon Fanshawe, came up with the title, and it was the *worst* possible name for a comedy event staged in Glasgow in 1988. An open invitation for a rough and rowdy crowd to heckle the shite out of me and Lily. It's where I came up with another of my personal mottos: 'Never work to an audience that's funnier than you.'

Recovering in a bar with Simon (these days an OBE) and actor Ian McKellen (now a Sir), I found a quiet corridor to phone home for news on how *Lake Lost* had been received. The word was good and my companions raised a glass, even as they wondered, with good reason, how a thirty-something, female stand-up comedian had scored a gig with the Australian Opera.

It was because of my indefatigable agent. I wish that everyone in the arts could find someone who believes in them as much as Hilary believed in me.

I heard that Cameron Mackintosh—who produced, among a long list of hit musicals, *Cats*, *Phantom of the Opera* and *Les Misérables*—had been interested in *Lake Lost*. But by then Baz was consumed with the stage show of *Strictly Ballroom*.

However, Baz wasn't done with opera. Not by half. In 1990 he returned to the rebranded Opera Australia with his wife and creative partner Catherine Martin to create a sensational version of Puccini's *La Bohème*. A huge, red neon sign spelling out L'AMOUR stamped their vision on the production. It made its way to New York via San Francisco, where it had been 'the most sought-after ticket in town'.

This time I didn't miss out!

In 2002 I was invited by Baz to the opening night at the ornate chocolate-box setting of the Broadway Theatre. Happily, the premiere coincided with a press junket to see *The Lion King* on its way to Sydney. On a snowy winter evening, my best friend Laura Waters and I arrived early at the theatre—1681 Broadway, New York, New York—and settled into what we thought would be the 'cheap seats'. For the next half-hour we sat, open-mouthed, as the gilded beau monde glided to their places.

We were seated directly in front of Leonardo DiCaprio and Anna Wintour. In the same row as them, Rupert Murdoch, Harvey Weinstein, Sandra Bullock and Hugh Grant. Cameron Diaz was over there. Donna Karan a few rows down near Regis Philbin and Kathie Lee Gifford. It went on and on, 'like a really weird dream', Laura remembers. 'It was epic.'

In an even more outlandish turn of events, at intermission Laura and I were marshalled to the VIP enclave. Not to where

Hugh, Cameron or Harvey were heading; they were directed to turn right. We were waved to the left, to somewhere even *more* exclusive. Huh?

We found ourselves in a roped-off corner next to a grand piano with Rupert Murdoch and Wendi Deng. Just the four of us. I attempted small talk. Then . . . even smaller talk. Minutes ticked by. Awkward.

We were saved by the arrival of Joe Cross, business partner of Lachlan Murdoch and best man at his wedding. I knew Joe from back home and our connection to the Manly Warringah rugby league club, along with Lachlan's wife Sarah. I fell on Joe like a tourist on a baked pretzel in Times Square.

'Wendy! Great to see you!' he exclaimed. 'Rupert, you know Wendy, don't you?'

This was met with a blank look and incoherent mumble. Actually, I had met Rupert the year before, at the premiere of Baz's movie *Moulin Rouge* at Fox Studios in Sydney where he'd greeted me with the same glazed expression. Laura and I escaped back to our seats as fast as was polite.

Later, in our hotel room, Laura and I pinched each other in disbelief and squealed with laughter. She accused me of sloshing a flute of champagne over Ms Deng's glamorous outfit, to her annoyance. I maintain it was Laura who dared me to introduce her to Harvey Weinstein, who we'd bailed up on a staircase landing and was even less impressed. These remain matters of dispute.

Not only did Baz so kindly give us the best seats in the house that night, but on his 1998 compilation album *Something For Everybody*, among the hits from *Strictly Ballroom* and *Romeo +*

Juliet, there is a small something Felix and I had written for *Lake Lost* a decade earlier. My lyrics for 'I'm Losing You' are a bit naff, but the tune is pretty and it survives where the rest has vanished in the mist.

*

A huge contingent of Aussie comedy and musical talent headed to the Edinburgh Festival Fringe in August 1988, funded by the Australian Bicentennial Authority. Mikhail Gorbachev's *perestroika* and *glasnost*, with their promise of reforming the Soviet political and economic system, had captured the world's imagination.

Riffing on the theme, promoters John Pinder and his partner Roger Evans assembled the assault on Scotland under the banner *OZNOST: From behind the XXXX curtain* (XXXX beer being a popular export).

There were seven acts from Melbourne: Circus Oz, Kate Ceberano, Rod Quantock, Sarah Cathcart, Julie Forsyth, and a double bill of impressionist Gerry Connolly and magician Doug Tremlett. I was on a triple bill with Magda Szubanski and Gina Riley as *Faking It 3*. We were all playing at the illustrious Assembly Rooms.

DAAS, now darlings of the festival crowd, and Adelaide's Glynn Nicholas had paid their own way there. Happily for Patrick and me, the Cabbages came along too and paired with Mark Trevorrow as Bob Downe for a night of sparkling home-grown cabaret.

Faking It 3 was a showcase for our various star turns. I performed stand-up and also stepped out in character as Jane, the Australian sister of Fergie, the notorious Duchess of York, which the Scots heartily approved of. Magda was there in all her grotesque, chain-smoking glory as Lynne Postlethwaite—'I said Love ... I said Pet'—which a review in *The Scotsman* recognised as being in the best tradition of cultural attaché Sir Les Patterson. Gina's vocal impressions of female pop stars—Stevie Nicks, Diana Ross and Suzanne Vega—were judged 'excellent'.

As for me: 'Wendy Harmer is one of that rare breed of vicious comedians who can successfully make you cringe—without disregarding her vitriol as the product of a really sick mind instead of a pretty clever satirist.'

Yikes! Was it something I said?

We made 'Pick of the Week' in *Time Out*.

The festival was the usual madhouse of late nights, too much drinking and not enough sleep. Hangovers cured with lumps of sugary dough bought at dawn from the bakery. Flogging ourselves in a game of rounders with Arthur Smith, and then an afternoon nap before doing it all again.

When the festival wrapped, Patrick and I spent a sublime, peaceful autumn in Europe. Caught the transcendent trumpet of Arturo Sandoval at Ronnie Scott's jazz club in London and cycled around Versailles with friends.

But a huge decision was looming. Should I pursue success in London? What would that look like? For Patrick? For us? How could we make it work? We often told each other, 'I can't imagine being with anyone but you.'

Hilary had found me a top London agent and my face was showing up all over the place as an Antipodean oddity. Interviews on breakfast TV and guesting on panel shows—once on a quiz team with Suzi Quatro! There was plenty more where that came from. If I wanted it.

At a dinner party I was seated next to a literary editor from *The Times*: 'So . . . Orstralian comedy? Where do you sheilas tell your jokes?' he brayed. 'At outdoor dunnies? Haw! Haw!'

I recall that exchange so clearly because it struck me that, as sexist as the scene was back in Australia, at least it was in your face and you could deal with it. In England there were more layers of discrimination to be going on with. My voice had been described as sounding like 'the brakes on a Melbourne tram' in *The Age*. But at home, almost everyone sounded like me. Only difference was: did you ring the bell to get off in Brunswick West or East Caulfield? In the UK, there was also the question: were you in the first-, second- or third-class carriage?

I auditioned and won a part in a new comedy sketch series for ITV's Television South, alongside Clive Anderson and the clever musical improviser Josie Lawrence. They both became national stars in Channel 4's *Whose Line Is It Anyway?* the following year.

I have a letter from a producer, dated January 1989, replying to a Christmas card I'd sent.

'We were all really disappointed that you couldn't be part of the team . . . You know how difficult it is to find intelligent, talented and funny female comedy performers—especially loud-mouthed, bitchy Australian ones! Anyway, you were a great hit with everyone. Clearly you are destined to be a star over here soon.'

After much deliberation, I'd concluded that in the UK, I'd always be a novelty act. That 'loudmouthed, bitchy' Aussie sheila direct from a sell-out season at an outdoor dunny.

All my cultural references—the jokes about Vegemite sangas, blue-ringed octopus at the beach, Sunday drives in the bush, Queensland coppers, politics, footy and eating roast turkey for Christmas when it was forty degrees in the shade—would be lost.

I'd be working with one arm tied behind my back. Always an outsider.

The producer signed off with: 'I hope your version of *Friday Night Live* is happening.'

It was. At last.

I packed up and came home to the biggest gig of all!

14

Bright lights and red dust

Dressing-room mirror
ABC studios
Gordon Street, Elsternwick

That was amazing.

How did we do that?

No, really. How did we make that happen?

Stop crying.

Everyone's sick of your crying.

Especially me.

You are pathetic.

*

Tuesday Night Live: The Big Gig almost didn't happen.

Ted had gone back to the ABC for one last pitch after being knocked back all over town. This time he was in front of Michael

Shrimpton, then head of Light Entertainment, who had created *Countdown* with director Robbie Weekes. That cavernous studio at Gordon Street was now empty, asking for it.

'I walked into the meeting and had nothing,' Ted tells me. 'I told them there was interest from the commercial networks, but I lied. I was bluffing. The meeting at the ABC was coming around to the idea, but again told me they didn't want a woman hosting and had a few suggestions for male comics who could do a better job. I got up from the table and started walking slowly to the door . . . slower . . . and slower, until my fingers were on the doorhandle.

'Then I heard from behind, "Well, *alright*. You can have her! But it's on your head. And does it *have* to be live?"'

It did, Ted insisted. That was the whole point of the exercise. At the time Australia was in love with brilliant sketch comedy on TV that had begun with *The Eleventh Hour*, then *The D-Generation*. The stars of those shows were about to hit out with *Fast Forward*. *The Comedy Company* had debuted the year before and was a smashing success.

Where did the *Gig* fit in? The difference was that very little was pre-recorded. The sketches, stand-up and musical numbers were played live to the studio audience, who became a vital part of the show. The aim was to showcase performers from the thriving live comedy and music scene and give them exposure, much as *Countdown* had done for the music industry for thirteen years. It had wrapped in 1986 after an extraordinary 563 episodes.

I had just finished up another Christmas show at the Laugh, managing pissed office parties. By this time, I must have been a world expert at handling an unruly comedy audience in a small room. The prospect of doing it on television was exciting. I knew I was built to host the *Gig*.

Ted and I put our heads together on who we'd like in the ensemble. Our shopping list included a house band. No contest. It was the Swingin' Sidewalks, an upbeat, jazzy outfit with an awesome brass section and backed by the accomplished Swing Sisters—Rebecca Barnard, Kerri Simpson and Shelley Scown.

I'd been hassling Ted about the Doug Anthony All Stars. He'd seen them on the tape I'd brought back from London but was 'unimpressed'. I hauled him to the Prince Patrick hotel in Collingwood to see them live. 'Blown away. Booked them on the spot,' says Ted.

He signed the Empty Pockets—Matt Quartermaine and Matt Parkinson—after attending a gig in a pub where no one turned up. The place was deserted. After a conversation with the boys, Ted knew they 'got it'. 'They were smart, knew the way to play a classic double act.' They were signed, their act sight unseen. Ted's instinct was right. Their signature physical, knock-about style was to become a crowd favourite.

Ted had caught Glynn Nicholas and Jean Kittson's shows. We were on the same page. They were in. We'd been huge fans for ages.

Jean had starred as Nurse Pam Sandwich in *Let The Blood Run Free* at the Last Laugh, an off-the-wall spoof of TV medical melo-dramas, set in St Christopher's Hospital. Jean, alongside the late, much-loved Lynda Gibson as 'Matron Conniving-Bitch', impro-vised brilliant slapstick comedy as part of the comedy collective

The Blood Group. (The TV version, produced by Ian McFadyen, ran here and in the UK for 26 episodes in the nineties.)

Jean, in the tradition of Lucille Ball's physical comedy, and I, more from the school of Joan Rivers stand-up with a line in acerbic commentary, made a good combination.

Patrick Cook and Phil Scott from *Gillies* were drafted for the writers' room with a roster of wits, including the talented Shaun Micallef who wrote with Glynn. Ted had assembled the ABC's finest floor crew, prop makers and assistant directors.

After a successful pilot, we were good to go on a Tuesday night at the 'adult' time of 9.30 p.m.

The first night the show went to air, the ABC executives were 'astonished', says Ted. 'But they reckoned they'd been dudded. They were sure the whole thing had been pre-recorded. No way had it gone out live.'

The next week, to prove the show *was* going out live, we crossed to a Billy Bragg concert that was happening simultaneously. 'It was a mistake, I realised, because it just sucked the energy out of the room,' Ted recalls. 'But they still didn't believe me and insisted the Billy Bragg bit was pre-recorded. It *must* have been a clip.' Finally, he exploded: 'Well, go and stick your head into the studio because the audience is STILL THERE!'

It was Ted's genius that made the show so different from other live comedy TV shows screened in the US and the UK. As a young man he'd been inspired by ABC TV's *Six O'Clock Rock*, where the bands performed on the periphery of the studio and the audience and camera 'hardware' was in the midst of it all. 'I'd always wanted to re-create that.'

He did just that with *The Big Gig*. The cameras were right there in the middle of the crowd, hand-held or on swooping cranes, creating a dynamic 'in the round' feel, as if you at home were really there . . . at a big gig. There were multiple stages for sketches, the bands and stand-up. When the whole thing cranked—with fog machines, pyrotechnics, multiple lighting rigs, huge swaying inflatable puppets, fly-in-fly-out graphics and dizzying camera effects—it was a surreal trip.

No wonder it became appointment viewing for every stoner in the nation.

A review from *The Age* after our first show: 'It is difficult to characterise this program . . . much of it looked made up on the spot. Yet *Tuesday Night Live* seemed fresh and natural, like Wendy talking about douche spray. I'll keep watching.'

Douche spray? Was that even a thing? He made that bit up, bless him.

I rang my father for his verdict. 'I thought your diction was quite good,' he said.

I look back at my opening monologue from that first show and see a young woman stepping out with extraordinary confidence. Sparkly black jacket, cute floral skirt, black tights, high heels and my merino perm scraped into an unruly updo.

Brash and in-your-face from the get-go: 'I'm Wendy . . . Shockingly daggy name. We're always Casper the drippy little ghost's sidekick or Peter Pan's fag hag.'

The message: I was a sister doin' it for herself. Out there, loud and proud.

But I was faking it.

There's a line that's a clue to my real state of mind: 'I'm single at the moment.'

Only days before opening night, my darling Patrick had left me.

Just as I remember where we were when we'd got together almost four years earlier, I remember too the moment it was all over. He was standing in our flat in front of the white-painted windowsill filled with framed photographs of people we loved and my pots of temperamental African violets.

'Don't you love me anymore?' I asked.

'No,' he said softly.

And the floor fell away.

*

More than fifteen years later, in my thinly disguised autobiographical chick-lit novel *Love and Punishment*, the lead character, Francie, is sitting in the office of her therapist, Faith Treloar, after a hideous romantic break-up. She is looking into a hand mirror.

'Now, Francie,' Faith says, 'I want you to look in this mirror and tell me everything you love about yourself. I want you to think of all the good qualities you have and all your talents. Tell me what *you* love about *you*.'

Francie looks at her image and tells herself: *'I hate you. You are an utter loser. A fat lump of nothing. Give up. Go home. Disappear from the face of the earth, evaporate into thin air. Just do everyone*

*a favour and fucking die. You will not be missed . . . by anyone . . .
ever.'*

It had been exactly my state of mind at the time. Not ideal for
the host of a live national television show.

The break-up hit me with a force I had in no way anticipated.
A sledgehammer blow. I was wreckage. I'd been through break-
ups before, but this time was different. I crawled around our flat
on my hands and knees, lived on vodka, hardly ate for weeks and
lost a lot of weight.

I was barely coping, had suicidal thoughts. I couldn't
remember ever experiencing such raw emotion. But, then, I'd
jumped off the garage roof when I was a kid, so I must have.

When I found out Patrick had left me for another woman,
sorrow escalated into rage. I cut up all his clothes with scissors . . .
and I enjoyed it. I plagued all our mutual friends with late-night
calls of hysterical crying and desperate pleas for more information. *Who is she? Why? When? Where? How?*

As I wrote in *Love and Punishment*: 'Francie's friends all told
her that if she didn't get professional help, they would hire a hit
man to kill her.'

When Francie is in the therapist's chair and has run out of
tissues and self-pity, her therapist says they are going to do some
'grief work':

'What if I told you that grief was something that crept up
on you? That if you didn't deal with it properly, it hid in the
shadows, quietly feeding on your pain and doubling in size
until it was immense and unstoppable. What if one day it

253

caught up with you and knocked you out? Don't you think you should be brave? Turn and face it now before that happens?

'I'd like you to go back . . . imagine yourself as ten years old. Tell me what happened that day. Can you see yourself there?'

Francie could.

I could.

I hauled myself into therapy, and the counsellor quickly identified that I had 'abandonment issues' from childhood which I'd never addressed. That made sense, and I joined retreats on weekends, signing up for all manner of New Age 'healing'—vows of silence, divination through tarot and numerology, scrawling my regrets on a rock and chucking it into a river. I found a lot of it nutty, but the visualisations, where I went back to childhood and rescued my 'inner child', had a profound effect. In one exercise I time-travelled to comfort that little girl back in Bendigo and sobbed my heart out. Afterwards, I did feel lighter and like I'd resolved some longstanding, subconscious fears I held of unworthiness, of being unlovable, and my deep dread of being left again.

The counsellor also suggested that Patrick and I had become so deeply connected through a shared 'pathology': the absence of our mothers.

In *Love and Punishment*, Francie's estranged lover attends a truth-telling session with her as Patrick had done with me in real life. Faith Treloar intones in 'therapy-speak': 'You recognised something in each other, you didn't know what exactly. I believe you came together not to hurt each other, but to heal each other. But truly, the healing has to be done within your own hearts.'

On the last page of the novel (spoiler alert), Francie looks into an enchanted mirror in a dream: *'Tell me what you see. Tell me why you love you.'* She replies: 'I'm beautiful. I'm happy, and I have nice hair.

'Next morning Francie got out of bed and walked, completely unaided, down the hallway towards a bright light, the smell of buttered toast and the sound of laughter.'

A review of the novel in *New Idea*, said: '. . . a quirky, painfully honest, yet hysterically funny account of one woman's journey towards relationship closure.' It took me a long time to get to forgiveness, friendship, and see, if not the 'hysterically funny', at least the 'ridiculous' in the unhinged drama I'd put myself and everyone else through. I wrote that book in hindsight as a happily married woman with two small children.

I lost a layer of skin in that break-up. It took me years to recover and, while I suppose an honest reckoning with the past was overdue, I don't subscribe to the myth that 'everything happens for a reason'. It's junk philosophy, shit theology, bad science and even worse advice.

Everything happens because . . . well . . . it happens.

The only thing I can add is that poor Patrick chose the wrong woman to dump. I must have been his worst nightmare when I became known as the comedic 'Queen of Broken Hearts'. He never once complained. He read my books. Apologised for the way he went about things and the hurt he had caused. Accepted the invitation to my wedding.

We still care for each other.

More than thirty years later, he's still with the woman he left me for.

PS: The cutting-up-the-clothes thing? Word got back to me that on surveying the carnage he said: 'Well, she's a passionate woman and that's why I loved her so much.'

*

In the early days after the break-up, I clung to the *Gig* like a life raft.

Over the first fifteen episodes, the weeks, then months, took on a familiar, reliable and comforting pattern—writing, memorising, rehearsing, putting the show to air, and then gathering the day after to watch what we'd perpetrated on the viewing public.

Sometimes we'd thought the show had been a triumph, but on watching it back realised it hadn't quite hung together. Other times it was the opposite. What had felt disjointed and clunky on the night had come out of the oven as a freshly baked, perfectly timed, exuberant, spicy extravaganza.

Ted's approach as a director suited me. If you asked him about your performance—'What did you think?'—he'd answer, with an inscrutable, 'Hmm,' and a stroke of his beard, 'Well, what did *you* think?' For those of used to critiquing our own work, it was the correct and only response. We were all self-starters and worked our arses off to make each outing better, and the show went from strength to strength.

I was now recognised everywhere I went. Two cops pulled me over in peak-hour traffic at a St Kilda intersection. I hadn't done anything wrong and was mortified as rubberneckers drove by, yelling my name out of their car windows. A police notepad and pen were thrust at me: 'Hey! Can we have your autograph?'

In Prahran market on a Saturday morning, I was stalked by an elderly woman giving me the side eye at the fruit and veggie stalls, through piles of bananas and carrots. Finally, I turned and asked, 'Can I help you?'

She hissed, 'I think you're vulgar,' and marched off.

Often asked how I dealt with that level of recognition and notoriety; my answer was always: 'At least I'm never lonely.' Maybe that very first motivation—'I'll give you something to stare at!'—had worked. I never quite knew why people were pointing at me.

I was back in a shared household, this time in a rambling old Victorian-era mansion, 'Himalaya', I'd found on Tennyson Street, St Kilda, opposite the botanical gardens. The joint was so massive that, even when divided into four flats, our portion on the ground floor was bigger than anywhere I'd ever lived. It came with a cloakroom, a cellar and an immense lounge room with a sprung wooden floor—perfect for dancing.

I took two rooms for myself—a handsome high-ceilinged bedroom and another for an office. Two friends—Michael Trudgeon and Dale Langley—moved in, and it all made for a congenial household. Between us we had a huge circle of friends in the music, design, fashion and art world and loved throwing open our magnificent front doors. (Dearest Dale was to succumb to breast cancer at just forty-five. Vale)

I collected cookbooks and slaved in the kitchen for regular dinner parties. On a Christmas morning, I woke to find three people sleeping it off in the cellar after a drunken festive rave the night before. I found another two comatose bodies rolled up in a carpet.

There was constant coming and going. A good thing. Otherwise, I was writing in a mad frenzy. Anything to fill up the time and distract me from wallowing in my own misery.

It turned out to be one of the most creative times in my life. My heartache became fodder for columns, books and routines. I couldn't help myself. Obviously, I wasn't the first to be ploughing the fertile ground of bad relationships, but maybe I was the first high-profile, noisy female comedian in Australia who wasn't taking it lying down:

'He says: "You mother me." "Mother you? What? I sewed a name tag in the back of your jumper—what more do you want?"'

'I asked him: "Do you love me?" He replied: "Well, I'm *here* aren't I?" Like he's got the option to be at Elle Macpherson's place, but is just doing *me* a favour, lying on *my* couch, emptying *my* fridge.'

In the very first rehearsal for the *Gig*, I'd alarmed Ted and the entire cast and crew with a highly personal, detailed monologue about my days-old breakup. He recalls being worried about my mental health. I had to assure him it wouldn't be going to air. I'd just needed to say it aloud and, after all, turning misery into laughs is the stand-up comedian's stock-in-trade. I had plenty to be going on with. Nevertheless, Ted tells me, 'I was genuinely fearful that you'd crack under pressure. But you rallied. Pulled it off.'

Cast and crew all have vivid memories of the *Gig*. Because the show was live, it was a high-wire act fuelled by an addictive mix of high-octane adrenaline and pure fear. Ted loved his pyrotechnics, and one night the set caught alight. I introduced the next act; even as out of the corner of my eye I could see actual flames and the crew frantically rushing over with fire extinguishers.

My opening monologue, often written with Patrick Cook, sometimes stretched to almost ten minutes, delivered without autocue or note cards. I would wander into the audience for a live Q & A and improvise with whatever I could glean for laughs. If one of my lines bombed, it bombed. There was no way to go back and fix it.

Going 'live' has always suited me. I'm the original 'one-take wonder'. If I have to go back and replicate a performance, it's usually worse in every subsequent version. Ask Ted and he'll confirm it. In pre-recorded sketches which required another take, I drove everyone crazy.

When I'm working to a live audience and really in 'the zone', I have this weird image of my forehead disappearing so that information comes in and is processed without me thinking about it. What then comes out of my mouth often surprises even me.

I remember one night performing with Jane Turner at the Laugh in a sketch as two Cockney leather-wearing punks when a strange high-pitched laugh from an audience member punctuated a momentary silence. Immediately I said: 'Yeah. I can 'ear the swallows migratin' back to Capistrano.' No idea at all where that had come from. Over the years, the workings of my brain and mouth—with nothing holding up the traffic—have often been a curse, as much as I've been lauded for my quick wit.

My clueless beauty pageant contestant Leanne, in a chiffon gown and sash, whose aim was 'to meet PR people from all walks of life', became a fixture on the *Gig*. She was useful for making political comment. The newly crowned 'Miss Southern New South Wales Woodchip Queen of 1989', with a circular saw blade as a tiara, announced a change to festivities. The chainsaw relay would be held in the disused fire-brigade shed . . . now that there were no actual trees left to catch fire. Commiserations also for those incinerated in an accident between a 4WD and a logging truck.

One of my favourite appearances was as an irate archangel, lowered from the ceiling and wearing an enormous pair of feathery wings. She'd been sent by God as head of Her property department (yes, God was a *She*) to review the tenancy arrangements on Earth: 'A two-hemisphere, one-moon, temperate planet with central solar heating and close to all amenities.'

The angel had a few items on her agenda. To begin with, the original lease had been signed by an 'Adam' and an 'Eve'. Would someone mind explaining the current occupancy of *six billion*? The 'condition report' also noted that 'whales were an original feature and not to be removed'. So where were they? The monologue ended with an eviction notice accompanied by a series of demands: the flora and fauna must be steam-cleaned, a new barrier reef installed, the hole in the ozone layer repaired and the keys to the planet handed over to the cockroaches. 'AND YOU CAN TAKE YOUR NUCLEAR WASTE WITH YOU!'

That was more than thirty years ago.

If only.

Jean Kittson and I teamed up as Sheree and Miranda, two slappers in outrageous teased wigs and the most garish of eighties-style sequinned taffeta frocks, downing cocktails and gossiping at a bar. (Amazing to look back and see myself puffing away on a ciggie!) In one pre-recorded outing, we were decked out in fascinators as bridesmaids throwing back flutes of fizzy. The alcohol was real, and we did take-after-take until we were legless. The punchline was us falling backwards off our bar stools onto a hidden mattress. I missed, fell onto the concrete floor and dislocated my shoulder.

Proof of the old adage 'Dying is easy, comedy is hard.'

The *Gig* ran for sixty-three episodes between 1989 and 1991 and, even more than thirty years later, everyone who loved the show has a favourite act: Glynn Nicholas as the children's TV host Pâté Biscuit with her bug-eyed puppet Bongo, or as fat-gutted Sergeant F'kn Smith. The Empty Pockets with their clever, choreographed cartoon violence. Jean Kittson as the snooty ABC newsreader Veronica Glenhuntly and her adoration of golfing legend Wayne 'Lightning' Truscott. Jean again as Candida Royale, the ditzy, pink-Lycra-clad fitness freak flailing on her exercise equipment, and also as the flight attendant Rose McCloud, with scarifying commentary on Australian businessmen flying to the 'fleshpots' of Bangkok.

As for the phenomenon of the Doug Anthony All Stars? From the moment DAAS stepped out, greeted by chants from the adoring faithful, they pushed the shock and awe as far as it was possible on ABC TV—which is a lot further than you could push it these days. Tim Ferguson says that, broadcast now, 'a lot of our material would see us burned in effigy in the inner-city town square'.

In rehearsal, I was appalled to see that DAAS planned to crucify the Easter bunny on Shrove Tuesday. It would be the end of us, I feared. I approached Ted, who told me to mind my own business. Fair enough, too.

'Even *we t*hought it might be a bit much,' says Tim. 'So we crucified ourselves instead, with Richard on the cross at the end complaining, "I shouldn't even be here. I'm high Anglican!"'

The question is often asked: could we have done our show today, in the era of social media and 'culture wars'?

It's difficult, or even pointless, to look back at the comedy of the past and judge it by today's standards. What's immediately obvious, though, is the lack of diversity in all the sketch shows of the era. We were predominantly white and mostly straight. There's no way that would fly now, and nor should it.

But as for the strident political commentary, the challenge to social mores and slaughtering of sacred cows?

On one hand, the relentless outrage machine cranked by radio shock jocks and Rupert Murdoch's News Corp brigade of Flying Monkeys would see us as Exhibit A in front of Senate Estimates on high rotation, accused as a bunch of ABC 'leftys' of offending public decency and contributing to the downfall of Western civilisation. (No matter that we bashed both sides of politics. On the opening night I likened the then PM Bob Hawke's interview with Jana Wendt on *A Current Affair* to a 'flasher peering through a hedge'.)

On the other hand, we would be attacked by the straighteners and wowsers of the far left for unconscious bias, misogyny, ableism, homophobia and myriad microaggressions.

Some in the 'concerned' middle would no doubt deem us 'inappropriate'—my least favourite word and today used to encompass any kind of behaviour: 'rude', 'crass', 'depraved', 'stupid', or even 'dangerous'. *Those* words are never uttered, because they're intriguing and demand more salacious detail. Also, they don't have enough syllables to make you sound well educated.

Maybe Dame Edna Everage had it right: 'It was quite *uncalled for*, possums,' leaving everyone none the wiser.

We would trend on social media today, become a battered football in the 'free speech' melee, and the ratings would soar as everyone tuned in to see next week's deplorable antics. I'm sure we would have obliged. Sex, politics, religion, drugs . . . there was no topic nor incendiary behaviour off-limits, including DAAS blowing the Australian flag to smithereens with a bazooka.

We were blessed to have the support of management. The ABC's managing director at the time, David Hill, was a fan. He was in the audience one evening and of course I made a beeline for him with my microphone and made jokes at his expense. He took it well. (Trivia: David Anderson started his career as a cable dragger on the *Gig* and became ABC managing director in 2019.)

We all felt bullet-proof, and in no small part because Ted was running interference on any negative feedback. He knew our performance was a confidence game. Maybe not so much for DAAS: 'We didn't get any complaints, so we just turned up the volume. If we *had* got bad feedback, we would have done what we wanted to anyway,' says Tim.

One day, looking for some stationery, I found a cache of letters addressed to me that Ted had hidden in his desk drawer. They were really nasty, calling me every vile name imaginable. One mentioned the scars on my face, asking: 'Hey, love, did you cut yourself shaving?' If those insults had been amplified on social media? Maybe I would have wilted and run away. Instead, back then, there were a few tears, a consoling talk from Ted, and nothing to be done but get out there again the following week.

The roll call of international performers over the three years was stellar: Ben Elton, Craig Ferguson, Pete McCarthy, Roger McGough, Lily Savage, Rich Hall, Greg Proops, Geraldine Doyle and, notably, Stevie Starr The Regurgitator, who swallowed the diamond ring from my finger to squeals from the audience . . . and then coughed it back up again.

We would have loved to feature more international acts, but were always in a pitched battle with what was then called Actors Equity. It was explained to them that this was a two-way trade, and the more overseas acts we featured, the more opportunities opened up for local acts when they travelled, but the union was immovable and often threatened to shut us down. It was incredibly frustrating.

The locals were world-class: Rachel Berger, Denise Scott, Richard Stubbs, Anthony Morgan, Greg Fleet, Angela Moore, Brian Doyle, Jimeoin, the Found Objects, the Umbilical Brothers, Scared Weird Little Guys. Paul Livingston, as His Weirdness Flacco, became a regular; likewise Anthony Ackroyd as Addam (two d's), the coke-addled advertising guru snorting lines off a table.

One more anecdote from Ted. Possibly my favourite. The *Gig* featured many bands, among them the Bachelors from Prague, Zydeco Jump, Vacation in Harlem and the Violent Femmes. Booking TISM (This Is Serious Mum) was always going to be a risk. They were an anarchic, controversial, seven-piece outfit who were playing wild gigs in Melbourne. Their debut single was 'Defecate on My Face' and their follow-up '40 years—Then Death'. Wreaking havoc was their MO. Most importantly, they always wore balaclavas and full bodysuits to maintain anonymity, crucial to their fanbase who'd signed up for their ironic nihilism (and probably saved them from serial defamation suits). The line-up was a moveable feast.

As Ted tells it, the lads turned up for rehearsal, unmasked, in t-shirts and shorts. Word got back to him they were planning to 'go feral' once we went live to air, and they did. During their first number, one of the band members jumped on a camera crane and was swinging off it over the audience.

'It was potentially lethal. Could have toppled the crane and killed someone. We had to keep cutting away. I was furious,' says Ted. 'The band was slated for a second number later in the show, so I went to their dressing room and told them if they didn't behave, I'd play their rehearsal tape and give away their identities to the world. They came out and performed like little lambs.'

Another, unexpected, advantage of going live to air.

(I've lately heard that there was no such 'rehearsal' tape. That Ted was, again bluffing. If so, well played.)

*

In between series, I toured the US with Los Trios Ringbarkus (Steve Kearney and Neill Gladwin) going to Chicago, Atlanta, Houston, Miami and Los Angeles. It was a steep learning curve. Part of Los Trios' act involved chucking bread rolls at the audience; they were used to them being pelted back, leading to an almighty, hilarious food fight. In America, the audience ducked.

My performances were nothing to write home about, until I had the measure of the crowd and realised that observations from an outsider on the weirdness of life in the US was where the laughs were. 'But enough about me. Let's talk about you. What do *you* think about *me*?'

Most of my routine was re-written for every place we played after wandering the streets and taking notes. I was a hit in Houston. (Which I've never had the chance to put into a sentence, until now.) 'Why, you're as cute as a speckled pup underneath a fire truck,' one local drawled at the bar.

Not so lucky at a midnight slot in a club in Miami where I asked, 'G'day, anyone here been to Australia?'

And the whole room answered: 'Que?'

*

I came home to host the second season of the *Gig* with a roll call of comedy stars who inspired those watching. One of them was a young Wil Anderson on his family's dairy farm in country Victoria. Wil says the show changed his life. He's now one of the nation's most successful comic performers.

You never know where your act will land. The impact it has. Like the night I saw those performers on stage as a journalist with my notebook—my life was never the same after that.

I apologise for leaving out the names of so many talented people I worked with. One reason why the *Gig* has never been re-screened is because it would involve hundreds of release forms from myriad performers.

And maybe it's better to let the show live on in memory, where it remains so vivid, larger in the retelling of it. Like that nightclub you couldn't get into or that rock festival where your car broke down on the way, but everyone told you they went and had the time of their lives.

The Big Gig was a show best viewed through the lens of the excesses of the late eighties.

It's lamentable that we don't have something like it now.

*

WENDY LIKES YOU TO LAUGH AT WOMEN
PROOF THAT WOMEN ARE FUNNY
GIRLS HAVE THE LAST LAUGH

THE RISE AND RISE OF THE FUNNY GIRLS
STANDING OV(UL)ATION
DID YOU HEAR THE ONE ABOUT THE FEMALE
COMEDIAN?
THE WIT OF WOMEN
YOU TELL 'EM LUV

In 1989, the Australian media decided that, yes, women were *actually* funny, and these headlines in the newspapers were a gift from the subs desk. The women in TV sketch shows were often outshining the blokes, rewriting Aussie humour as they saw it, and we couldn't get enough of them. The timing of my first book, *It's a Joke, Joyce: Australia's Funny Women*, was perfect.

I'd been approached by Pan Books editor Penny Hueston, who'd picked up on the zeitgeist. It was a project I'd had in mind for some time, but I thought I'd be lucky to sell it to any publisher. Instead, it dropped into my lap.

For those who don't get the reference, 'It's a joke, Joyce' was coined in the 1960s on Channel Nine's TV variety show *In Melbourne Tonight* by scriptwriter Freddie Parsons in the famous sketch of an elderly couple, the Wilsons—George (Graham Kennedy) and his wife Joyce (Rosie Sturgess). Whenever the irascible, constipated, toothless George uttered an innuendo that went over his wife's uncomprehending head, he'd pause, stare at her with exasperation and mutter: 'It's a joke, Joyce'. It was a hugely popular catchphrase that became part of the Aussie vernacular for decades.

I was always asked in interviews: 'Why aren't there more funny Australian women?' I was puzzled by the question. There were lots. I'd grown up watching Rosie Sturgess. Also Judi Farr's perfect deadpan delivery in *My Name's McGooley, What's Yours?* and the fabulous Noeline Brown drawling, 'Piss off, Bruce,' in *The Naked Vicar Show.* Maybe everyone had forgotten them? And who else had there been? Who had come before them? I had to find out.

The enterprise, driven by frustration and curiosity, produced a work of no great literary merit, but it was the first anthology that looked exclusively at our funny sheilas. I found the history fascinating and could have spent years pulling it together. As it was, I fitted it around my live comedy work and, thankfully, reviews acknowledged both the book's serious intent and scrappy, ratbag charm.

I included scripts from vaudeville days, performed by Bubby Allen, Kitty Bluett, Florrie Forde, Lillian Colenso, Ida Newton and Ada Reeve, to name a few. Many Australian women had become stars of English music hall when they exhausted opportunities at home. Sadie Gale, the wife of Roy 'Mo' Rene, was celebrated in her day. Likewise Jenny Howard, the wife of George 'Onkus' Wallace, a giant of comedy in the 1920s. The phrase 'whacko-the-diddle-oh' was popularised on radio by the legendary comedy duo Ada and Elsie.

I count myself enormously privileged to have been granted lengthy sit-down interviews with some of the greats of the 1950s and 60s—Ruth Cracknell, Val Jellay, Jan Adele and Rosie Sturgess. (Rosie told me that my approach to comedy reminded her of her own, a treasured compliment.) Toni Lamond and Tikki Taylor sent me written recollections, which I included.

In a Norwich tearoom, over copious cups of tea, I caught up with Barbara Angell, a prolific contributor to Channel Seven's *Sunnyside-Up* and *The Mavis Bramston Show*. Barbara had started out in the Tivoli as a 'chi-chi soubrette'. She abandoned Australia after being passed over for a producer's role on 'Mavis' by a male TV executive. In the UK, Barbara became a successful scriptwriter, playwright and wrote jokes for Ronnie Corbett and Dave Allen.

A long chat with Rosalind Hollinrake—married to Barry Humphries for fourteen years, mother of two children with him, and his writing partner—was an eye-opener. She spoke of years in London spent in 'soul-destroying menial jobs in order to establish Barry in the West End theatre'. Who knew that one of Humphries' most famous characters, Sandy Stone, was based on a friend of Rosalind's father, and that the old fawn-and-brown-checked dressing-gown Sandy wore on stage was from her father's wardrobe?

Jan Adele reminded me that long before women took to the stage in stand-up, she'd been performing 'patter' in between songs in her nightclub act. She didn't write her own material, but said: 'I never told a joke that didn't make me laugh the first time I heard it'.

Not long after I began at Le Joke, Rhonda Carling-Rodgers was working the Sydney comedy clubs as the only woman stand-up on the circuit. Here's an intro she received: 'Ladies and Gentlemen . . . our next act is different because it's a shiela.

Ya don't get many women up here tellin' jokes . . . not that we mind . . . means we comics get someone to iron our costumes for us. She's backstage right now givin' one of the blokes a head job. Make her welcome.'

Rhonda said comedy room managers were reluctant to book her when they found out she wasn't a stripper, and asked, 'Can a woman be funny?' And when it was proved that, yes, a woman could make an audience laugh, they'd ask: 'Well, what is she then? A slut or a lesbian?' It's not surprising that I quickly developed a hard-edged style of humour, says Rhonda. Her comeback to the drunken male hecklers: 'Whatsa matter? You never seen a woman without a bruise before?' There was plenty of abuse from the women too. 'Keep ya eyes off me boyfriend, ya mole.'

It's a Joke, Joyce spans the decades with contributions of cartoons, scripts and songs. The numbers tell the story—profiles of ten women from the 1970s and, in the 1980s, thirty-six. Once women got their hands on the scriptwriting, the characters they invented were no longer those staples of vaudeville—saucy French maids or harridans in hair rollers. They were schoolgirls, beauty therapists, TV hosts and bitchy executives. Waitresses, politicians, doctors, nuns, cross-dressing cabaret singers and street kids. Depressed, repressed or ditzy housewives and mothers . . . you name it. The female condition in all its gloriously funny variety.

In 1989, in the wake of my book, an episode of Peter Couchman's ABC TV chat show featured some twenty women comedians from across the decades—from vaudeville to New Wave. In a *Sydney Morning Herald* review next morning, Peter

Luck wrote: 'It seemed every funny woman from every generation was there—a cornucopia of comediennes, a super abundance of soubrettes, led by den mother, Wendy Harmer.'

'The evident camaraderie and understandable mutual compliments did not quite serve to mask some fairly deep differences of opinion. We can talk about movements in women's comedy, but not about a women's comedy movement,' continued Luck. A perceptive take. When putting my book together, the older generation had shuddered at the 'crass' and 'explicit' content from the younger women about menstruation, although their own work, with jokes about sexual harassment, even rape, was shocking by modern standards.

'In the studio was the greatest collection of female comics yet gathered . . . a significant event in Australia's theatrical history' said Melbourne's *Sunday Herald*.

To have witnessed and been a part of that blossoming was deeply satisfying. To hear the voices, at last, of our talented women comedians? It's hard to imagine an era when they were mostly silent. Their lines written for them and policed by men.

In the preface of a 1993 reprint of *It's a Joke, Joyce*, I was able to say that no one had asked me lately: 'Why aren't there more funny women?' I noted the success of Judith Lucy and Jane Kennedy on the D-Generation's *The Late Show*, Libbi Gorr as Elle McFeast on *Live and Sweaty*, Mary Coustas as Effie from *Wogs Out of Work* and Cathy Wilcox as a political cartoonist.

'Funny women are everywhere you look,' I noted. 'We have been here all along. We were just waiting for a break in the conversation.'

15

Love gone wrong

Mirror backstage
Hilton Comedy Club
East Melbourne

What have you got yourself into this time, Harmer?

This is ridiculous.

There is *no way* you can pull this one off.

Big mouth.

Just don't say 'fuck'. Not even once.

Remember . . . it's fucking Christmas!

*

I'd been performing downstairs at Melbourne's Hilton Comedy Club, a step up from the usual comedy dives in the inner city. Supported by Simon Palomares and the Tiboldi Reception Band—stars of the wildly successful *Wogs Out of Work* ensemble—we were the first locals to be booked at the swish venue, which usually featured international acts of the calibre of Ben Elton and Rita Rudner.

Our reviews had been five-star—'Harmer sparkled', said one—so that's probably why, full of my own dazzling self-importance, I'd agreed to a mad proposal and headed upstairs.

A snippet from *The Sunday Age* written by Lawrence Money, published on Christmas Eve 1989, tells the story:

> Just a mite ominous was the managerial contingent waiting in the wings for larrikin loudmouth Wendy Harmer the other night when she stepped down from the stage at the Hilton Hotel's Comedy Club. Did someone take offence at her more acidic jibes, pondered a jumpy Harmer as she was led off to see the boss. To the lady's great relief, she found they were actually seeking her help in a crisis: Neil Sedaka had fallen ill and could not perform upstairs in the cabaret. Could she fill in?

Neil Sedaka, superstar singer of 'Happy Birthday Sweet Sixteen' and 'Calendar Girl'. *That* Neil Sedaka! Can you possibly envisage an audience—swathed in pearls and sequins, wearing best suit, collar and tie—*less* likely to be pleased to see me? *And* in the festive season?

I have no recollection at all of what transpired out there, but it must have gone down well enough, because the newspaper also records: 'Post performance, Harmer was ushered to a special room set up with strawberries and French champagne and the staff were told: "Give her anything she wants."' I assume this was out of sheer relief that I wasn't pelted with mince pies and didn't say 'fuck', even once.

I performed a few times at the Hilton after that, most thrillingly as a support act for my comedy idol, Joan Rivers. A Peter Weiniger review in *The Age* records: 'Where Joan Rivers is pure New York mega-bitch, Wendy Harmer is the definitive Australian larrikin . . . she expresses the ratbag in all of us that refuses to lie down and mature gracefully.' One thing that rankled: 'Harmer commands the stage with her broad grin and ill-fitting clothing that is the antithesis of chic.'

(*Excuse me?* That Italian Romeo Gigli gold jacket was the height of fashion and had cost me two weeks' wages! I admit to squandering a fortune on designer clobber back then, probably enough to put a deposit on a flat. With real money in my pocket, I indulged in every frippery I had been deprived of as a kid, especially shoes. I was not good with my finances and lived as an expensively shod grasshopper.)

I got to meet Joan Rivers briefly and was surprised at how small she was. Just a tiny thing. Demure, softly spoken and kind to starstruck me. That uber confidence can make an audience believe you are ten-foot tall.

When I look at my old recordings, I ask myself: *How did I do that?* I'd often agree to do gigs I had little hope of pulling off. While I can trace my steely self-belief to childhood origins, the often reckless 'crash or crash through' mentality I came to develop is more difficult to understand. I just would not be told . . . or tell myself . . . 'No'.

I was to be taught the hard way, many times, that I wasn't quite as clever as I thought I was. There's always a fine line for the artist: for some, self-confidence turns into arrogance, while for others humility becomes crippling self-doubt.

For many years it was my brother Noel who kept my ego in check. He'd come to my shows and heckle me with withering put-downs. When I confronted him and asked why, he replied: 'Well, some bastard had to.'

I miss Noel.

*

Debuting in March 1990 on ABC TV at 9.30 p.m. and with just ten episodes, the chat show *In Harmer's Way* barely registers as a blip in the annals of Australian television, but perhaps deserves more attention for the sheer audacity of its format.

First there was me—a thirty-something woman hosting a chat show. Unheard of. There was an extended guest interview, music, a session or two of improvised theatre sports with the four male comics of Chawfest—Simon Rogers, Andrew Goodone, Tim Smith and Greg Fleet—and, to finish, three guests were asked to wrestle with a few tricky questions in a cooked-up scenario. My guests ranged from David Williamson, Jeff Kennett and Barry Jones to Andrew Denton and Kaz Cooke.

'It's about the moral dilemmas that people face in real life— a sort of B-Grade *Hypothetical*,' I told the Melbourne *Herald* TV guide. 'Yes, a cross between *Hypothetical* and *Juke Box Jury*,' added Patrick Cook, giving an example: 'It's raining and your neighbour's newspapers are closer to your door than his . . . Do you take his, or get your own? Put that to an archbishop and you can get a very interesting answer.'

Indeed, and in one session I recall asking Rene Rivkin, the controversial entrepreneur and investment adviser, if he was able to cut up the *Mona Lisa* and sell the pieces off for more money than he could get by selling the intact painting, would he do it? Deprive the world of a masterpiece revered by generations?

He answered, 'Yes.'

Each show had a theme—celebrity, fashion, media, poetry, the 'clever country', the 'future'. The audience of almost 200 sat in a semicircle around the stage and were invited to join the fray. 'If not within touching distance, then certainly within spitting distance,' director Ted Robinson told the *Herald*. 'It has enormous potential for lying down and just dying. We know that. But I think there's nothing wrong with honest failure as long as you can pick yourself up and keep going.'

That was ominous.

Did I say the format was audacious? How about 'foolhardy'? Or 'not quite thought through'? It was certainly unpredictable. Thank Christ it was pre-recorded.

'Why leave *The Big Gig?*' I was asked.

'I probably need my head read,' I replied.

I could have stayed for another year as host, but I've always believed where there's a chance, you have to take it . . . or invent it. Besides, it was time for Glynn Nicholas to have a shot at hosting, which he did with aplomb.

In Harmer's Way was a modest success; but marshalling all the disparate elements of the show wasn't easy. I'd perhaps bitten off more than I could chew this time, although I received plaudits for my ability as an interviewer from people I respected. Not from radio jock John Laws who, writing for *TV Week*, found it 'unwatchable': 'Wendy, I fear, is suffering from over-exposure and too much adulation from a small, but noisy band of followers.'

When I was offered a second series, I declined. To set the record straight, the show wasn't axed—but I'd looked at the whole shebang and realised it needed to be rebuilt from the ground up and that Ted, with a raft of new, exciting projects on his slate, wasn't able to hold my hand to start again.

It was time to fly the ABC nest.

So, just weeks later, I piled into a minivan with the lads from Chawfest and we travelled almost 2000 kilometres north up the West Australian coast from Albany to Karratha. Our *Wendy and the Lost Boys* tour took us to workers' clubs, hotel bars and mining camps, sometimes driving almost eight hours between gigs.

'G'day' to anyone who stood on the side of a remote highway watching that van drive by filled with noxious dope smoke, looking like a giant bong on wheels. My face was pressed up against the window, with the words 'HELP ME!' drawn in the condensation.

I wanted to kill those boys!

To while away the time, Simon, Tim, Andrew and Fleety devised an interminable game of 'cricket' with tedious, ostentatious sports commentary and two whole teams of imaginary players. (I remember W.P. Basket being a featured spin bowler.) Kilometres rolled by for hours . . . then days . . . to a soundtrack of clacking dice and cries of 'Out!' 'Snicked it!' 'LBW!' 'Caught, silly mid-on!' I was almost delirious with boredom.

Motel notepads and beer coasters with written scores were passed from the front seat to the back in the world's longest, most excruciating, fantasy test match . . . until I demanded the van stop. I snatched up their stupid bits of paper and chucked the lot out the window into the scrub.

Simon, the cricket nut, was particularly peeved, but Tim admits to being secretly relieved.

The locals were thrilled that we'd got red dust on our boots and brought our show to where they lived. The lads took no prisoners, 'killed' every night, and we were shouted enough drinks to replenish the Great Artesian Basin. In the mining town of Karratha, where tough women drove the bestial monster trucks in the pits, I had the best time ever. Even got a marriage proposal! It was just the antidote to the rarefied atmosphere of ABC recording studios that I needed.

Heading back south, *Wendy and the Lost Boys* harassed Mount Gambier, Whyalla, Tumby Bay, Port Pirie, Bordertown, Wangaratta and Shepparton. Somewhere along the way, Tim reminds me, we all ended up naked in a hot tub, with Fleety shouting at us, 'C'mon, people. Get your gear off. TONIGHT COULD BE THE NIGHT!'

'It was a case of "white line fever" by then,' Tim recalls with a laugh. 'We'd lost all sense of decorum. Time to go home.'

We wound up with a gig in Launceston. There we were photographed in front of a billboard for a 'cabaret room' advertising us, Colleen Hewett, Col Elliott and Rolf Harris. We'd made it!

John Laws was wrong about a 'small, but noisy band of followers'. In fact, because of the extraordinary reach of the ABC, people knew us everywhere we went.

(Reminds me of the time my husband Brendan and I stayed at the remote El Questro cattle station in the Kimberley region. The then property owner, Englishman Will Burrell, took us on a long, dusty, drive to visit a camp of locals in the far-flung reaches of his property. He pulled up under a gnarled old tree, I got out of the car, and an elderly man ambled over from a campfire and greeted me with: 'Hey! Aren't you that bird off the television?' Will was utterly gobsmacked. So was I. *There's* the reach of the Australian Broadcasting Corporation for you.)

Wendy and the Lost Boys restored my belief that live comedy was where my heart lay. A heart that was still raw and in bloody pieces after my break-up with Patrick. How could I recover from my deep, underlying sadness? Despite being crowned Australia's Queen of Comedy, I felt I was wearing the undergarment of a sad, pathetic clown. It itched. Wore away at me. Chafed. Didn't suit me. I was not that person.

My soul was being ground to gravel by my neurotic, incessant self-talk that I was not young-pretty-smart-thin enough, and so unlovable that I'd be single for the rest of my miserable life.

You've heard of Sigmund Freud's 'talking cure' for treating trauma and restoring mental health? I embarked on the 'telling jokes and singing cure' in a new one-woman show I wrote called *Love Gone Wrong*.

This, surely, would do the trick.

The show remains my most accomplished outing on a stage and was to fetch me up in a London theatre as one of the Perrier 'Pick of the Fringe' winners in the Edinburgh Festival of 1990.

*

I could deliver a one-hour monologue almost in my sleep. But there had to be a new way of going about things. The experience of seeing Lily Tomlin's one-woman show *The Search for Signs of Intelligent Life in the Universe* on Broadway in 1985 had never left me. Written with her partner Jane Wagner, it had brought me to tears of sadness and then uproarious laughter within a sentence. In that magical moment, stuff happened. Perceptions changed. Attitudes shifted.

Not that I thought I could do the same, but it was something to aspire to. I decided to chance my arm, daring to juxtapose quiet melancholic notes alongside my usual 'boom-tish' comedic rim shots.

I'd always wanted to explore the possibility of music in my act. I loved UK comic Victoria Wood and knew all her hilarious songs word for word. I'm not a player of any instrument, besides a strum on a guitar; as a singer, I have good pitch and phrasing, but sadly my voice is not blessed with that special quality that makes it memorable. Serviceable enough for parody songs, though. Done plenty of those.

Here are the lyrics for one of a handful of songs I wrote for *Love Gone Wrong* and sang, accompanied over successive seasons by stellar jazz pianists Christian Sommerville, John McAll and Alexander Nettelbeck.

I've been driving round and round the block
Watching your house since ten o'clock
You had the nerve to change the lock
I've got my eye on you.

I nailed a rat to your front door
Took to your car with a circular saw
And I'm sure you know who the bomb was for
I've got my eye on you.

Her hair is blonde, her name is Jane
She better not stand too close to a train
And she'll never see her cat again
I've got my eye on you.

Your dumb new girlfriend, what a mess!
She fakes orgasm, that's my guess
I've got it all on VHS . . .
I've got my eye on you.

Ahem. Cough. A tad 'stalkerish', sure. But funny at the time. *Love Gone Wrong* began, tentatively, with an experimental run at the Laugh. A brief outing at Mietta's, where, ironically, Patrick and I had met. Then I hit the Assembly Rooms for the Edinburgh Festival.

'Imagine a female comic who's something like a cross between Ben Elton and a much more radical Terry Wogan (how could it be otherwise) and you have some idea of what to expect from Aussie comic Wendy Harmer,' said *Time Out*. 'Her current full-length show, *Love Gone Wrong*, combines comedy and songs, touches on topics like where you meet people and start relationships, the things that go wrong with love affairs, getting old and the new breed of "sensitive" men. She also interviews the audience about their love lives . . . it's a perfect show for her particular comedy talents.'

'The content of the show is so polished as to be sparkling— the blending of song and stand-up routines is seamless . . . it oozes class and style,' said *The Edinburgh List*.

Class? Style? Who, me?

The Perrier pick won me a spot in a showcase in London, and I'll never forget peeking out from the curtain backstage at The Place theatre to see faces I recognised from British TV settling into their seats. I had to pinch myself that it wasn't all a dream.

Again, there were offers of work in the UK, but why would I stay when I could be feted by the likes of Brisbane's *Courier-Mail* as 'the knock 'em down, drag 'em out, stand-up comic who castrates holy cows with a laser-like wit and who could be counted on to drop the "F" word in front of the Queen Mother'?

Have to admit: it *was* likely I'd swear in front of royalty.

I flew back to Australia.

Knew which side of my buttered bread was slathered in Vegemite.

*

In the spring of 1991 I performed at Melbourne's comedy festival, back at Mietta's, which felt like home—if your home was down an inner-city laneway, though a marble foyer, and in a swanky room with plush velvet chairs and amber lamps set on petite tables . . . and had a bar that served a cocktail named after you. (I can't recall the recipe of the concoction, but it was lethal. Pink, fizzy and flavoured with rosewater. You could only ever drink two. Three and you lost the power of speech.)

Mietta's was a cultural hub. Unique. It attracted the beau monde of Bleak City. On any given night there were opera recitals or jazz concerts in the upstairs ballroom—an opulent space, set with white linen-covered tables and golden candelabra and home to French-inspired fine dining. The downstairs rooms were given over to nights of poetry, play readings and the occasional season of ratbag comedians—one of whom was me.

My relationship with the enigmatic Mietta O'Donnell was a slow burn but deepened over time and we became close. I came to trust her considered judgement. An odd couple, for sure, but it was Mietta who encouraged me to wear a classy, low-cut velvet jacket, which showed my cleavage to its best advantage as I draped myself over the grand piano. (One male friend told me it was a definite improvement: 'When the songs are boring, we can just look at your tits.') There are not enough pages in this book to do justice to the impact of Mietta and her partner, Tony Knox, on the city's cultural awakening, or how much I valued the constancy of their friendship.

Mietta's death in a car accident in January 2001 came as a terrible shock.

Grief-stricken accolades and glowing tributes flowed from the nation's food and arts scene. A requiem mass was held at St Mary Star of the Sea in West Melbourne. Her family accorded me the great honour of delivering her eulogy.

The church was filled to overflowing and her coffin was resplendent, covered with a carpet of fragrant, full-blown roses.

She was only fifty when she died.

*

In October 1991, my glamorous, clever pal Jean Kittson launched not only a season of *Love Gone Wrong* at the famed Kinselas nightspot in Sydney's Darlinghurst but also my book of the same name.

I treasure that little book. It's a gem. Superbly illustrated by inspired animator and my good mate Bruce Currie, the cover depicts a withered red heart impaled by a massive, menacing spear and wreathed in barbed wire. The endpapers are a battle-field in which a host of fat cupids unleash their arrows at hapless humans whose skeletal remains are picked at by crows. Perfect.

Inside, I'd compiled every rancid piece of advice I could think of for the broken-hearted. The humour is satirical, dark and cata-logues all manner of aberrant behaviour. Among the 'Recipes for One': 'Tipsy Vegetarian Salad. Gather healthy salad vegetables on kitchen bench. Play with sharp knife, drink bottle of vodka and think about life. Collapse on kitchen floor. A good recipe for the diet conscious.' The book struck a chord with the dumped and despondent. Got rave reviews and made the bestseller lists.

The live show, in the cavernous performance space of Kinselas upstairs, did equally good business. Played to packed houses. The initial run of two weeks turned into five. It was a 'hot' ticket.

It was after the show one night that I was given what I regard to be the best critique of my comedy career. The celebrated actress Kerry Walker, whom I'd performed with in Adelaide in *Shepherd On the Rocks*, told me she'd seen the show, enjoyed it and had returned with a table of friends. But the second time she was disappointed.

Why?

'Well, it was the same as it was the other night. I thought you'd made up a lot of it on the spot.'

Who said I couldn't act? Hah!

Another stint back at Mietta's for Christmas with pianist Christian, this time a hotchpotch of 'greatest hits' with a few new seasonal songs chucked in. (Two-course lunch and show for $25. Three-course dinner and show for $40.)

There was no mention of my broken heart. None. I'd finally reassembled the pieces and never wanted to speak of sex and relationships again. I was heartily sick of the entire topic and my status as Patron Saint of the Lovelorn.

I was now thirty-five, 'with marriage on my mind and a body clock on burn out', as I liked to say. I was to find that the prediction I'd made in *Love Gone Wrong* about the men I would date was accurate: 'People who like you more than you like them. People you like more than they like you.'

You'd think by then I'd have known better than to pile into a car to go on tour with a bunch of blokes. Not so. This time it was on a holiday to Europe with two of my piano players and the outrageous all singin', all dancin' gay icon Ignatius Jones. As lead vocalist with the punk band Jimmy and the Boys, he had taken to the stage at Sydney pubs in studded leather corsets as ringmaster in displays of sadomasochism, transvestism, drug abuse and every variety of degenerate behaviour that only former students from one of Sydney's most prestigious private schools could have dreamed up. I adored Mr Jones. His waspish one-liners and acute eye for every nuance of underground culture made me squeal with laughter. He made it his personal mission to take me to every gay bar, dance club and drag show in town. An education, for sure.

My overseas trip began in Paris with me and my musician *bons amis*, Chris and John. They behaved just as you'd expect jazz pianists to behave—congenitally late, self-absorbed, dreamy and not taking responsibility for any damn thing. I'd made a date to meet up with Ignatius in Spain, so rented us a car and we drove down to Madrid. He took me to a bullfight, which he explained in great, enthusiastic detail as I peeked at the gruesome spectacle through splayed fingers.

Juan Ignacio Rafaelo Lorenzo Trápaga y Esteban, Filipino-born, spoke Spanish. So why then did he not know that on the evening of the bullfight we would be travelling smack in the middle of Spain's most hectic holiday long weekend? Soon things went to total *mierda*. There was no accommodation to be found anywhere. We drove for hours—and debated sleeping rough in a field. Eventually, we found a place to stay . . . in Portugal.

Yes, that's right. In an entirely different country.

We smuggled Ignatius over the border in the car's boot because he didn't have his passport with him. We headed back into Spain on his promise of an idyllic stay in a coastal village in northern Galicia.

Reading from his travel guide, Ignatius raved about 'old lace-makers, wrapped in shawls, sitting on the shore with their traditional crafts as they greet the fisherman in their rustic boats'.

It was a sardine cannery.

The 'old lace-makers' were long gone. The women we saw outside the factory wore rubber gloves and plastic hats.

We were all crammed into one room. It was all we could find. I was with three farting men who reeked of alcohol. Stinking, boiling hot, with giant freezer trucks thundering past our window until dawn. When I did catch a few moments' sleep, I dreamed I was in a Turkish prison.

Tearing back to the closest international airport, we couldn't find anywhere that was open on the weekend to leave the hire car, so I left it just outside the wire-fenced depot. Back in Australia I was informed that the vehicle had been stolen, stripped and set on fire.

It seemed a good metaphor for that holiday.

The perfect disaster for a comedy outing.

In my new one-woman show, *Please Send (More) Money*, I was joined by consummate musicians George Washingmachine on violin and Ian Date on guitar. It was a sweet, affectionate offering that played in venues across the country, mining my travel experiences—from soccer hooligans in Scotland and 'five-star' hotel construction sites in Crete to the ill-fated trip in Spain. A veritable baggage carousel of complaint, all set to music.

Ignatius gave me his blessing via postcard:

'DEAREST PALOMA,

I see from the Melb. Festival program that you have turned our spiritual journey to the shrine of St Imelda the Alcoholic into a COMEDY ROUTINE! The least you could do is invite me to the opening night and ask me to sanctify your living room floor by sleeping on it for three weeks. Besides, you're going to need an open-minded interpreter to help you chat up the hordes of cute LATINOS who will be thronging on the streets of Sodom-on-the-Yarra. You know the number of my convent. Yours in Christ. *Sister Ignatius of the Holy Rear End of God*'

The show was directed by the inspired, enfant terrible of Australian theatre, Nigel Triffitt (*Momma's Little Horror Show*, *The Fall of Singapore*, *Tap Dogs*), although my outing was *so* low-rent, his 'direction' mostly consisted of: 'Puh-lease. It's fine. Carry on!'

Extraordinary, wondrous Nige was 'openly gay', as they say, and one of my closest friends and confidants. He was always dressed in shorts, wore round tortoiseshell glasses and looked like an overgrown naughty schoolboy. We'd gossip and laugh on the phone for hours when we were both hyped up after a show and sleep was elusive. He, my agent Hilary and I took holidays together. Both gone now. Miss them dreadfully.

(In 1993 I was invited to appear on the lead float of the Sydney Mardi Gras parade with the UK comic Julian Clary.

What to wear? It was the biggest style crisis of my life. A big meringue wedding dress? No, I'd just look straight and desperate. Nude with body paint? No—think of the rear angle. Flashing fairy lights? *So last year.* In the end I opted for a black trouser suit, beret, cigar, dog tags . . . like a female Fidel Castro, or . . . ? Very odd. On the night, Mr Clary turned up in a white Lycra bodysuit encrusted with fake rubies and with a plaster cast on one arm. Of course! *Darling, it was so obvious!*)

During the time I was close with Nigel and Ignatius, they always pushed me out of my depth.

Consoled when things got rough.

Rescued when I was sinking.

Re-floated me.

*

A few reviewers complained that in *Please Send (More) Money* I'd lost my comedic 'edge'. I'd become 'tame', 'lacked bite'.

At the same time, I was getting the most generous notices of my life as a performer 'at the peak of her powers'.

But like Mr Toad of 'Toad Hall' I had a new fascination.

Poop! Poop!

Live radio was where it was at.

And it would be—for almost two decades, on and off.

16

The secret sound

Bathroom mirror
The Beverly Hilton
9876 Wilshire Boulevard, Beverly Hills, CA 90210, USA

Not even an hour to get ready for *THE OSCARS*?

This is ridiculous!

Bet Kate Winslet isn't looking into a bathroom mirror right now with wet hair and wearing a maternity bra.

I'll just give my fringe a tiny trim . . .

OH NO! *What have you done?*

It's sticking out. Horizontally.

Like the fringe on a cushion!

AAARGH!

*

In 1998 I was off to the seventieth annual Academy Awards at the Shrine Auditorium, Los Angeles. The film *Titanic* had bagged fourteen nominations that year. Billy Crystal was hosting for the sixth time.

It was my second visit to LA in awards season with the *2DayFM Morning Crew* co-hosts Paul Holmes and Peter Moon. A year earlier, we'd broadcast back to Sydney from a broom cupboard at KIIS-FM, a powerhouse of American commercial radio. We'd stayed in the San Fernando Valley at Universal Studios and watched the Oscars go live to air from a local restaurant.

This year, management had wrangled tickets for the three of us to attend the real, live Oscars ceremony, and we were upgraded from three-star to deluxe. We even had an entourage of two producers!

The *Morning Crew* was broadcast from a conference room in the Beverly Hilton. Hotel owner Merv Griffin dropped by, intrigued by the sudden flood of hotel bookings coming from Sydney.

I mean, of all people, *Merv Griffin*! The creator of *Jeopardy!* and *Wheel of Fortune*. The host of *The Merv Griffin Show*. Showbiz royalty. They didn't come any bigger than Merv. I'd walk to the poolside breakfast room in the Beverly Hilton and linger in front of photos on the walls featuring Merv with a bevy of big-name stars. Names that boggled the mind—Elizabeth Taylor, Orson Welles, John Wayne, Judy Garland, Sammy Davis Junior, Richard Burton, Doris Day, Sophia Loren, Grace Kelly, Clint Eastwood, Andy Warhol, Muhammad Ali, Martin Luther King Jr, John Lennon.

During its twenty-five-year run, his talk show hosted 25,000 guests, including four US presidents. He'd interviewed all my comedy heroes—Lucille Ball, Steve Martin, Andy Kaufman, George Carlin, Phyllis Diller and Richard Pryor. Jerry Seinfeld made his debut on *The Merv Griffin Show* in 1981.

And now here he was, sitting across from us behind a microphone. He was then in his early seventies, fit, tanned and sleek with success, a silver fox. I was beside myself as he told stories of his friendship with Marilyn Monroe. Even if our listeners didn't have a clue who he was, I was transfixed. As mine host at the Beverly Hilton, Merv took us under his wing and often swung by to see how we were getting on.

Ally McBeal was a huge TV show in 1998, and Dyan Cannon—who starred as Judge Jennifer 'Whipper' Cone—was our guest. She even baked us a tray of her famous muffins. I recall coveting *the* most divine, yellow ostrich leather vintage handbag I'd ever seen, which she'd placed on the seat beside her. I had to ask. 'Oh this?' she drawled. 'Cary gave it to me.' That would be her ex-husband, Cary Grant. I reached out and touched a handbag that had been touched by Cary Grant. It was all I could do to stop myself from snatching it up and sprinting down Wilshire Boulevard.

Paul and I reported on American culture: tales of bizarre menus in fast-food restaurants; odd characters we met in the street; the crazy traffic; visits to the real-life places where hit TV soap operas like *Beverly Hills, 90210* and *Melrose Place* were filmed. Meanwhile, Peter had whiled away the hours in some obscure antique shop and purchased a seventy-million-year-old fossilised insect in a lump of amber.

Typical Moon.

We bickered and traded stupid insults—the usual carry-on which had become our trademark act as Sydney's most dysfunctional family. It was all grist for the commercial breakfast radio mill. Hundreds of thousands tuned in over their breakfast tables and on their daily commutes to hear us squabble like a box of ferrets.

On the day of the Oscars, we finished broadcasting around midday and were due in the limo barely an hour later to attend the ceremony. The night before, I'd unearthed a crumpled ball of grey georgette fabric from my suitcase to iron as my red-carpet dress. I discovered it was perforated with tiny moth holes. *Fabulous. SO chic!*

At this time, I was breastfeeding a four-month-old baby. Had barely recovered from an emergency caesarean. Was starved of sleep, weepy and hormonal. In hindsight, I shouldn't have been on a train to Dubbo, let alone working in LA. There was no way I could have pulled together a glam outfit for entertainment's Night of Nights. At that time I could barely manage shoes that matched. Often didn't. I wasn't fit to be attending the Oscars; I must have just nodded 'yes', too exhausted to think about it.

Marley, our newborn son, had come along on the trip. So too had his father, Brendan, and our nanny, Julie. She was 'Mistress of the Breast Milk', which I pumped furiously at 3 a.m. in our bathroom before I drove the forty-five minutes to work every morning. Brendan, Julie and baby Marley all headed off to watch the live broadcast from some Hollywood TV museum I can't recall the name of. Brendan was seated that night in

Captain Kirk's chair on the plywood and plasterboard bridge of the starship *Enterprise*, Marley in his arms.

Meanwhile, out the front of the Beverly Hilton, I piled into the limo with Peter and Paul. Moth-eaten dress, too-short fringe and tear-stained make-up. It would have to do.

After circling the block of the Shrine Auditorium for hours in an endless cavalcade of limos—past homeless people and unemployed actors on median strips holding up signs begging for work—it was finally our turn to alight.

The atmosphere is almost indescribable. Let's just say it was 'HOT'. With dozens of helicopters buzzing overhead, the screaming of fans in the bleachers and a thousand searing lights all trained on a few metres of red carpet, I felt I was standing on a pinhead of blazing brilliance that was radiating heat to the entire universe. The epicentre of 'hotness'. At the time, it was the most-watched telecast in Oscars history.

A few steps forward and . . . wrong way! Not *that* side of the red carpet. That side was for the movie stars. We were to walk the *other* side, with the industry types—the crews, technicians, agents and entertainment writers who oiled the cogs of Tinseltown.

I was halfway up the carpet with the rest of the Neville Nobodies when I heard my name called—'Wendy! Wendy Harmer, over here!'—and saw Kerri-Anne Kennerley holding out a microphone. She was host of Channel Nine's *Midday* show, there to catch the big names for a few words.

I quickly ducked under the velvet rope, a camera was thrust in my face and I babbled . . . something about looking forward to star-spotting, but also suspecting that 'the real action will be in the ladies' powder room'. The camera swivelled off me. Plunged back into obscurity, I went on my way.

Later I heard that my sister Helen's three children had been watching the red carpet arrivals on TV at their farmhouse in country Victoria. 'Ooh, look, there's Kate Winslet . . . there's Leonardo DiCaprio . . . THERE'S AUNTIE WENDY!'

My friends told me they couldn't believe I'd made a joke about cocaine on national television. I protested that when I'd mentioned the 'powder room', I'd actually been thinking of the contortions required to manage glamourous gowns and too-tight undergarments and hadn't want to offend with the indelicate word 'toilet'.

'*Sure,*' they laughed.

My biggest worry that night, as I sat in the nosebleed section of the auditorium, was that I was thirsty. Breastfeeding-mother thirsty. The thirstiest thirst of all thirsts. We'd been hustled into our seats, barely catching a glimpse of the trays of champagne not destined for the riffraff.

Midway through the ceremony, I sneaked out of my seat and into the corridor, a parched desert creature in search of moisture.

I ran into the very famous Shirley Jones.

Now, Shirley Jones was a past winner of Best Supporting Actress for her role in the 1960 movie *Elmer Gantry* and the star of musicals like *Oklahoma!*, *Carousel* and *The Music Man* but, most importantly to me, she was the mother in *The Partridge Family*. As a teen I'd decorated my bedroom with posters of

David Cassidy. I was besotted with him. Watched every episode of that show.

Surely 'Mrs Partridge', widowed mother of five capable of salvaging any sticky situation, could help me find a glass of water! She did. She was gorgeous.

We got to talking and it was when I was raving about my beautiful baby son that I felt . . . uh-oh . . . let-down. As the milk leaked, I could almost *hear* the shrivelling of fine georgette fabric around my nipples. In my rush to get out the door, I'd forgotten to put absorbent pads into my nursing bra.

Holding an evening bag over one breast and a souvenir program over the other, I saw out the ceremony in the dark and then, as fast as humanly possible, fled the Shrine Auditorium.

I declined the next invite to the Oscars in 2000. Now, as mother of daughter Maeve, not even two months old, I'd learned my lesson, but the *Morning Crew* was back for the 2002 Emmy Awards. It was a year after the 9/11 attack, and this time our limo was checked for bombs by US Marines in full riot gear.

We were directed down a labyrinth of corridors. I got lost and eventually spied a set of stairs topped with a sparkly gold curtain. I stepped through . . . and that's how I ended up gate-crashing a live interview between an *E! News* reporter and Kelsey Grammer.

*

My trajectory to being 'the highest-paid woman in radio' was a rocket that failed to launch, twice, before I achieved take-off.

It was often a bumpy ride, but I floated back to earth with a 'golden parachute' of more than a million dollars in the new millennium.

My first experiment with the medium was in 1986, when Melbourne's 3AK and Sydney's 2UE stations embarked upon a shared talkback format. Jane Clifton and I took evening shifts at the weekends and the direction was: 'Never mention which city you're broadcasting from. Imagine you're on a station on the moon.' At the time, when AM radio was all about familiarity— the weather, traffic and 'parish-pump' issues—this was indeed lunacy.

On Saturday and Sunday nights the talkback phone line was as dead as the proverbial duck and doornail. I drafted in every comedy colleague who could spare some time to share the three excruciating hours on air. Fellow stand-up and always-lovely gentleman Glenn Robbins came to my rescue as a regular guest and we'd shoot the breeze, talking silly stuff. Laughing our heads off.

There was only one track in the entire music library that suited my taste, Paul Kelly's 'Before Too Long', and I played it over and over. When I'd ask my producer what he thought of the show, he'd just shake his head and say: 'I'm not sure what management wants *exactly*, but that *definitely* wasn't it.'

The axe fell when I introduced a live in-studio performance with, 'This could be blasphemous, but what the hell,' and Tracy Harvey sang, 'I Was a Surfboard for Jesus'. After a flood of listener complaints, I was threatened with an appearance at the Australian Broadcasting Tribunal.

It was gratifying in one way; I mean, who knew anyone was listening?

The entire, strange enterprise was a short-lived failure.

*

In 1991, Norman Swan, as the manager of ABC's Radio National, offered me a thirty-minute shift in the afternoon 'drive' hours, wedged between heavyweight international news reports and the current affairs show, *PM*. I was an avid listener to the station, had it on from morning till night when I was at home.

Around the same time, Norman employed Geraldine Doogue and Phillip Adams. They're still there behind the microphone, decades later, with the Australia-wide network now rebranded as RN. I was lucky to see out the twelve months.

'There was no comedy on Radio National, just serious, po-faced offerings. And I decided the station could do with a bit of entertainment and exploration of new frontiers,' Norman tells me. 'I loved your work and thought you'd be ideal for a bit of disruption.'

In the show I named *Kaboom!* I disrupted, exactly as ordered.

Asked what the show would offer, I answered in a press preview: 'At no time will it have any live crosses to the National Press Club or Parliament House. Nor will it invite talkback on how to deal with teenage stress at exam time.' Instead, I said, listeners could expect such divertissements as 'a look at the music in gangster movies and why the car dashboard is designed the way it is'. That was the least of it. I'd met my producer Laura Waters through music circles. She was married to Michael Waters, trombone and keyboard player with Hunters & Collectors. Tall, with a tumble of tangled chestnut curls, an easy laugh and a Colorado country gal take on life, Laura and I clicked. She'd worked in daily broadcast news in America. Knew her stuff. Together we crafted a daily show that often gave Norman Swan 'heart attacks' on his drive home. 'I remember the night, after a scandal in Parliament, you interviewed a sex worker in Canberra and asked her the going rates for politicians. I almost drove off the road.'

Instead of the usual roster of 'experts' to comment on the day's events, we'd call remote towns and hit up the publican to ask how the drinkers in the front bar were taking the news. I knew where to find lively guests with something to say—academics in obscure disciplines, experimental artists, activists—all 'disrupters'. Laura could ring anyone, anywhere, and talk them into coming on air. We'd segue from the semi-serious to the completely ridiculous—like the lady in California who had a thriving business selling hats for dogs: 'If you have a spotty dalmatian, I wouldn't put it in a floral. I think a block colour is better, and of course plaid looks real good with the Scotty dogs.'

'What about a dingo?' I asked perceptively.

'Well, that's a challenge—maybe something in yellow 'cos it's a sunny country. Maybe something with a brim?'

Laura and I paid our way to the US and spent a week broadcasting from Los Angeles. We're still proud of those shows.

One interview took place in a helicopter with Hollywood's most notorious paparazzo, Phil Ramey, who earned a fortune for his celebrity snaps, which filled Australia's women's magazines.

The day we hitched a ride, we swooped over the exclusive neighbourhood of Laurel Canyon in the mountains of Santa Monica, with Ramey hanging out the door of the chopper catching movie stars by their swimming pools with a long-lens camera as big as a baseball bat.

I interviewed autograph hunters who'd camped out for hours to waylay their idols outside nightclubs. Talked to limo drivers, valets, doormen. We visited Fred Hayman, aka Mr Rodeo Drive, the flamboyant creator of the famous fragrance, Hollywood. He gave us a giant bottle of his perfume, which I accidentally broke in our hire car. We then had to drive everywhere with the windows down.

Laura and I worked for hours to gather the audio, and then she'd edit and package up the shows to send home. The music stings were from Looney Tunes cartoons like *Bugs Bunny* and *Wile E. Coyote and the Roadrunner*, composed by Carl Stalling for Warner Bros. Those programs were a rare inside look at how the celebrity machine worked—something Radio National tragics had never heard before, that's for sure.

Let's just say the reaction was 'mixed'. One high-profile critic declared *Kaboom!* to be the nadir in the history of Australian public broadcasting. 'Well, it's good to be the best at something,' Laura deadpanned. We kept at it, undaunted.

Norman was stoic in the face of a barrage of criticism—not only from many listeners, but from our fellow program makers, who thought I was lowering the tone of the entire station. I have fond memories of *Law Report* host Jon Faine, stopping by with encouraging words.

Norman had no comment on our work on *Kaboom!*, apart from sometimes offering encouragement in his lilting Scottish accent: 'I thought your time out before the news was quite good.'

His abiding memory of me is of a staff meeting where he was addressing the station's ratings. 'A music producer said, "But I thought the audience doesn't matter on Radio National." You threw yourself, bodily, out of your chair onto the carpet in protest. I'll never forget it.'

I wasn't sacked. The evening my year's contract was up, I just packed my stuff in a box, walked out the door and caught the tram home.

Laura went on to establish the wildly successful Princess Pictures production house, winning many awards for her television and film work with John Clarke, Chris Lilley, John Safran and Peter Helliar. In 2019 her company was nominated for an International Emmy award for *Wrong Kind of Black*, a series commissioned by ABC iview.

I wasn't finished in radio.

Only seventeen (and a bit) more years to go!

Stay with us. After the news, we'll reveal your next clue in 'The Secret Sound' and YOU could WIN BIG!

*

All my most important career breaks have been afforded to me by men. It makes sense. They were always in charge of things.

I don't think of myself as a 'man's woman', but I've always been relaxed in male company. Just as well, because journalism, comedy and radio were male-dominated industries when I first worked there. I would ignore the sweary banter, or join in, but drew the line at demeaning 'locker room' talk. 'Oi! Enough!' and a baleful look was usually enough to put a stop it. Once that boundary was established, things went fine.

When I joined Sydney's *2DayFM Morning Crew* in 1992 as a co-host, it was again a first for a woman. The station's program director, Brad March, says he hadn't heard my short-lived run on Radio National. 'I had no idea you were on radio. I'd seen you on *The Big Gig*, you were very funny. I was amazed a woman had a key hosting role like that.

'When I hired you, there was not one single woman hosting an FM radio show—not that I was aware of anyway. Certainly, no woman at the "centre" of a show. My reference was *Oprah* on television—the power she had and the huge female audience she had. It wasn't being catered to by anyone in radio.'

Sydney's Triple M breakfast show had ruled the breakfast airwaves since the 1980s. Hosted by 'Uncle' Doug Mulray, it was an institution—as 'Sydney' as a midnight meat pie at Harry's Cafe de Wheels. As 'Sydney' as a truck getting stuck in the harbour tunnel or a traffic jam on the M1.

With a cast of beloved fictional characters—many voiced by the incredibly talented Dave Gibson—Andrew 'the Boy Wonder from Indoor Cricket' Denton and Liz 'Miss Lizzie' Muir dropping by, a generation of schoolboys had grown up listening to the show in the back seat of Mum and Dad's car.

Brad March saw an opportunity. 'Doug Mulray was an extraordinary talent with very high ratings, but his following was more male leaning . . . Right there was the gap in the market. It was time to do something different.'

Brad—tall, blond and Sydney tanned—came down to Melbourne and took me to a fancy lunch in Toorak Road, South Yarra. We got on so well, and racked up such a huge drinks bill, that he totally forgot to offer me the gig.

When he later did, I immediately said yes. I'd been bitten by the radio bug. Loved the immediacy of it, the adrenaline rush, the requirement to come up with something new every day. It took me back to everything I'd been addicted to in newsrooms.

Then there was the money, which was more than double what I'd been earning. Hilary drove a hard bargain, including regular flights back to Melbourne and a clause in my twelve-month contract in the event I wanted to return there permanently.

I was done with Melbourne. After twenty years, I'd played every venue in town and spent too much time at late-night dance clubs, in shithole pub band rooms. Woken up in more than my fair share of strange beds, wondering what I was doing there. Was always looking over my shoulder, in case I ran into my ex, Patrick, and his partner. I'd been planning to relocate to London, had even bought my plane ticket.

Instead, I travelled north to the Emerald City.

My farewell party at Mietta's was bittersweet. Both my exes, Steve and Patrick, were there toasting my departure. I was smothered with love and affection by friends who'd been so supportive, always in my corner. It was such a wrench to say goodbye. Heading to Sydney for a job that started at 4.30 a.m., with a radio station that no one had ever heard of, I may as well have been going to Siberia.

I fetched up in a splendid, huge, sunny flat in Elizabeth Bay with a view of the harbour, all paid for by my new employers. The first night in my new place, I took a bath and encountered a massive cockroach . . . then another . . . and another. Who knew that the exclusive suburb was also known as 'Roach City'? I'd never seen a cockroach. It was almost enough to get me on the next plane south.

With my fortieth birthday looming, and thinking I'd always be single, instead I went out and bought two cats.

*

'Doug Mulray calls it "a very odd marriage—Wendy Harmer and a puppet".' So ran the quote in the *Sunday Telegraph* on the day before I started my new gig in February 1993. 'From tomorrow when she joins the *2DayFM Morning Crew*—Paul Holmes, Jamie Dunn and Agro—she's in the big time, the tough, rough, highly competitive world of Sydney commercial breakfast radio.'

Uncle Doug wished me 'the best of British . . . or should that be Australian,' adding that I was a 'nice lady'. Doug Mulray was a nice man, and we became friends after our FM radio days were behind us. He was giant of the medium and paid tribute by Andrew Denton as a 'true original' after his death in 2023 at the age of seventy-one.

I hadn't known just how toxic the rivalry between the two breakfast shows had become. 'It was a full-on war,' Paul Holmes recalls. 'It got totally out of control.'

One ditty aired on 2DayFM, to the tune of 'That's Amore', went: 'When your gut starts to sag on the wheel of your Jag . . . that's a Mulray.' In another stunt, a couple of obnoxious blokes driving trucks full of rubble abused commuters in their cars. The banner on the trucks read: 'Another load of old rock on its way to Triple M.'

The low point came when 2DayFM aired a promo that included Doug Mulray's ex-wife. Paul remembers protesting: 'I'm *not* playing that.' To no avail. Mulray responded that 'in the graveyard of radio . . . I will piss on their corpses'. It took years for Paul to mend his friendship with Doug. Thankfully, the ugly conflict was an uneasy truce by the time I got there.

To be fair to Doug, co-hosting with a puppet never made a lot of sense to me either. Agro, the 'talking bathmat', was the alter ego of Jamie Dunn. Brad had brought Jamie to Sydney from Brisbane's B105 FM following his success there.

Brad says that, from the outset, he knew Jamie and I were 'far apart as people'. I was a lefty from Melbourne; Jamie was from Brisbane and conservative in his political views. 'You were polar opposites,' says poor beleaguered Holmesie, who sat across from us, operating the panel. When we were supposed to be entertaining listeners with light-hearted, fun banter, we went at it like the fabled Kilkenny cats. 'One morning it was about capital punishment. String-'em-up Jamie on one side and Rehabilitation

Wendy on the other. I was stuck in the middle and threw to a track when you took a breath.'

All the while, Brad was attempting to teach me the finer points of commercial FM radio. After years of rambling rants on stage, to get my thoughts down to a few pithy sentences and a punchline—between ad breaks, promos and music—seemed impossible. We had blazing arguments. I slammed doors.

One day I went into his office to find he'd pinned on the wall a guide on 'How To Deal With Difficult People'.

'You *were* difficult, but you were a good learner,' he says. 'I knew I was working with someone smarter than me, but I knew radio better.'

He did. Brad March has the best 'radio ears' in the business. A student of radio shows worldwide and forensic in his listening, he often spent a day at home to hear the station in the way an audience heard it. That was invaluable feedback. He was a hard taskmaster, insisting on interminable, daily air-checks (where we'd listen back to segments of the show) and then giving us a mark out of ten.

In the early days, I reckon we barely got more than a six. I was exhausted by the hours, felt permanently jet-lagged and, yes, it got 'heated'.

'But it was respectful; we were just trying to get it right. You and I were a bit like an old married couple, I thought at the time.'

I owe much of my 'radio chops' to Brad.

For the newlyweds in the studio, things were rocky. Paul and I 'got' each other instantly. He was a country kid, like me.

We shared a sense of humour and I found him fair and respectful. That boundary I set about talk that made me uncomfortable? Jamie crossed it repeatedly with his tracksuit pants around his ankles. I saw his penis more times than I care to remember.

'He called it "doing his Nadia", after the Olympic gymnast Nadia Comaneci,' Paul explains. 'He'd drop his dacks, exposing his penis, raise his hands in the air and strike a pose. He did it a lot. It was a good way to change the subject. You'd say, "Oh my God, Jamie, put it *away*!" And on we'd go.'

One of Jamie's characters was Hector Pascals, a stereotypical, flamboyant 'gay': '*Oooh*! Mr Holmes, Mr Holmes! The American fleet is in Sydney and the harbour is full of seamen!'

'It was all a bit "Benny Hill" and out of date,' Paul recalls. 'I'd see you behind Jamie, rolling your eyes, but you never shot down or sabotaged his act.'

We quickly made some good gains in the ratings. 'What Harmer has done is shift the demographics . . . so now the station is attracting more women in the 18–40 sector,' wrote Richard Ackland in *The Sydney Morning Herald*. 'Music, gag, dream-come-true giveaway, ad, skit, music, gag, giveaway etc. on an endless roll. It's a very effortless-sounding flow of persiflage, that could only be as slick as it is because of a great deal of effort.'

By April we were within striking distance of Mulray's show, but with 2WS moving to the FM band, things were only going to get tougher. Surprisingly, it was Triple M that took the greatest hit in the ratings, and in the middle of the year we overtook Doug's show for the first time.

In December, Brad made the decision to send Jamie back to Brisbane: He and I just didn't see eye to eye. 'It was a difficult conversation. Jamie is a legend, but I had to choose,' Brad says. 'I wanted the female perspective. Strategically, that's where I wanted to be. So, I went with you.'

On his exit, Jamie told Sydney's *Sunday Telegraph* that he'd never come across anyone in the business who was tougher than me. 'She's so super-strong. She is the dominant force. A mild-mannered force like myself didn't fare too well, I just faded away.' He added, 'We didn't leave on bad terms,' but acknowledged that the studio wasn't big enough for the both of us.

Under the headline AGRO'S GONE TO QUEENSLAND—MOANING, the furball said it was 'too easy to blame the puppet with ping pong balls for eyes'. And in a list of 'Ten things the puppet hates about Sydney', five of them were 'Doug Mulray'.

For the record, Jamie Dunn did not 'fade away'. With Brisbane's *B105 Morning Crew*, he topped the ratings for a phenomenal 115 surveys until the end of 2004 in the 'City's Greatest Breakfast Show'. One of the biggest station promotions was 'International Nude Day', when he and co-host Ian Skippen broadcast in the buff.

(Brad March is now an agent for radio talent. Among his achievements as Austereo chief programmer in the 1990s are bringing to the airwaves: Tracy Bartram in Melbourne; the Sydney partnership of Andrew Denton and Amanda Keller and the legendary, national Tony Martin and Mick Molloy drive shift.)

*

In 1993 and into 1994 I was also appearing in ABC TV's *World Series Debating* with fellow team captain Andrew Denton, playing to huge live audiences all over Australia.

After a performance in Melbourne, *Sunday Telegraph* journalist Sally Macmillan came along for the ride. 'It's a night flight. The Terrier of Talk and the Queen of Comedy are coping with crises in their own peculiar fashion as they wing their way home to Sydney. Wendy is convinced she has fluffed it. Andrew is hoping he bluffed it. Wendy didn't. Andrew did.'

We'd just debated 'That TV Is Bad For You' in front of 2000 people in the State Theatre and, as Andrew told Sally: 'We're sitting here like two limp pieces of lettuce. We're both bloody crazy to be doing this thing.'

This 'thing' was a television outing devised after the success of the Melbourne Comedy Festival debates; it was co-produced by Andrew and Ted Robinson. With the dry wit of Campbell McComas as moderator and an extraordinary cast of debaters chosen from the fields of media, the arts, science and politics, all under Ted's expert direction, the show was an instant smasheroonie.

Among the propositions we debated: 'That Football is Stupid', 'That God Has No Sense of Humour', 'That Beauty is Better Than Brains' and 'That Sex Has Killed Romance'.

The most memorable, 'That Australia Needs the Royal Family', was staged in Canberra. In Andrew's corner for the affirmative were Senator Bronwyn Bishop and senior press gallery journalist Paul Lyneham. In mine, for the negative: Senator Graham Richardson and internationally renowned lawyer, merchant banker and future prime minister Malcolm Turnbull. So daunting was the occasion that Richo, a seasoned headkicker, admitted to being 'very nervous'. For her part, Bronnie—Australia's own Iron Lady—confessed to 'butterflies, a *lot* of butterflies'. Malcolm was as cool as a cucumber.

Andrew's team won the majority of the debates we co-hosted. He memorised his arguments and roamed the stage in a bravura display of showmanship that got the most applause on Campbell's 'clap-o-meter'. I just didn't have the bandwidth to do the same and stuck to my lectern reading my notes, but I gave him a run for his money nonetheless.

Comedy debates became the fashion for charity fundraisers and corporate events for years. I did dozens of them. There is one that stands out.

'That Polo is Better Than Sex' was the title of the debate Kerry Packer hired me for. He'd rung my agents with the directive: 'Get me that bird off the television!'

Husband Brendan and I drove to Ellerston, Packer's pastoral station of 30,000 hectares in the Upper Hunter region of New South Wales, near the township of Scone. We were speechless at the life-sized statues of African wildlife installed along the majestic drive and, beyond them, vast expanses of emerald-green polo fields watered by sentries of sprinklers going full bore. Housed in the station manager's home, Brendan immediately turned on the Channel Nine cricket telecast and was thrilled to see the feed came 'ad-free'. Now, this was living!

In the foyer of the small theatrette furnished with plush leather armchairs, I was chatting, nursing a drink before we got underway, when Packer's gruff voice in my ear said: 'Everything that happens here is private. Remember that.' Ergh! If I hadn't been nervous before, I was now.

I can't remember whether it was 'polo' or 'sex' that won the night, but there were enough sexy polo players in attendance that it was probably a draw.

I sat and chatted with Kerry until the very early morning hours. He was a fascinating raconteur and, unexpectedly, most charming. At one point he explained the difference between me and Andrew Denton in our approach to comedy, as he saw it: 'Denton tells a joke, and you don't laugh . . . but if you think about it for a moment, you realise it was very funny. Then you laugh.

'You tell a joke. You laugh . . . and then, when you think about it, you realise it wasn't that funny and have no idea why you're laughing.'

I'm not sure who comes out best in his critique.

*

Our new co-host on the *Morning Crew* was Peter Moon. I'd worked with Peter a decade earlier in the sketch show *Carnival Knowledge*, and by the time he joined Paul and me, he was a national comedy star as a cast member of the TV sketch show *Fast Forward* and its successor, *Full Frontal*. You might know him best as cock-eyed, gurning Viktor—the Soviet anchorman (with Sveta, played by Jane Turner) on *Good Morning Moscow*. 'A very unattractive man.'

He'd been dabbling in radio with our sister station Fox FM in Melbourne and been a 'big hit' when he was hired by Brad March. 'Again, you and Peter were quite opposites as people,' says Brad. 'But you both came from that Melbourne comedy scene. You were brilliant together.'

When Peter left the *Morning Crew* nine years later, he said that behind our success as a constantly bickering duo had been a real animosity. 'From day one, Wendy and I irritated the hell out of each other,' he said. 'But it made people laugh. It was like everyone's bad marriage. It makes me wonder what the state of relationships in New South Wales is that it was such a popular show.'

Peter thought of us as being chalk and cheese, even in our first years at the Comedy Cafe. That's not how I remember it. We got on well, even pairing as lovers, in bed, in a couple of skits. Shared a comedic sensibility. But our social circles were very different; we didn't ever 'hang out' together.

I had an upbeat in-your-face personality while Peter was sardonic and self-contained. I'm sure I got up his nose. But how could we have been comedy partners for those long years if we'd had a real 'toxic chemistry', as he later claimed? Beats me.

Peter Moon made me laugh every morning when we were together on air. Paul and I could throw anything at him, and he never failed to come back with an inspired line or unhinged rant that cracked us up. Our listeners fell in love with mad 'Moonie', and no one can quite believe that Peter operated remotely for all that time.

Broadcasting up the line from a small studio in the backyard of his home in Melbourne's eastern suburbs, sitting there alone, I'm not sure he ever realised just how much he was adored. And I'm not sure he would have liked it much, even if he did. Peter was, at heart, a serious person and felt conflicted in his role as a radio chucklehead. As Ian McFadyen says: 'He found himself on an unexpected trajectory, he couldn't help but be funny. That side of him is irrepressible. Everything he found insufferable and crazy about the world became comedy.'

I couldn't go anywhere without being asked: 'Where's Moonie?' I never replied: 'Actually, he's in Melbourne.' That would have torn it.

In its heyday, the *Crew* was a tightly disciplined operation. We would prepare for hours after the show, but if something more compelling presented itself in real time . . . on the morning? All our planning would be thrown in the bin and we would go with what was in front of us. From the on-air studio to the producer's airlock, music library and production, the pace was feverish. People *ran* through corridors as they shouted instructions to each other and no two days were ever the same. Exhilarating when we pulled it off. If we didn't?

The next morning was only hours away.

I took my mantra from A.A. Milne's Christopher Robin: 'And the look in his eye. Seemed to say to the sky. "Now, how to amuse them to-day?".'

As a woman in a hosting role, I was able to bring a female per- spective to the airwaves—celebrity gossip, parenting, relationship stuff. Rehashing the TV shows our audience never missed, like *Ally McBeal* and *Friends*.

Our best-loved segment, 'Battle of the Sexes', became, in radio lingo, 'appointment listening'. The set-up was simple: male and female contestants were asked trivia questions that the opposite sex surely couldn't answer. (This was when the book *Men are from Mars, Women are from Venus* was a bestseller.) A running tally was kept and the winning side announced at the end of the year. Our female audience was totally invested in handing the men a flogging, and usually did.

We were always on the hunt for that magic caller who'd generate 'water cooler' office talk—a very big thing with radio programmers in the nineties. On the topic of 'When did you know your partner was having an affair?', a gem of a call came in from . . . let's call her Jessica.

Jessica: 'Well, I knew Matthew was having an affair when he told me he was at the football with Danny.'

Morning Crew: 'And how could you be so sure?'

Jessica: 'Because I was in bed with Danny at the time.'

In the eleven years I was with the *Morning Crew* we won eighty-four out of eighty-eight surveys in Sydney FM radio, with Alan Jones outright number one on the AM band. As Brad March had predicted, women listeners were a 'gap in the market'—that's if you can characterise half the population as a 'gap'.

We interviewed all the big-name movie stars who came to town—something I never really enjoyed, because it was obvious most of them were on interminable press tours to promote films they'd made years before and could scarcely remember. They were sick and tired of the inane: 'And what was it like to work with . . .' or, 'What do you think of Australia?' Some were also quietly seething because, back in the US, they did the rounds of national television talk shows and weren't required to visit tinpot radio stations in far-flung lands to be quizzed at eight o'clock in the morning. I was sympathetic.

The cast of *Spider-Man*—Tobey Maguire, Kirsten Dunst and Willem Dafoe—were in studio one morning and lovely Ms Dunst did most of the talking. Afterwards we totted up the number of words Willem Dafoe had uttered. We could almost count them on two hands. Often I'd be bussed to fancy hotel rooms and sit in a queue of interviewers, each of us allocated a strict ten-minute slot. Producer Gemma O'Neill and I once waited . . . and waited . . . for the cast of the movie *Charlie's Angels* to arrive in a sumptuous room at the Park Hyatt. When they finally turned up, we were caught out jumping off the headboard onto the bed and sproinging onto the carpet. *Oops!*

Many of the A-listers, though, were fabulous, realising that we were all stuck in the same hellscape hamster wheel of 'publicity' and trying to make the best of it. The locals who'd become internationally famous—Hugh Jackman, Nicole Kidman, Russell Crowe, Heath Ledger, Kylie Minogue, Bryan Brown and Sam Neill—were always forthcoming and playful. Inevitably, when Russell and I were together we sparred about rugby league and the two Sydney teams we followed, who were mortal enemies. That *was* a lot of fun.

Of all the years on radio speaking with celebrities, the high-light for me was a 'phoner' with Paul Newman, arranged with the help of Nicole Kidman. As a teen, I'd had a poster of him on my bedroom wall from *Butch Cassidy and the Sundance Kid*. Worshipped him. I can date when I spoke to Paul (here's me saying 'Paul', like we were on a first-name basis) to 2001 because it was just after Monica and Chandler were married on *Friends*.

After a lovely, meandering chat—him speaking from the verdant garden at his home in Connecticut—I dared to ask what he thought was the secret to a long-lasting marriage. He'd been with Joanne Woodward for forty years by then, and their longevity as a couple was something to aspire to in fickle Hollywood. In fact, Chandler had said on *Friends*: 'The only one who can make marriage work is Paul Newman.'

He paused and then replied: 'Well . . . Joanne and I have an agreement. She looks after the "small stuff"—like where we live, where our kids go to school, where we go on holiday, what we eat. I look after the "big stuff".' He then reeled off a list that included his passions as a campaigner against fossil fuels, nuclear weapons and for gun control and migrant workers' rights. 'So far, I'd have to say she's doing a lot better than me.'

A lifelong supporter of humanitarian causes and left-wing politics, Paul Newman died in 2008 at the age of eighty-three. The year before, he'd nominated as one of his 'life's proudest achievements' making it onto Richard Nixon's 'hit list' in 1971: 'More than the films, more than the awards—finding out that I was on Nixon's enemies list meant that I was doing something right.'

*

Anyone who's worked in daily radio will tell you it's a greedy maw that chews up content. The more you throw into it, the more it demands. 'Breakfast' on FM is the hungriest baby of them all. By the time I'd done the show and finished planning for the next morning, watched a special screening of a new-release movie in the afternoon, got home, written gags and then stayed up late past my bedtime to watch a popular TV show . . . many workdays were sixteen hours long.

Not complaining. I was rewarded with the big bucks.

For those eleven years, I could have told you what time it was to within a minute—from the moment I woke up until the moment my head hit the pillow. It became a joke with friends and family that I could fall asleep mid-sentence.

One summer I watched a currawong feeding an enormous chick, almost bigger than she was, that had been smuggled into the nest by a channel-billed cuckoo. Mumma bird wore herself ragged as she flitted back and forth in a frenzy, trying to keep the baby fed as it squawked hungrily, never satisfied.

It was exactly how I felt.

In my forties, and a new mum, every day presented a new challenge and I took on a lot of 'mother guilt' in those years when I was working such crazy hours and the kids were young.

When Maeve was born in January 2000, I spent a month broadcasting from home. Breastfeeding Marley had been a breeze, but Maeve was a fussy babe at first and often refused to latch onto the nipple. I could only make it work if I lay down on the floor and she was put on top of me. We managed that way, sort of upside down.

When we finally got our act together, I'd be sitting in front of the microphone in our sunroom, topless, breastfeeding while I was on air and the whole of Sydney could hear Maeve noisily slurping away. Brendan would keep toddler Marley corralled in the rest of the house, but sometimes he'd escape and burst through the door shouting, 'Mumma! Mumma! Thomas! Thomas! Toast!' until Brendan could catch him and plonk him in front of the television with breakfast and the latest episode of *Thomas the Tank Engine*.

One morning we crossed, live, to Geoffrey Rush in LA for the Oscars and I realised I'd been holding my hand over Maeve's mouth to stop her from crying. Had I really almost suffocated my own baby? I was horrified. Time to head back to the studio. I will admit that I often breathed a huge sigh of relief as I crept out of the house in the dark, leaving Brendan to manage the chaos.

It became my ritual to find a quiet corner in the studio before I went on air, stand face to the wall and administer myself a stern talking-to: 'Now. Remember why you're here. You're here to entertain people. Give them a good start to their day. That's what you are paid to do. No one wants to hear any of your bullshit.'

I also had a script for self-talk to get over the creeping, crippling tide of sleep-deprivation. 'Get a grip! You're *not* going to die. I will take care of you. Trust me. We will get some sleep. There's all the time in the world for us to sleep. *It's just not now.*' The trick was to persuade the brain to convince the rest of the body to 'calm down', 'relax'. Not to let emotions get the better of me. It was a self-taught soothing technique I'd used for as long as I could remember.

It worked, more or less.

*

The *Crew* was so much more than the hosts, of course. There was, inevitably, a turnover of staff in that decade—all of them dedicated, highly skilled, creative and professional. Also a roster of comedy writers, including Gary Eck, Adam Hills, Anthony Mir and Des Mangan, who supplied us with first-rate jokes, ad and song parodies and clever scripts for radio soap operas. Our recollections usually begin with, 'Oh my God! Can you believe we actually did that?'

We did.

We pulled some crazy stunts. Having the idea was one thing. Figuring out the 'mechanics': the logistics of delivery and the on-air 'imaging' for the audience was another. We got better at it as the years progressed.

Here's a sample:

Dash for Cash: Frank Vincent was our 'man on the street'. We pinned $10,000 worth of banknotes on him and gave him a head start. How long would it take to catch him and nab the cash? It should have provided an entertaining few minutes. Within twenty seconds he was caught by a group of highly trained athletes and all we heard was 'EEEAARGH!' *One star.*

The Perfect Man: They were in short supply in Sydney, so why not make our own 'perfect man'? One you could win? Damien, renamed Damon, took etiquette lessons, was educated in household tasks and given a full makeover. Women who won keys had the chance to break his chains and padlock. One 'lucky' woman got to take him home. Can't recall what happened after that. *Two stars.*

A Rude Awakening: Know anyone who habitually sleeps through their morning alarm? How about we give them a 'wake-up' call they'll never forget? Michael 'Sydney' ONeil, who took charge of our escapades outside the studio, organised a fireworks display, earth-moving equipment, a speedboat with a V8 engine and even a full brass band underneath bedroom windows. Classic morning-radio stunt. Really annoyed the neighbours. *Three stars.*

Secretary's Day: In the nineties it was a big-ticket item on our calendar with early-morning cocktails, prizes and staggering stories of bad male bosses. I'll never forget the broadcast from a CBD venue when a couple of hundred female secretaries (and a few men) stormed the airwaves singing Shania Twain's feminist power anthem 'Man! I Feel Like a Woman!' a cappella and word-perfect. *Four stars.*

Morning Crew to the Rescue: Listeners nominated a person or a cause worthy of a good turn and we did our best to deliver. Everyone in the station helped with the 'rescues'—from the hardworking sales and promotions staff through to the front desk. Our loyal advertisers always came through with donations of flowers, catering, travel . . . we only had to ask. It's difficult to nominate any one 'rescue' above another, but there were a few weddings at hospital bedsides that it was a privilege to be part of.

Arranging meet-and-greets with celebrities and toy drives at Christmas was a *Crew* speciality. Good stuff. *Five stars.*

There were some awful promotions suggested by management that I drew the line at, like giving away plastic surgery. That wasn't going to happen on my watch. Another was a competition to send a listener into 'space'—which would turn out to be an anti-gravity training centre. Our listeners would have been furious. We did try to make our competitions fair, with a chance of winning something of value.

Peter was particularly unhappy with our offer of a free private detective, although our producer Gemma says she was inundated with women keen to take up the offer to track down errant partners. After some salacious details came to light, we decided the content was too dark for morning radio and quickly abandoned the idea. There were, after all, kids listening in the back seat of the car.

But it wasn't all silly stunts and giveaways. Two mornings stand out for me. On the day Princess Diana died, I cried along with our callers, all of us unable to comprehend the distressing news.

On September 11, as Sydney awoke to the terrifying events in New York, we asked our listeners to switch on the lights in their homes or car headlights in solidarity. Before dawn, from our broadcast studio in a tower in Bondi Junction, we watched as the City lit up before our eyes.

*

On my office shelf, I keep a 'Raward'—the gongs handed out annually by Commercial Radio Australia (now known as the ACRAs). It's an ugly pyramid-shaped lump of resin and reads: *1999. FM's Morning Crew.* Two Strangers and a Wedding. *Best Station Promotion. Metropolitan.*

'Austereo promotions are starting to resemble elaborate socio-logical experiments,' said the *Sunday Telegraph.* Over at Triple M, breakfast hosts Andrew Denton and Amanda Keller had run 'House From Hell', a forerunner of *Big Brother.*

Did this radio stunt of ours spawn television reality shows like *Married At First Sight*? It could well have done. It was certainly copied by radio stations all over the world—in New Zealand, the UK, the US, Canada, Ireland, South Africa and even in Hungary and Estonia—with most using our original branding. The press clipping book I have from that time runs to a hundred pages.

I remember very clearly how it all came about. I'd read an odd snippet in a newspaper that reported a mother in rural America had taken her adult son to a County Fair and announced on stage that she'd marry him off to the first woman in the crowd she approved of. Prospective brides had formed a queue, she'd brought along an authorised public official, and they were wed on the spot.

Hmm. At the time, there were so many 'desperate and dateless' women in Sydney that newspapers had resorted to printing maps of the suburbs where the most single men resided. Our talkback line was full of women moaning that it was impossible to meet someone. (Remember, this was back when meeting someone 'online' was barely socially acceptable.)

Perhaps we could explore the whole topic of attraction and relationships for our legion of female listeners if we came up with a new wrinkle on 'arranged marriage'? We hashed it out over a few meetings. Too weird? How could it work on radio? It would be sight unseen. But maybe that was the hook: Theatre of the Imagination. That's what radio did best, after all. Unethical? It was probably too weird. Hmm.

It was when Paul came up with the title 'Two Strangers and a Wedding'—a riff on the title of the beloved rom-com *Four Weddings and a Funeral*—that the idea started to take shape. As everyone in FM radio knows, coming up with a witty title is the hardest part; after that, everything falls into place. Like 'Traffic and Weather . . . Together'.

The selection process for the 'bride' and 'groom' was exhaustive. Facebook was years away. It became an administrative nightmare as hundreds of hopefuls stampeded to take part— some ninety men and 300 women.

It was imperative that we exercised due diligence to weed out stalkers and exes with an agenda. That was uppermost in our minds. One night we eyeballed and spoke with a group of prospective male contestants over a game of snooker in a pub.

We whittled our lovebirds down to two. The question was popped, live on air. By this time, the saga of 'Two Strangers and a Wedding' had transfixed Sydney. Callers rang, sobbing, from underground car parks where they'd stayed listening to the radio, making them late for work.

The stunt caused national, then international, uproar. Church leaders weighed in, fulminating that the 'sanctity of marriage' had been traduced. After this degradation of all things holy, where was society headed? (Little did they know.)

The chosen couple, Glenn and Leif, both twenty-somethings, hadn't set eyes on each other before that morning in the grand ballroom of the Sydney Hilton on 4 September 1998. Kate Ceberano sang. Glenn was smart in a dark suit, white shirt and tie with a pale rose in his lapel, Leif lovely in an ivory satin gown with a sweetheart neckline.

The ceremony was a tear-jerker. Traffic on the Harbour Bridge slowed as callers jammed the switchboard. 'Everyone in every car I can see right now is crying.'

On the morning, Glenn said: 'God, she's beautiful. I couldn't have picked a better bride.' Leif said: 'It's romantic. More romantic than marrying someone after going out with them for three years.' Then they were off on a honeymoon in Paris, trailed by reporters from current affairs shows, with a stopover in London to appear on breakfast television. Their 'marriage' had made front-page news there too.

It wasn't a *real* wedding, rather a 'commitment ceremony'. Australian law stipulates that notice of legal marriages must be registered at least one month in advance—a convention reality show watchers are now familiar with. As for how Glenn and Leif's story unfolded? I've read various accounts so I'll leave that for them to tell. We staged two more weddings, neither of them as noteworthy as that first one.

Was 'Two Strangers and a Wedding' the inspiration for the current plague of even weirder, more outrageous dating shows?

If so, someone owes someone a royalty cheque.

But don't send it to Glenn's mother who, unlike that 'mom' at the County Fair, is quoted as decrying the whole award-winning spectacle as 'an appalling stunt'.

*

Peter Moon hadn't been happy with what he saw as the 'Jerry Springer' direction the show was taking when he left the *Morning Crew* in 2002. He was more at home with his scripted comedy characters, the Guru and Clive Pompous-Arse. The 'confessional' style of radio we were doing didn't play to his strengths. Paul and I knew that. So did management. He'd made his many grievances heard.

There was some mischievous myth-making around Peter's departure that cast me in the role of the Wicked Witch who had summoned mighty forces and commanded that he be 'axed'. 'When Harmer made it clear she wanted Moon out of the show, Austereo didn't hesitate,' ran a story in *The Sydney Morning Herald*.

First I'd got rid of Jamie Dunn, and now Peter Moon! It was inferred that I was a difficult woman, ignoring the fact that almost a decade had passed in the interim and that radio line-ups elsewhere were changed with the regularity of pairs of old socks. Also, that Paul and I had been co-hosting from the beginning, and we were still getting on as well as we ever had, him as my faithful radio 'husband'.

Even worse, one story went that I'd schemed to dump Peter so I could replace him with my former 'boyfriend', Greg Fleet. I was furious when I read it. Fleety and I had once regaled 2DayFM listeners with our disastrous attempt at a one-night stand back in the nineties. Hardly an enduring romantic relationship. (I'd attempted a few liaisons with fellow male comic performers over the years. They were always ridiculous. It's impossible to achieve erotic sex when it starts with a stifled giggle and ends with you both rolling on the floor, on opposite sides of the bed, laughing.)

Fact is, at the end of 2002 Peter was over it, as those who were there at the time will attest. When sounded out on whether he wanted to stay, he'd been non-committal. I probably should have walked too, but I agreed to two more years. It was for the money. By now, it was a phenomenal sum I felt sure I would never earn again and, considering the still-excellent ratings, why would I walk?

In the years we were co-hosts, Peter and I never spoke about our contracts or future plans. Either of us could have been replaced at any time, for all we knew. We were always jumpy on survey days, knowing that we lived or died by the numbers. If they were good, you'd be left alone to get on with it. If they weren't, you'd have someone in your ear with often inane suggestions like, 'The funniest bit is the punchline—why don't you put that first?' Or, 'If you could just make the jokes seventeen per cent funnier.' Peter Clay, a long-time *Morning Crew* producer, remembers a procession of managers who were always quoting Sun Tzu's 'The Art of War' in the relentless battle for ratings, to the amusement of all.

Decisions made in the boardroom were always opaque. My theory is that radio management enjoy executing dramatic exits.

It's a payback for all the times the talent takes the piss out of them and they're unable to barge in when the 'on-air' light is glowing. A friend of mine who was a senior manager and has since left radio is even harsher in her assessment: 'There is always scheming behind doors. Skulduggery. Always a group of men conspiring. And they just seem to relish pulling the rug from under people.'

I have no doubt the way Peter found out he hadn't been re-signed was totally shit. Demeaning and unforgivable. I know, because the same was done to me a year later.

Much as I regarded Greg Fleet as a brilliant comic talent, and one of my most cherished friends, it was an open secret that he was using drugs heavily when he was given the job as co-host with me and Paul in 2003. Greg is a wildly lateral thinker, and it was hard to find a rhythm on air. I often likened our efforts to him driving our car into a cul-de-sac, jumping out, running away and leaving me to do a fifteen-point turn to get it out, even though our listeners enjoyed the madness.

The *Morning Crew* was on borrowed time after more than a decade, and our younger listeners were drifting to Merrick and Rosso on Nova FM. We'd started the year on top, but our dominance was waning. I was called into a meeting room by Austereo management, who showed me the numbers—still huge in the older female demographic. 'We don't want these people,' I was told. 'Get rid of them.'

'And how am I supposed to do that?' I asked. Tongue-kiss Britney Spears, like Madonna had just done at the MTV Awards?

It was a bizarre directive.

With still a year to run on my contract, I was at lunch when I took a call from my agent Hilary. 'Darling, you can go home,' she said. 'They're letting you go.'

I was stunned.

I rang Paul Holmes, who'd had no inkling. He commandeered a microphone in the foyer and announced to the entire station: 'This is Paul. If anyone in management is listening? I QUIT!' Then he went off and finished his round of golf.

Brendan's response when I called him? 'Yahoo! You're coming home!'

The press release from Austereo was a masterpiece of confection—a veritable croquembouche of saccharine profiterole puffery.

> We have known for years that women rule at breakfast (and some say lunch, dinner and the rest of the day) and there is further proof at 2DayFM, where Wendy Harmer has decided to pass the Breakfast baton ... or is that the Breakfast Berocca ... to good friend Judith Lucy.
>
> Michael Anderson, CEO of Austereo, said: 'When Wendy came to us and said that after 11 years at the top, all the changes in the team, and the various things on her plate, she wanted to have a big talk about next year, it made sense. And it made even more sense to both of us when we started talking about what a brand-new breakfast team could look like. All the talk led to Judith Lucy being the one.'

Well, all this was *very interesting*, because I'd had no idea that negotiations were taking place to replace me with Judith.

She and I knew each other from around the comedy traps; she'd been a guest a few times on the show, and there was talk of her appearing more regularly. But that was the extent of it, as Paul and I recall.

Here I will defend Judith, who, I am reliably informed, had no idea either that I hadn't been fully consulted on this jolly baton change. All the quotes supplied by me—'Every now and again you get that perfect moment when you get what you wish for' and being 'thrilled' that a 'great mate' was taking my job—were a frantic exercise in face-saving. I brought my own shovel, excavated my own shallow grave and filled it in with a steaming pile of self-serving nonsense.

That's radio for you.

There are precious few graceful exits.

*

'The Morning Crew has left the building!' Paul's final words echoed through the city streets from our stage in front of St Andrews Cathedral in the Sydney CBD, where a thousand people had turned out for our farewell on a November morning in 2003.

Premier Bob Carr and Lord Mayor Lucy Turnbull were there to send us off.

Australian Idol winner Guy Sebastian sang the Louis Armstrong classic, 'What a Wonderful World'. Jamie Dunn called in from Brissy as Agro. Brendan brought Marley and Maeve along . . . and, yes, I sniffed back tears.

One last 'Battle of the Sexes'. The final question: 'Who hosts *A Current Affair*?' That would be Ray Martin, who was with us that morning.

Ray and I went back a way. I was the original whistleblower in 1995 on the 'Cash for Comment' scandal that rocked commercial radio. Hilary Linstead had been approached by an ad agency on behalf of Telecom—now known as Telstra—with a clandestine deal. All I had to do to get the cash—a fee of up to $500,000 was suggested—was to speak positively about Telecom whenever I had the chance: 'Excellent company. The best . . . blah, blah, blah.' I would deflect anything negative that arose from callers to the station. As proposed by the agency: 'initially agreeing with the comment but then stating a positive comment in reply'.

There was one vital stipulation: I wasn't to tell my employers. Hilary and I immediately knocked back the offer. I told Ray, and a story ran on *A Current Affair* tipped off by an anonymous broadcaster. Four years later the scandal 'broke' on ABC TV's *Media Watch*. An Australian Broadcasting Authority inquiry estimated the value of such arrangements—where paid advertising was disguised as editorial comment—at a whopping $18 million dollars. Alan Jones and John Laws were revealed to have been rewarded for favourable comment on radio 2UE for some of the nation's biggest companies, including Qantas, Optus, Foxtel and Mirvac. The practice was defended with claims that they were not employed as journalists but as 'entertainers' and 'radio personalities'. The same could have been said of me, but I had a fundamental set of ethical principles intact: regard for my employers and, most importantly, the listeners.

I'm quoted in *The Age* in 1999 about that initial offer: 'If you haven't got your independent views in broadcasting, then you're nothing. Without your credibility, you're stuffed. You can only sell it once. How much is it worth?'

A shitload, as was later revealed.

*

'After 11 years as one of Sydney's most successful broadcasters, Harmer will end her $2.2 million a year job in two weeks,' said *The Sydney Morning Herald*. Knock a million off and it was close enough. I walked away with a huge sum and a clause that I couldn't work in radio for a year. Suited me.

'I'd just like to take all the clocks in my house and throw them in the bin, go out and get drunk, watch late-night television, and go to bed at the same time as my husband.'

Now, that *was* an accurate quote.

But, I loved my time in that gig. I laughed every morning. *Really* laughed. Not too many jobs where you can say that.

An insider told me that it cost Austereo many millions in lost advertising revenue after the new team took over and ratings quickly faltered. It doesn't illustrate anything about their undeniable talents, but says much about how radio management often underestimates the loyalty and trust listeners invest in the disembodied voices they choose to admit into the intimate spaces of bedrooms, bathrooms and kitchens or in cars and headphones on the daily commute.

The ephemeral nature of daily radio has always appealed to me. Like a live comedy gig, it's done. It disappears.

Remembered as a familiarity which soothed in times of distress.

Was there to share celebrations.

A soundtrack to life's milestones.

Forever tied to a place and time.

17

Hearts and flowers

Brendan James Donohoe
St Canice Church
Rushcutters Bay, Sydney
Friday, 2 December 1994

He's the mirror I always want to look into.

The one that reflects my image as I see myself.

He sees me true.

He says, 'I'll never leave you. Ever.'

*

It was just months after I'd lobbed into 'Lizzie' Bay in 1993 when my old flatmate from St Kilda, Dale Langley, rang and nagged me to go to her sister's place in nearby Edgecliff to attend an election night party. Didn't think I'd know anyone there but forced myself to go. Turned up on the doorstep, pale-skinned, all in black. Very 'Melbourne'.

It was the 'unlosable' election. All Opposition Leader John Hewson had to do was stay upright and victory was surely his. Prime Minister Paul Keating was weary, swinging at shadows; the polls and pundits had all but written him off. Cheers, my fellow voters! Drink up. Settle in for a sure defeat. I'd be going home by midnight to two cats, no matter who was in power.

To the beat of Midnight Oil, Lenny Kravitz, Pearl Jam, Hunters & Collectors, the frenetic throng was crammed on the balcony dancing. It was a beautiful, balmy March evening. After a desultory perusal of the dips and chips, I settled in front of the teev with a warmish bottle of Riesling in the only quiet corner I could find. My dates for the night would be Kerry O'Brien and Antony Green from the tally room in Canberra.

And then he walked in . . . tall, broad-shouldered, sun-kissed blond curls, tanned from his head to his toes. He must have come with someone. I looked about, couldn't see anyone. He sat down next to me, smelling of sea salt, and whispered the magic bellwether words, 'Eden–Monaro'. His knowledge of politics was encyclopaedic and, as the results rolled in from across the nation, he knew the name of every player on the field and had a witty take on all of them that kept me laughing.

That night, Keating said his win was 'the sweetest victory of all . . . a victory for the true believers, the people who in difficult times have kept the faith.'

Then we danced.

Brendan James Donohoe was also sure that I'd arrived at the party with a date so, reluctantly, we left each other.

A week later, after finding out my address, he made his way to my gate. It so happened that my other dear friend from share-house days back in St Kilda, Michael Trudgeon, had rolled up in his vintage Porsche to visit at exactly the same time.

Thinking that it was the end of any romantic overtures, Brendan left his box of organic fruit and vegetables outside my door: including a calling card from his home delivery company 'Cleanfoods' and a flyer on a forthcoming information night on the danger of pesticides. I might want to mention it on radio?

Ah-ha! So that's what he was after. Free publicity! I knew a man like him wouldn't be interested in me. I stepped over that box on my way to work. Left it to rot, then threw it all in the bin.

It wasn't the first time I'd sabotaged my love life. One night at an ARIAs after-party, I was talking with Jimmy Barnes when James Reyne interrupted our conversation. 'Want to know some-thing, Jimmy?' he said. 'Wendy would never go out with me, because she thought I was too dumb.'

In Melbourne in the mid-eighties, James Reyne, then the lead singer of Australian Crawl, was the most desirable man in rock, a national pin-up boy. I was a lowly, plain-looking stand-up comedian. We'd sometimes find ourselves backstage together and he'd ask me on dates. *Seriously?* I suspected he must have been doing it for a bet and turned him down.

Only recently, we laughed about it. 'I really did want to go out with you,' he reassured me. 'All the people in the comedy scene were so *alternative* and *cool*. I had this thing where I thought no one took me seriously because I'd come from *Countdown* and everyone thought "fuck him".'

And in another, much-regretted failure of confidence, when my good friend Deborah Conway invited me to be in the music video of her mega-hit 'It's Only The Beginning' in 1991, I declined because I thought I'd look too fat in tartan golf pants.

I watch that clip now and want to hit myself over the head with a 9-iron.

There you go. The foolish scripts we write for ourselves when we are young.

It was a few months after the election night party when Brendan and I met again. I was MC for a fundraiser in aid of writer Bob Ellis after his house had burned down. Brendan had spent money he didn't have to get there. He was even lovelier than I'd remembered. Again, I couldn't tear myself away from his amused bright-blue eyes. We sorted that we were both single.

At the end of the evening, as he walked me to my car, he held out his arm and I stepped under it. A thought came to me unbidden. *I'm home.* It was an insistent voice. I'd never heard it before, with anyone.

We woke up together next morning. No more entrants—we have a winner! The judges' decision is final and no correspondence will be entered into.

Within three months, in my flat in Elizabeth Bay, Brendan got down on one knee and proposed marriage, proffering a plastic ring from a soft drink bottle.

'I'm a faithful old dog,' he said. 'I will never leave you. Ever.'

This time I was certain it was true. They were the words I had waited my whole life to hear.

He was so different from the musicians and writers I'd been dating, who were often self-absorbed and given to bouts of melancholy. Brendan's outlook was always 'clear, sunny, with a slight chance of rain'. His belief that the future was bent in the arc of justice, and that we could all make a difference, was infectious.

From the passenger seat of his battered avocado-green Renault 16, I could see the road below through a giant hole in the floor. He lived in Collaroy, on the Northern Beaches, in an old shack on the side of a hill he shared with a couple of mates. Over his bed he'd strung up a fishing net containing all the treasures he'd collected from the beach—bits of driftwood, shell-encrusted buoys, bleached bones. The walls were adorned with Bob Marley posters and surfboards were stacked in every corner.

On still nights the sound of thundering surf lulled me to sleep. In the morning I was woken by the cacophony of rainbow lorikeets in the Norfolk Island hibiscus.

A 'drifter surfie', you may be thinking. Not a bit of it. Brendan was a qualified town planner and had recently finished up after ten years with the National Trust of Australia (NSW), campaigning against the demolition of priceless heritage buildings, bridges and wharves. (He was the first to nominate the Sydney Opera House for heritage listing.) On weekends he drove me around the Sydney suburbs, knowing that on the radio I'd need to be acquainted with my new city. We discussed plot ratios, setbacks, height limits and rezonings. We had lots to talk about—the surfie town planner and comedian urban affairs reporter. Other times we'd take off from the city to the country and spend our time poking about in historic churches, courthouses, jails, gardens and homesteads.

I mean, what's the likelihood of falling in love over the headstone of the bushranger Ben Hall in the Forbes Cemetery on Bogan Gate Road?

Brendan came with me to visit my old haunts in Melbourne, and I was struck by how 'vivid' he seemed—Sydney blond sandstone and sparkling blue ocean in contrast to drab grey bluestone and the brackish brown Yarra River.

All my friends approved and it wasn't too long before invitations came with the hopeful inquiry, 'And will Brendan be coming too?'

But I did miss my old town. One night I took him to the top of Mount Dandenong to survey the glittering carpet that was Melbourne. 'Look at it—so beautiful,' I breathed. He muttered, 'What a total dump!' and stalked back to the car. Sydney born and Katoomba bred, like a mollusc on a rock he will never move south.

Brendan's friends were gobsmacked. Their treasured, eccentric mate going out with some big-time, smart-mouthed celebrity? It wasn't until I started turning up at dinner parties and barbecues that they believed we were a real thing and conceded, 'Well, it *might* work.'

Before I agreed to marry him, a giant obstacle: Brendan had never seen me perform stand-up live.

He'd watched me on the *Gig* and thought 'nice legs', never missed the show. But this was a test. So many men didn't want to take me out for breakfast after I'd eaten them alive for dinner.

This would probably be the end of it. Backstage afterwards, there he was, with an enormous bunch of red roses and declaring that if he'd only seen me years before, he would have found me and proposed.

I said, 'Yes.' Mad if I didn't.

*

There was one final impediment to our union and it rested in the hands of Pope John Paul II.

Brendan was educated by the Jesuits at St Ignatius College, Riverview. You'll know the school from its famous alumni, which include former PM Tony Abbott and Deputy PM Barnaby Joyce.

A boarder there from the tender age of eleven, young Donohoe was a good student and excellent athlete—he was in the First Eight in rowing and the First XV in rugby. He revelled in his schooldays and still counts his friendships from that time among his closest.

His father, Jim Donohoe, was a renowned publican who was running the famed Carrington Hotel in Katoomba when Brendan was born, the middle child of three brothers. Jimmy also presided at the Forbes Tavern in the city and the Windsor Castle Hotel in Paddington. He was a larger-than-life character at Royal Randwick racecourse, where he knew everyone by name and everyone knew him—from the members enclosure to the trainers, jockeys and strappers. In the hallowed chairman's car park of the Australian Jockey Club, there was always a space for 'J. Donohoe'.

As a boy in the 1920s, Jim had attended Riverview and, as a lifelong adherent to the Catholic faith, was determined his three sons would follow him. In the 1970s and 80s, when Brendan was there, almost all his instructors were priests, novitiates or lay teachers from religious institutions. He recalls the uproar when the first-ever woman teacher was appointed.

Riverview wasn't as posh then as it is now, but many of the boys who boarded would be collected for weekends and holidays in Mercedes or Range Rovers. Brendan's father cruised down the drive in a bronze, two-door Chrysler Valiant Hemi Pacer, covered in bird shit and scratched from headlight to tail-light by the pissheads who'd 'coined' it outside the pub.

'That car was a complete disgrace,' Brendan remembers with pride. 'And there would be Dad, elbow out the window, waving cheery greetings to all. I'd be thinking, *Are you fucking kidding me?*' When the car boot was opened on the sideline of a sports field, revealing a bounty of his mum's homemade quiche and roast chicken, 'boys came from everywhere'.

Sadly, I didn't ever get to meet Jimmy; he died before Brendan and I met. But his mother Shirley was an enduring presence in our lives until she died at the age of ninety-two. A Kiwi, she was the daughter of the 'Uncrowned King of New Zealand'. Born in Ireland, 'Big Jim' Roberts was a hugely influential figure in the union movement, a member of the New Zealand Legislative Council until it was abolished in 1950, and president of the New Zealand Labour Party. Shirley emigrated to Sydney as a secretary in the fifties. Was late to marriage and motherhood, like me.

Nicknamed the 'Creamy Pony' in her time, Shirley was a tall, elegant figure. She welcomed me without question and was the best mother-in-law you could wish for. Brendan doted on her. There were regular hour-long phone conversations in which the two of them rehashed the politics of the day. The calls were even longer during the John Howard era, when I would hear: 'Sorry for swearing, Mum, but . . .'

The Donohoes are part of a big Irish family that has its fair share of horse trainers and one priest; Brendan's cousin, Father Michael Kelly SJ, would marry us. He would also become one of my closest friends and confidants.

The aforementioned obstacle was that I'd been married before, and so I met the nuns to take 'instruction' while we waited patiently for a papal annulment. I'd been very young at the time of my previous marriage and so the dispensation was granted on the grounds of 'diminished capability'. (I always tell my husband that if I ever decide to divorce him and remarry in the Catholic Church, I'll get off for the same reason.)

The church was full at 6 p.m. on a Friday for our December wedding, with 250 guests—our families, my friends from Melbourne, his mates from school, and a 'who's who' of the entertainment industry,' according to the *Telegraph Mirror*. I was 'stunning' in 'a layered cream and off-white silk and chiffon dress she designed herself'. In a very exciting moment before the formal nuptials, Father Kelly, with his robes flying, charged down the aisle towards the rear of the church and kicked the paparazzi off the premises.

Many on my side of the aisle were surprised that it would be a Catholic ceremony, with (almost) all the bells and whistles. There was one concession I asked for on the evening—that there be no Holy Communion. I didn't want one of our first acts as a married couple to be one I couldn't take part in. Brendan agreed. (I also asked that he didn't take his surfboard on our honeymoon in Morocco. He agreed to that too. Last time that ever happened!)

After we said our 'I dos', I turned and punched the air and the congregation stood, cheered and clapped madly. It was *that* kind of wedding. As we signed the register, Deborah Conway, heavily pregnant, sang 'Forever Young' with future husband, Willy Zygier. Sublime.

We walked from the church in a long procession around Rushcutters Bay to the reception at the Cruising Yacht Club of Australia in Darling Point; Sydney had put on her best shimmering dress for us on a still, warm evening. We'd decided against a stuffy sit-down affair and went with a fabulous cocktail party. Brother Phil played MC to perfection; Gerry Connolly delivered an impromptu speech as Paul Keating that had us all in hysterics; Hannie Rayson's heartfelt words had everyone crying into their champagne.

She was outdone only by my father, Mr Brown The Headmaster, who addressed the assembled with a booming, vintage, grammatically correct, ode that could even be heard by the strag-glers right at the back of the room.

I kept it, and it reads, in part:

The circumstances of Wendy's growing up have made her a complex and interesting personality along with some insecuri-ties, like the rest of us.

She pivots around a core of confidence, and inner source of sustenance which she has built up for herself and this has given her a great sense of self-reliance and a sense of purpose.

She is emotionally liberated, or what I choose to call, 'non-dependent'.

We are delighted by Wendy's marriage to Brendan; for he has the capacity to bear with her uncertainties and doubts. He lovingly supports her curiosity, adventure and risk-taking that her chosen career path constantly sets before her.

We trust that they will continue to interact so that the one helps the other to feel *beautiful, confident, joyous, loveable, smart, worthwhile* and *whole*.

When the Sydney All Star Band with Ignatius Jones out front struck up the opening chords of 'In the Mood', every guest hit the dance floor.

Magda Szubanski hoisted her dress and played her knees.

*

There is simply no way I could have achieved everything I have in my career for the past thirty years without Brendan. Every word written in every column, book or play is half his. My television appearances and the long hours spent on morning radio or podcasts are half his too.

We have created this life together in equal partnership. I said that I'd earn the money that would allow him to continue his work as a passionate environmental activist. And if children came along—something that we and all our friends and family doubted would ever happen—he would stay at home with them while I went off to work.

'After all,' I said, 'I earn enough money. Why should both of us be miserable?'

(The number of men electing to be 'house husbands' has barely changed in decades; still below ten per cent. It takes two wages to maintain even a modest family household. We were most privileged to have that option.)

Perhaps Brendan's greatest talent in life is for friendship. He has a multitude of friends and acquaintances, collecting them everywhere he goes. Never misses a celebration, attends every funeral and wake—even for those he barely knew—and is always the last to leave. So many times I've seen a gathering light up when he walks through the door—'Brendan's here!'—knowing that he'll be doing the rounds and engaging all the guests in animated conversation or spirited debate. And when he's not out with friends, they're here at our house. 'I've invited a few people over' quickly turns into an impromptu party and I've learned to cater on the run for when a 'few' quickly turns into twenty. I'm amazed our front doorsteps haven't completely worn away by now.

Our home in Collaroy is perched on the side of Mount Ramsay and, on a clear day, you can see through the Norfolk pines to the Long Reef headland in the south and far up the coast to Bouddi National Park in the north. Before us stretches the magnificent Pacific Ocean, rolling away to the horizon.

It's a view I've come to love over the three decades I've lived in this old wooden house. It was built in 1914 as a holiday home with just two small rooms in the days when Collaroy was an escape from the city. The house is a real 'beach classic' with heaps of old-fashioned charm. Anyone else would have knocked the joint over when they renovated, but Brendan, with his love of heritage, knew the house had 'good bones' beneath some ramshackle fibro additions. We tore them out and built new extensions, replicating as much of the original style of window frames and ceilings as we were able.

It's all mellow shades of wood, inside and out, with an octagonal kitchen that resembles a yurt (one of Brendan's fanciful follies), a deck to die for, and is crammed with bric-a-brac from our many travels and (too many) books. Like my father, Brendan is an incorrigible scrounger and much of our furniture has been rescued from the side of a road or a junk shop. There are barely two chairs that match. It's a bugger to dust.

You might think I would have chosen a spot with a view of the ocean to set up my working space but, as a kid who mostly grew up inland on flat, dry country, I found the ocean too restless. Too unsettling. Instead, I set up my computer in a corner at the rear of the house, next to my (treasured) walk-in pantry, with my only view out an old back door, down a set of stone steps to trees where the kookaburras visit. Not even a glimpse of water.

Now I was married to a 'seaweed head' who had first hit the waves at Coogee, aged six, on his Surf-o-Plane rubber mat. Brendan takes off surfing most days, even in the dead of winter, or at dusk, when I'm certain he'll be eaten by a shark. He's travelled the world on his surfing adventures, intrepid in his search for a wave.

We surf widows and widowers do it tough. There's no off-season for surfing. We live at the beck and call of the wind and tides with partners who always have one eye peering out the window and become increasingly antsy when the sea is a flat, featureless pane of glass for the third week in a row. If 'surf's up' we're lucky to have happy salt-encrusted creatures walking through the door. If we're unlucky, we get foul-tempered gorgons with dinged boards, fin chops and bad backs . . . who live for the moment they can walk out the door again.

Brendan's activism with Surfrider Foundation Australia, a not-for-profit dedicated to 'protecting waves and beaches', has been a constant in our lives. In that long association he has served on the board and as chairman and been president of the Northern Beaches branch (still is). There is no discarded sheet, tablecloth, random bit of cardboard or broken surfboard that hasn't been press-ganged into service with a spray-painted slogan and carted off to a rally. The one half of the sunroom that's his is piled with banners, donation buckets, raffle books, flyers, posters, boxes of stickers and a row of filing cabinets stuffed with government and council documents and his lengthy, meticulous submissions in reply.

As any environmental activist knows, there may be a victory here or there, but the battle is never won. How he maintains his optimism, I'll never know.

Optimism.

It's such an attractive quality in a human being.

One you can easily fall in love with.

And then there's the football . . .

*

I've always followed my partners' passions. With Michael it was cycling, with Steve it was Formula 1, Patrick made a jazz-lover out of me and with Brendan it's rugby league.

I should be allergic to footy but, brought up in a house where a match always droned in the background, I long ago surrendered and nominally followed the Richmond Tigers.

On a literary tour with the crime writer and AFL aficionado Peter Corris, he asked the audience: 'Has there ever been *anyone* who switched their allegiance from Aussie Rules to rugby league?'

I raised my hand. 'Me.'

Brendan had followed the Manly Warringah Sea Eagles since he was a kid and I liked the game from the first kick-off. Two smallgoods trucks colliding in a back paddock in the middle of winter? What wasn't to love?

Long story short, in 2002 the club was facing bankruptcy. The supermodel Sarah O'Hare (who was married to Lachlan

Murdoch and had followed the team since she was a teenager) and I staged a fundraiser—even performing a two-handed comedy routine I wrote for us as hosts.

Me: My husband bought me a lovely nightie in club colours for Christmas, Sarah. What did your husband buy you?

Sarah: The LA Dodgers.

The evening was such a hit it attracted a sponsor, Max Delmege, who set the club back on its feet.

We were dubbed the 'Eagles Angels' in the sports pages, and over the next seven years some twenty high-profile sportswomen—including Layne Beachley, Zali Steggall, Melinda Gainsford-Taylor, Laura Enever, Kerri Pottharst, Naomi Flood, Debbie Watson, Louise Sauvage, Anne Sargeant, Shelley Taylor-Smith and Nici Andronicus—joined us in 'what is believed to be the first and best-known female supporter group of its kind . . . the gold standard for female supporter groups in Australian sport,' according to *The Sydney Morning Herald*.

We achieved a first with a women-only corporate box at the Sea Eagles' home ground, Brookvale Oval. With sponsorship from Domayne, the powerhouse homewares chain, we installed a chandelier and Florence Broadhurst wallpaper, offered tarot readings and manicures. Sarah recruited designer Collette Dinnigan to create a female jersey for 'merch'. Through renting out our 'ladies lounge' and hosting numerous lunches, debates and events, we raised a lot of money for the club and local charities. Our manager, Mary Finkelsen, ran our outfit like a boss.

One evening in 2005, Katie Page—the CEO of Domayne—visited our Angels' eyrie along with David Gallop, then the head honcho of the National Rugby League (NRL). Mary was there when Katie said to David: 'The NRL has to do something for women. This is fantastic!' From that conversation, Mary says, we were encouraged to put a proposal to the NRL, and the Women in League round was born in 2007. It's going strong to this day.

Because I did so much national media as a rare, recognisable female face who followed League, I was always approached by fans of the game—even in Aussie Rules-mad Melbourne. 'Onya, Wendy!' they'd shout, despite Manly always topping the poll as the most-hated team in the competition.

The Eagles Angels folded in 2015, when the club's new owners and the NRL didn't show much interest. I just gave up trying to demonstrate our worth.

'How many wives have saved their husband's footy team?' says Brendan.

For that alone, he should never divorce me—although now, disillusioned with club management at Manly, he goes for the Auckland Warriors.

So I guess you never know.

I've pretty much given up following footy.

It's broken my heart one too many times.

*

I'd always wanted to have children. Having them without a partner had been an option but didn't appeal to me. I keenly felt the judgement that I was one of those selfish 'career women' who'd wanted to 'have it all' and 'left it too late'. But like so many women I knew, finding a partner who could deal with a successful woman hadn't been easy. I'd been told, more than once: 'I could never be with someone who earns more than me.'

I'd made a joke of it on stage: 'I want to achieve a few things in my life before having children: a career, financial independence . . . menopause.' But I felt great sadness about missing out on motherhood. Newlywed at the age of thirty-nine and now past forty, it seemed to be a far-fetched notion.

Brendan and I found ourselves sitting in front of a desk at an IVF clinic.

We'd drive from Collaroy and back, with me inconsolable. The verdict was plain. I was too old and our chances of conceiving were negligible to none.

We'd just begun a round of fertility-boosting drugs, with Brendan regularly stabbing a nasty needle into my backside, when the call came: 'You should come into our office. We have some news.'

The 'news', I was sure, was that my ovaries had spontaneously combusted and there was no chance I'd *ever* give birth.

Instead, we were informed that I was pregnant. Somewhere between delayed pathology results and a holiday, we'd conceived.

'I told you! I told you!' Brendan whooped, chucking the drug paraphernalia in the bin. 'I knew it, but you didn't believe me.'

Our son was born on a scorching-hot, forty-degree summer's day. As we drove around Narrabeen Lake at dawn, the cicada chorus was deafening and the air-conditioned maternity ward at the Mater Hospital seemed a good option, even if I wasn't in labour. Brendan, in his panic, had unpacked my carefully packed maternity bag, and I hadn't made a birth plan, figuring they never worked. My 'no birth plan' hadn't included an emergency caesarean, so I was vindicated. Him, when I had no nighties or lip balm? Not so much.

Marley James (I'll leave you to figure out the provenance of his name) had been due on Christmas Day in 1997, but came four days earlier. On Christmas Eve, I was still at the Mater, out of my head, happily delirious on strong painkillers and wreathed in flowers, when there appeared at the end of my bed's snowy counterpane a host of angels, all in white, singing 'Silent Night'.

Fuck me! I thought. *I DIED! I died during childbirth!*

Then I realised they were festive choristers. I saw baby Marley alongside me in a crib, snatched him up, felt his heartbeat, and gave thanks we were both alive.

The staff at the Mater kindly looked after Marley for an hour or so while Brendan and I went off to a local cafe to have breakfast as a couple—the last we would have without a baby in tow for quite a while.

I sat at the table and sobbed: 'One day he will grow up and leave us!'

'Oh, for Chrissake sake,' said Brendan. 'He's five days old!'

Our fertility doctor said there was no hope of a second child. 'Enjoy your son,' he said. 'At your age you're very lucky to have him. Goodbye.'

Our daughter Maeve Louise (her middle name after my sister's) was born less than two years later, when I was forty-four. We had again conceived naturally against all the odds. The good doctor, very happy for us, advised on a second caesarean, given my 'geriatric' womb. All I had to do was nominate a day for the procedure.

Pardon? This seemed to me to be an ill-advised meddling with the fates. What about her numerology, her star sign? That couldn't be for me to decide. I left it as late as I possibly could, until it was insisted that I pick a date.

On the morning I'd reluctantly nominated, I went into labour.

Mother and daughter in concert from the very beginning.

*

In the early days, me working and Brendan at home with the kids, I was approached by a group of his mates, worried that as a 'house husband' Brendan was 'losing his identity'.

He laughed for twenty-four hours straight.

Our role reversal hasn't always gone smoothly.

Me: 'Where is my good black bra? I put in the wash *two days ago*. You've LOST IT!'

Him: 'I am *sick and tired* of you bringing all your shit home every day. ENOUGH!'

Me: 'It's a BIG DEAL charity event in a BALLROOM! Could you wear some fucking decent *shoes*? ANY SHOES, AT ALL?'

Him: 'It's a *lunch order*, Wendy! You write the name and order on the paper bag. The prices are on the pinboard. EXACT CHANGE PLEASE!'

Brendan was a dedicated, 'hands-on' father who took being at home with the kids in his stride, even when he was the one to get up in the middle of the night to attend to them so I could sleep.

In my one-woman show at the Sydney Theatre Company in 2001, *Up Late and Loving It*, when the kids were tiny: 'I swear I could tell him I'd been captured by Somali pirates and he'd say: "Well, at least you didn't have the kids screaming in your ear all night!"'

*

Brendan didn't want to buy into the growing inequality he'd observed between public and private schools and nor did I, so our kids went 'local' and 'public'. With the skills he learned from a permaculture course run by the pioneering biologist Bill Mollison, he built a frog pond, chook shed, orchard, veggie patch and flower garden with the students at North Narrabeen PS. Coached footy teams with Manly legend Geoff Toovey.

I'd been MC for Riverview's glittering annual art auction and was presented with a magnum of Moët and inscribed champagne glasses. At Narra North Public, MC-ing a trivia night to raise funds for twin-flush toilets, I was given a bottle of low-fat Tia Maria and a mug inscribed with the school motto: 'Be Sensible'. (I complained to the school principal that it was more of a 'nag' than anything. It's now: 'I Aspire. I Achieve'.)

*

Our children have been an unalloyed joy and remain extremely close to us. Pittwater High School alumni, Marley holds a science degree in Sustainable Agriculture and Food Security from Western Sydney University, while Maeve graduated from the University of New South Wales with a Bachelor of Design (Hons). They are fine young people, kind, generous with a strong social conscience, and able to converse with anyone—qualities we value very highly.

Being an older mother has had its advantages. I sailed through my forties then fifties while raising them, although teenagers and menopausal women were never meant to share a house.

While my friends dealt with the misery of being 'empty-nesters', now they are experiencing the giddiness of becoming grandparents. 'Even better the second time around,' they declare.

Once again, I hope I don't miss out—but as a friend of Brendan's father once said: 'Life is like turning the pages of an interesting novel. When you have children, it becomes a thriller.'

*

You may be wondering whatever happened to my stepmother Alison. When our kids were small, Noel and Helen travelled from Victoria with their families to spend Christmas at our place. Dad and Alison joined us. We go big on a traditional Christmas: a huge, fresh, decorated tree, the house festooned with lights and tinsel garlands, 'the whole nine yards'. The day started with champagne and presents, then a dozen or so of us around tables pushed together for a lavish, traditional turkey dinner. Charades and games with a tribe of cousins. A happy gathering.

On Boxing Day, sitting on our deck recovering with a drink or two, an argument broke out between Noel and Alison about—of all banal matters: Does the week officially start on a Monday or a Sunday? Noel and Alison went at it furiously. They'd always fought bitterly and here they were, at it again.

As the disagreement escalated my father made a headmasterly attempt to adjudicate: 'Well, you're both right. It largely depends on which calendar you follow. For the working man it's a different matter . . . blah, blah, blah.'

In the middle of this explanation, Alison suddenly stood and pronounced to the assembled: 'I don't know WHY I have put up with being in this fucking family for the LAST THIRTY YEARS. I'm leaving.'

Within the hour a plane ticket was secured, she packed her things, Graham drove her to the airport and none of us kids ever saw or heard from her again.

Brendan relates this as the most astonishing vignette of family life he has ever witnessed. 'If you put it in a movie, no one would ever believe it. Just like that. She was gone.'

It's only now, on writing, I learn that Alison died in 2013 at the age of 66. I do not know of what cause. Her death notice says: 'Now free from pain. Rest in Peace.'

18

Velvet curtains

Mirror
Luxury suite
Crown Melbourne
Southbank

Hilary was right: I shouldn't be here.

I want to go home.

Too late now!

*

On the night of the 44th Annual TV Week Logie awards in 2002, Brendan was sitting next to actor Frankie Muniz from the sitcom *Malcolm in the Middle*. He recalls they both enjoyed my turn as host. Laughed at my jokes. But says, in hindsight, if he'd known the ferocity of the criticism to come, would have set the table on fire to create a diversion. Pity he didn't.

When I accepted the gig, Hilary advised me against it. '*Really*, Wen? Are you *sure*?'

I was. The chance to be the first woman to host since the inaugural awards in 1959 was one I couldn't pass up. I felt confident I could do it, but slowly became aware that there was a lot of chatter about me in Melbourne, where the awards were to be held. None of it complimentary.

I wasn't on television, I was on *radio*; and even worse . . . in *Sydney*. I should have taken note of David Letterman's fate in 1996, when he travelled from New York to Los Angeles—from television to the movies—to host the Academy Awards and made jokes about Hollywood A-listers which bombed, big-time. He was seen as an 'outsider' and nominated that night as the 'single biggest professional embarrassment of [his] life'. The 2002 Logies would be the same for me.

Writers Patrick Cook, Phil Scott, George Dodd and I had initially come up with a much gentler opening routine, but we were encouraged by the Logies producers to sharpen the barbs. It had been a horror year for television in 2001. Every second show had tanked. The producers thought the industry might be up for a bit of teasing to lighten the mood in classic 'stand-up' comedy style. This, as it turned out, was crapper than crap advice. I hadn't realised just how fragile many were feeling.

Sitting on the tarmac, waiting for the plane to take me south, all my 'Spidey-senses' were tingling, urging me to storm the door and flee my impending doom.

The rehearsal at the Crown Casino went well enough. Everyone laughed. Why wouldn't they? They weren't the target of my jokes.

Upstairs in my room, another portent. The worst teased and sprayed updo I'd ever seen. I grabbed a hairbrush and redid it myself. I did love my outfit, though: a bespoke, beautifully tailored, mid-length, crushed velvet coat-dress in a deep claret hue and fastened with satin ribbons. We'd decided against black. All the male hosts had only ever worn black.

The best thing I can salvage from that night is a 'good luck' kiss from Beyoncé, there to perform 'Bootylicious' with Destiny's Child. Shakira shook things up with 'Whenever Wherever'. I didn't get to meet Elton John, but did witness a meltdown as two assistants argued over a floral display. Was it *only* white flowers or *no* white flowers in his dressing room? Careers seemed to be riding on it.

When the curtains opened, I performed an impromptu 'twirl' to settle my nerves and opened with: 'Everyone is looking really fabulous tonight. It's not easy for the stars to get ready for a big night like this. It takes a punishing six months of being starved, shaved, soaked, slathered, perfumed, powdered, plucked, waxed, exfoliated, derma-braded, injected and implanted. And that's just Jamie Durie . . . imagine what the women have been through!'

When that joke fell flat, I knew I was in for a rough evening.

Looking back at that routine, some of the gags were too mean, some poorly targeted and others just begging for me never to be seen on television again.

'And tonight I really want to wish Happy Birthday to the ABC, which is 70 years old this year. Things are often tense between the ABC and Communications Minister Richard

Alston. But then, it must be hard dealing seriously with someone who played one of *The Thunderbirds*.'

Ergh! It hadn't gone well. I knew that. Bert Newton was backstage and offered condolences: 'I did the Logies fourteen years in a row and people forget there were a couple of years there where everyone in the entire country wanted to kill me!'

Lovely Bert.

Next morning, I was back on the *Morning Crew*, broadcasting from Melbourne. *The Australian* newspaper was scathing. Television 'showbiz reporter' Peter Ford called me 'an ageing, unfunny shrew who looked like her dress was made from the curtains of the Regent Theatre'.

In an ill-advised radio interview I likened the experience to 'slowly cutting off my own arm with a blunt chainsaw'. I'm also remembered for the immortal line: 'Yes, it's crap television, but it's *our* crap television.'

On the Melbourne talkback radio shows hosted by Neil Mitchell and Steve Price, the condemnation was unrelenting and ran for hours. I know this because my brother Noel, working as a house painter, had been listening all day to caller . . . after . . . caller—and rang to tell me. He'd been amused by it mostly, but when Price called me a 'nasty, negative woman' and 'as funny as a box full of spiders', Noel told me he rang his show and gave him an on-air talking-to.

Thanks, Noel!

When Brendan and I arrived back at Sydney airport next afternoon, a photographer jumped out of a pot plant and snapped me, as if I was attempting to sneak in incognito, rather than simply coming home for work the next day. Attending a post-Logies lunch party with showbiz types, I entered the room to hushed silence. *Who died?* I thought. It was me.

In the ensuing media pile-on I learned a lot about 'friendship' and 'loyalty'. Who was worthy of trust and who wasn't.

In *The Daily Telegraph*, I was quoted by Michael Bodey: 'It's my responsibility. I failed to hit the mark. The big story of the year was the axing of programs, but I just underestimated how bruised people are feeling.' He also wrote: 'Two things conspired against Harmer—the venue and the audience. The cavernous Crown Casino ballroom is no place for stand-up comedy, particularly when half the crowd is out smoking or in the powder room.'

Hmmm. Was that a 'powder room' joke?

As always, the *Morning Crew* listeners were supportive and sent kind emails. One from 'Queen Jess' ended with: 'PS You looked amazing. You did those old curtains proud!'

I punished myself for a long time after the Logies, was the first to bring it up in any conversation and was often told: 'Move on! Are you *still* thinking about that?'

I was.

Failure was not new to me, but this time it had happened on a grand scale. It was a hard lesson.

*

The first book in the *Pearlie in the Park* children's series was published the following year. I'd been reading fairy books to Maeve—who, like me, was entranced with magical beings—but found myself irritated by a host of vain, drippy fairies flitting off to balls in frocks.

Hilary and I met up for morning tea and she said, 'Wenno, darling, if you were to write a children's book, what would it be about?'

It was something I'd been musing on but never said aloud until that moment: 'Well, how about a fairy who's a bit bossy? With a bit of derring-do? She's in charge of a park in the city, runs the place sort of like a CEO. Part detective? She could live in a shell, maybe? Maybe a carved stone shell on a fountain?'

And there it was, the entire scenario, just waiting to be written.

I was thinking of Little Obelia, one of my favourite May Gibbs characters, a baby mermaid who lived in a shell. I was also thinking about city kids who would never get to visit a fairy dell in a forest or even the bottom of the garden, like I had. It would be fun for them to look out for fairy folk in the local park.

'Righto,' said Hilary, and within months she'd made it happen with Random House.

Those little pink books, beautifully illustrated by Mike Zarb then Gypsy Taylor, have sold almost a million copies. The final and seventeenth was published in 2016, and by then they'd been translated into Hebrew, Greek, Portuguese, Spanish, Dutch, Japanese, Catalan, Turkish and Bahasa Indonesia. It was a thrill to take Pearlie's distinctively Australian setting to the world, with possums, lilly pilly trees, a summer Christmas and a best friend, Opal from Rainbow Ridge, who rode a frill-necked lizard.

I adapted the books, with Phil Scott, for a musical staged by the Sydney theatre group Monkey Baa, who took it to schools and regional theatres. The animated television series wasn't all it could have been. It was co-produced between Sticky Pictures in Australia and the huge production house Nelvana, in Canada. 'Roots and Twigs!' Pearlie lost her Aussie accent. Collaborating with Canadian writers was often hilarious, with one line written for Opal: 'G'day, mate. Jeez, I'm knackered!'

The snobby types in children's *literature* haven't ever had much regard for *Pearlie in the Park.* The books' covers are lolly pink and written by a—gasp!—*celebrity.* Not that I cared when they were selling like hot wattleseed cakes.

The best reviews came from teachers, who reported that there was often a frenzied race to the library to be the first to bag the *Pearlie* books and they'd have to referee the scrum. Also from a generation of fathers who told me that when they played the roles of the two naughty rats, Scrag and Mr Flea, their children shrieked with delight.

The dedication of the final book reads: 'For my father, Graham Frederick Brown, who inspired my love of reading.'

*

I was enticed out of my hidey-hole on the side of the hill in 2005 for another shot at radio with an exciting project from media company DMG. Vega FM, big sister station to Nova FM, was hyped as a new concept of 'talk/music' for an older audience that would be broadcast to both Sydney and Melbourne.

As *The Age* reported: 'Here at last was a commercial FM

outfit promising intelligent analysis, interesting discussion and an eclectic playlist.'

The on-air talent they'd assembled was impressive. There were to be separate breakfast shows—in Sydney, Angela Catterns, the former darling of ABC 702 who'd ruled the airwaves for a decade, and in Melbourne, Denise Scott and someone named Shaun Micallef. (Him again?) They'd hand over to me, doing the morning shift and beaming into both cities. The money was much less than I'd been offered elsewhere to return to radio, but the chance to be part of a format that I'd always thought was missing on FM was irresistible. Likewise for my long-time friend Helen Thomas, who came from Radio National to be my producer.

Helen had been executive producer of RN's breakfast show for seven years and at the time was a senior journalist with the highly regarded investigative program *Background Briefing*. We'd known each other since the days of covering the magistrates court in Melbourne—her from *The Age* and me from the *Sun News Pictorial*. I had the utmost regard for her talent and knew I was in a safe pair of hands. 'I was loving my job, but the chance to start something as exciting as a "talk/music" network was too good to pass up,' says Helen.

We arrived at the new studio in Pyrmont to find an absence not only of vital pieces of equipment—a clock in the studio and phones that worked—but also on-air 'furniture', like station IDs and music stings. Nevertheless, we took up the challenge and Helen recruited some big-name journalists, including Bruce Guthrie and Helen Trinca as media and finance analysts. James

Reyne was our book reviewer, terrifically smart and well-read. (So much for being a 'dumb muso' from *Countdown*!)

Things soon went downhill. 'It was obvious from the outset that the "talk" element of the equation was completely foreign to those setting up the joint,' Helen says. 'Conceptually, they were building a two-city network that could lure listeners from Triple J, RN and ABC Local radio as well as commercial rivals . . . but when it came to actually doing it, they didn't appreciate what it involved.'

We worked hard to strike the balance between 'talk' and 'music', but management kept shifting the goalposts. We began with an allocation of an hour of 'talk' over the three-hour shift, but that was slowly reduced to ten minutes. Helen says: 'I knew we were in strife when I was told that ninety seconds could be regarded as an interview. I said, "No, that's a grab."'

The most confusing direction I can recall: 'We want more listeners on the air, but we don't want talkback.'

Huh?

It had got to the point where I looked at our whiteboard, which was supposed to be filled for the next morning, and burst into tears. I had no idea what was expected of me.

I lasted six months before I was sacked as 'a disruptive influence', told to clear out my desk. Didn't even get to say 'farewell' to the loyal listeners who had found me. Not long after, Helen was recruited back to the ABC, where she managed NewsRadio for twelve years. She now freelances and is the author of bestselling books on horse racing and true crime; she is also a top-rating podcaster.

The good ship Vega FM slowly sank under the airwaves with a roster of presenters either being tossed overboard or jumping when they had the chance—flotsam *and* jetsam. It was scuttled in 2010.

One human I found in the fallout was Angela Catterns. We'd hit it off during the handovers from the breakfast to morning shifts. Our banter had started off as ten minutes and had stretched to almost half an hour. The chemistry was instant. We made each other laugh and, judging by the feedback, our audience was laughing along with us. Could we do a show together? we asked. It would be a smart move as the first all-female breakfast show— two top-rating hosts from both AM and FM.

Er . . . that would be a firm 'no'.

Instead, we teamed up as 'the Early Girlies' over the summer break on ABC Local radio and were a huge hit. The radio journalists predicted we'd score a permanent gig. Somewhere, anywhere? But, as one radio dinosaur told me, 'Think of the blokes! They've spent the weekend being nagged by their wives and then they turn on the radio for a bit of peace and are nagged by *two* women?'

Instead, we became podcast pioneers in 2008 with *Is It Just Me? A podcast for fertile minds.* It was initially funded by the ABC but, despite doing excellent numbers, was ditched by a senior executive who said the ABC was after a younger demographic.

Again, *too old!*

Oh, well. Off to crochet myself a knee blanket, I guess.

*

I could afford to freelance, not knowing what was coming next and usually had a few projects on the go in case the *next* thing turned out to be *no* thing.

I was in demand as a novelist after my first effort for Allen & Unwin, *Farewell My Ovaries*, made the bestseller list in 2006. Next came a chick-lit offering, *Love and Punishment*, and two novels that were more for women of 'a certain age'—*Roadside Sisters* and *Friends Like These*. My text-and-cartoon book *Nagging for Beginners* always brought the house down when I read from it on stage.

There were two young adult novels—*I Lost My Mobile at the Mall* and *I Made Lattes for a Love God*. And for the littlies graduating from *Pearlie in the Park*, three readers in the *Ava Anne Appleton: Accidental Adventurer* series for Scholastic.

Perhaps I could have made a bigger name for myself as an author if I'd stuck to one genre and one age group.

But honestly, who'd resist the chance to write for *all* the girlies?

*

In 2007, long before Marie Kondo was a thing with her 'KonMari' method of throwing away possessions that don't 'spark joy', Laura Waters and I made the four-part television documentary *Stuff*, with her company Princess Pictures.

The aim was to examine the human urge to acquire. Not a showcase of 'collectors', nor a guilt trip about over-consumption, but something deeper. What 'stuff' means in our lives—our complex human relationship with objects. We began with a visit to a baby shower and finished at an auction for a deceased estate. Along the way we spoke to psychologists, prisoners, students in share houses, monks, 'hoarders' and 'chuckers'.

Screened on ABC TV, it got rave reviews from critics and a huge reaction from viewers, who all felt a little less guilty about their cupboards overflowing with junk.

It was an excellent series. Thoughtful. Stands the test of time.

Buoyed by the reception, Laura and I pitched for a new project, but were rejected. It's like that at the ABC.

Sometimes you're 'in' and others most definitely 'out'.

I was the latter desk tray.

*

What Is The Matter With Mary Jane?, a play I wrote back in 1995 dramatising my friend Sancia Robinson's harrowing journey through anorexia nervosa and bulimia, was often restaged and required updating. It's still being performed and is lately applauded as 'a journey of survival, resilience and hope presented using pithy humour, palpable energy and stirring pathos' in the online site 'Stage Whispers'. Elsewhere as 'powerfully intense, yet darkly comic'. Sance and I are very proud of our creation and the contribution it has made to understanding this pernicious disease and its effect on mental health. I'll always be grateful to Sancia for trusting me with her story.

In 2008, invited by Bill Shorten MP from the Gillard government, I served for six years on the National People with a

Disability and Carers Council (NPWDACC), where we paved the way for the revolutionary National Disability Insurance Scheme (NDIS).

Did I have a 'disability'? I'm lucky enough to have had a father who made my diction his personal mission, so I've never claimed so. But many kids with serious clefts require ongoing hearing and speech therapy and still fight for assistance under Medicare.

In 2014 the NPWDACC (worst acronym ever) was sacked by the Abbott government, along with seventy other advisory boards in a decision made with the blinkers of ideology and sheer political bastardry. Now we pay millions to 'consultants' for the advice we once got for free.

There was also lots to be going on with in stoushes in my neighbourhood—truly bad proposals for development in bushfire zones and on precious beaches—where I used my journalist skills with community groups to notch up a few wins. I even organised a ticket to run for local government. But we lost more than we won, despite our hard-fought campaigns against the local council and state planning authorities.

*

One constant was the long list of newspaper and magazines I wrote columns for. I'd gathered more than a hundred of them in my book *So Anyway . . . Wendy's Words of Wisdom* years earlier. For a time I had my own page in the *Australian Women's Weekly*, the magazine that was always on kitchen tables of every house I visited as a kid. After Dad died, I discovered a collection of my articles he had kept. My poor grammar highlighted in fluorescent markers.

On the merry-go-round of new media management, changing editors and shuttered titles, I got dumped . . . hired . . . given a raise . . . sacked . . . rehired . . . axed . . .

Which brings us neatly to the enterprise I loved the most. It cost me a small fortune and, if I won the lottery, would gladly use every cent of my winnings to go around again. On a business card there is a picture of a lady acrobat, with one foot balancing on a highwire and the other twirling a hoop.

It reads: *The Hoopla. Wendy Harmer. Editor-in-chief.*

In 2010 Jane Waterhouse, a visionary marketer and publisher, proposed we start an online site. She'd worked for twenty-five years in ad agencies, magazines and web design; she understood how to cater for and, most importantly, sell to women aged forty-plus—another one of those mysterious 'gaps in the market'. We launched *The Hoopla* as 'news through the eyes of women' . . . not 'women's news'. (There's a big difference.) Our founding editor was the very talented Caroline Roessler, former managing editor of the *Australian Women's Weekly* and editor of *Notebook*. The night we pressed 'GO!' on our beautiful, circus-themed site was one of the most exciting moments of my whole working life.

In our four years online we published some 5000 articles from 300 writers—and we paid them. Not the least of our achievements was securing accreditation for our own correspondent in the press gallery at Parliament House, Canberra—a first for a women's online publication. *The Hoopla* had front row seats during Julia Gillard's tenure as our first woman Prime Minister.

I mastered the 'back end' of the site, edited, wrote headlines, commissioned writers, moderated as the comments rolled in— sometimes hundreds at a time. Maybe it was my true calling, 'editor-in-chief', ever since the days of the *Greenwell Gazette* in Selby.

Two years in and Jane, Caroline and I were out of money. We raised some capital from wonderful investors Deanne Weir and Cass O'Connor, but we just couldn't attract the advertisers. God knows, Jane and I pitched hard at agency meetings. Often we'd be faced with a room of mostly men under thirty; once we mentioned 'perimenopause' they'd slide back in their chairs and slink under tables.

With little revenue, our product shamelessly copied, our writers and staff poached by a host of big media players, we introduced a 'hard' paywall that saw our engagement plummet off the highwire and into the sawdust. The technology of a 'soft' paywall, which would have tumbled our readers safely into a net, came too late.

As Jane wrote in *The Guardian* when we closed in 2015: 'It's a sad day for independent women's publishing. I was asked to write a post about why *The Hoopla* didn't work. But we think it did work, and very well in fact. We see it as a brilliant success and it's a story we are proud to tell. So why are we closing? Two reasons: we were pioneers, and too early for this market, and our pockets are not as deep as our competitors.'

A decade on and still, no one quite knows how to make an online news and opinion site pay its way.

You cannot find *The Hoopla* online.

We took it down.

Like all the best, most magical things, you had to be there.

Alley-oop!

*

What could be next? I was staring at a wall recovering from the burnout and personal financial hit of *The Hoopla* when I was offered the job of hosting the morning shift on Sydney's ABC 702.

What the . . . ?

Never thought I'd be back at the ABC and on radio again—not at the age of almost-sixty!

Brendan and I always rubbed along well enough when we were both in the house, but I could sense he was more pleased than he dared let on when it was back to pre-dawn alarms. Back to him packing my breakfast every morning. More than that, he knew I was a 'people person'; sitting at my desk, alone, wasn't good for me.

Again, I was thrilled to be driving across the Sydney Harbour Bridge just as the sun was rising, with the roads empty, watching the first house lights switch on and knowing I'd be a part of it all. I presented for two years in the morning shift and was back on my hobby horse of urban affairs, which suited me just fine. Ratings were solid.

It was then decided by the powers-that-be in the ABC that I join Robbie Buck for the breakfast shift on the now rebranded ABC Sydney. My alarm was reset for 3.45 a.m. I once counted how many cars I saw on the road during the thirty-kilometre drive from Collaroy to the studios in Ultimo. It was twenty-seven.

Robbie had been in the brekkie chair for four years when he was asked to move over a bit and make room for me. The listeners on the studio 'text line' weren't happy—'This will never work!' 'Why do we need *two* presenters?' etc.—but Robbie could not have been more accommodating, and it wasn't long before the two of us discovered a shared ratbaggery that spilled onto the air and listeners warmed to. Robbie, an incredibly knowledgeable music aficionado, invited lots of musicians to play live in the studio. What a blast it was to have Paul Kelly, Josh Pyke and Missy Higgins playing so close you could reach out and touch them. And I never thought I'd get to speak with not only Micky Dolenz from The Monkees, but also Christopher Knight who played Peter in *The Brady Bunch*. I was beside my teenage self with excitement.

Robbie's mastery of the panel astounded me, never failing to end a music track just as the 'pips' sounded for the news.

I often gave him a standing ovation of one.

We made a most congenial partnership, teasing each other, laughing together. On the dreaded text line, which I monitored, there were silly messages: 'Wendy! Leave Robbie alone!' followed by: 'Robbie! You owe Wendy an apology!'

Over time, sadly, the comments became increasingly politically partisan and nasty. It wasn't unusual after an interview with a politician, academic, activist or expert to read we'd gone both 'too soft' and 'too hard'.

The ABC had become a political football and we were kicked from end to end. The insults were often personal. I was 'too old', 'too white', 'too left', 'too right', 'too uneducated', 'too opinionated' and used the word 'amount' when it should have been 'number'. (Although my pronunciation of 'February'—with both 'r's—was widely acclaimed.)

Brendan often had to talk some sense into me when I got home and related the most offensive comments to him. 'Let it go. It's all bullshit. Just people with too much time on their hands.'

The daily onslaught became corrosive. I was enjoying myself less and less. As the ABC's budget shrank, staff were always asked to do 'more' with fewer resources—antiquated equipment, technical support slashed and miniscule or non-existent budgets to pay contributors. It was a daily struggle to deliver the product we knew our loyal listeners both expected and deserved.

*

In October 2021, Robbie and I announced we were leaving after our four years together. During terrifying fires, disastrous floods and the coronavirus epidemic, we'd found ourselves fielding distressed calls from those who were suffering. We did our best to console and find help, with the aid of our brilliant, dedicated producers, but it all exacted a toll. I worked remotely from home for months during the height of the virus, with Robbie in the studio at Ultimo. It was a real test to work live every day with no vision, just audio. I found myself concentrating on his breathing to anticipate where we were going next. Often after our four-hour shift, I flatlined. Could barely speak. Like so many others, we were just plain worn-out. We agreed. It was time to go.

When Robbie and I left, our highest rating, at 15.9 per cent was, according to an ABC Sydney spokesperson, 'believed to be the station's highest breakfast share on record'.

Like I say, there are few gracious exits in radio, but Robbie and I executed a perfect reverse one-and-a-half-somersault with four-and-a-half twists off the three-metre board . . . and away we swam in synchronicity.

*

To the astonishment of all my radio colleagues, Brendan had always packed my breakfast for every morning I was on radio. He'd be up late, long after I'd gone to bed at 8 p.m., filling a container with freshly cut tomato, veggies, cheese and ham slices, dry biscuits and miniscule pots of chutney, salt and pepper. He would also leave a little handwritten note on the kitchen bench for me to discover. Often those notes were the only reason I hauled myself out of bed before dawn, and I now have boxes and boxes of them, written on anything he could find.

Thousands.

I have kept them all.

One for every single day that I went to work before dawn.

I've often been told I should put them in a book, so here are just a few. The unwritten part is *I love you more than . . .*

the magic that is Cliffy Lyons
is humanly possible (almost)
all the tears shed in all the movie houses in the world
how orange oranges are

moonlight on the waves
ants' feet
the junk at a council clean-up
all the birds that visit our garden
how blue a blue-tongue's tongue is—should be on a paint chart
all the buttons on all the shirts ever made in Hong Kong
petals on flowers
the resilience of the brush turkey
the ticks of clocks (cumulative)
geckoes in the kitchen
how scrumptious you are
the pings and pongs of ping-pong
the number of smiles you have caused
the exhaustion of the firies
every beat of a wing of every hummingbird
more than how much work you do . . . A.T.A.V.L. (And That's
A Very Lot)

Many of them were about the politics and news of the day, and it's easy to date when I left breakfast radio, because one of the last notes I have reads:

more than Scomo lies
A.T.A.V.L.

Epilogue

Rear-vision mirror
My car
Narrabeen North Public School No. 3096
Northern Beaches
Sydney

Look at you.

No, not in the mirror.

As your husband, children and friends see you.

Like your mother promised: 'You will be just as beautiful as anybody else. It's just going to take time.'

*

A few days after *Australian Story* aired; I dropped my two young children at school. The photographs of me as a baby, a 'disastrous-looking thing', had been confronting.

I was dreading what they'd say about it.

Two little voices piped up from the back seat.

Marley: 'So, what *did* happen to your face, Mumma?'

Wendy: 'Well, sometimes when babies are being made in their mums' tummies, something goes a bit wrong and no one quite knows why.'

Marley: 'I've heard of that. Sometimes babies are born with no arms, or legs!'

Maeve: 'Or heads!'

Marley: 'The doctors made you better, didn't they, Mumma? They did a very good job. Your face looks very nice to me. I think you are beautiful.'

Maeve: 'Yes! You are the most beautifullest Mumma in the whole wide world. You are a queen! Our sparkling, diamond heart. We love you *all the day*.'

Marley: 'Can we have an ice cream on the way home?'

*

My mother remembers the day she told me to stand in front of the mirror and find 'something to complain about'.

'You were a terribly unhappy little girl,' she says. 'When you came away from that mirror and said, "Nothing," I bawled and bawled my eyes out. Bless your little heart for saying that. I look back and think how harsh that was. I wish I could have been softer.'

This is one of the few instances of my childhood where my mother's and my own recollections tally. She was there. I was there. She tells it this way. I do too. So, it *must* have happened.

When I've spoken of my childhood in public, at even the mere mention of either her presence or absence, Margaret Elsie has bristled, sulked or just gone missing . . . then turned up again whenever it suited her, to challenge my recollections or embellish as she'd prefer things were told.

Frankly? It's been a long and often tiresome charade.

An interview with Andrew Denton on ABC TV's *Enough Rope* in 2005 is just one of many examples of how I have tried to navigate the tricky terrain of my mother's feelings:

'I thought my mother had left because I wasn't very lovable, because of the way I looked. So I kind of deprived a family of its mother. My mother had her own reasons for going, but that's a big thing to take on as a girl—that you've driven your own mother away and you're unlovable. So they were sad times.'

I had another run at it in 2009 with Peter Thompson on ABC TV's *Talking Heads*:

'Mum is a very, very gregarious sort of person, and it was a real shame that she felt that she couldn't cope and had to leave the family. You know how a lot of people think that there's a man in the moon? I always used to think that my mother was in the moon.'

None of this careful treading around past events, with my ears pricked for the cracking of eggshells, has ever appeased my mother.

She says I've never told 'her' side of the story. Problematic, since she's only ever revealed it to me in fits and starts. So much of what you have read here is the first time I've heard it too. For her part, she would say that she has told me everything, but it never suited my carefully constructed 'narrative'.

At the heart of my mother's story is her overwhelming shame and enduring grief at leaving four young children. This has warped our every interaction. 'It's been my burden all my life,' she tells me. 'I have always carried a huge amount of guilt that won't go away. And it can't, no matter how many times I say "sorry".'

Now in her mid-eighties, Margaret Elsie has, at last, gone at least some way towards understanding that little girl, Margie Wicks: 'She could never cope with life. Life wasn't kind in general, so she always hid. I'm so sorry for her.'

All her recollections told to me have come after careful, persistent cajoling. Infrequent emails where she puts down a few hundred words or so, or from my note-taking during lengthy phone conversations—although it can take her days to reply to my messages.

I'm always wary of what she reveals, as she bends things to suit herself or, given her age, forgetfulness. One day, a story I've long believed about my past, or hers, just . . . vanishes. It's airily replaced with another, as if of no consequence.

She is a shapeshifter.

I can't remember much of those tumultuous times with my mother in the house in California Gully. The dates of when she left, came back and left again are all mixed up in my head. I remember some details of the emotional and physical punishment she exacted, but she cannot. When I visited her in Tasmania, about age sixteen, I remember that she said, through tears at Launceston airport: 'Forgive me. I always knew you were the strong one and I took it out on you, and I shouldn't have. I'm sorry.'

It makes sense that Mum took out her frustrations on me. Not only was I the eldest, but I was also actually *there*, standing in front of her, when my father wasn't. It was better she hit me than murdered him.

She must also have recognised that I'd become a stoic, unbreakable child. I was not rude or defiant, but there was a part of me that was inaccessible to her. Just as, when she was young, she walled off her emotions from her own mother and grand-mother. Must have seen in me a reflection of herself.

She says: 'The way I was brought up was, you didn't talk. You were either "bragging" or "snivelling", so you kept your thoughts to yourself. I could only bring you up as I was brought up.'

She says: 'I was hard on you because I knew you had to be strong, stand up and take it.'

She says: 'I always felt like a loner, an outsider looking in.'

She says: 'We are the same.'

But we are not.

Mum didn't ever remarry. 'Your father and I were always friends. We'd be on the phone, laughing about old times.'

Ah yes, the *old times*. Through the lens of modern mores and expectations, I have often found myself wondering how they could have been so reckless as to drive into a wall, at speed, with four little kids in the back seat.

Mum and I are in contact more often now than we've ever been. We talk about the weather, her beloved moggies, her garden. She lives in Launceston, where she's been for decades. She's a lively and profane narrator of her quiet, mostly solitary life and her laugh is still as light as a schoolgirl's. Her stories are droll and engaging. She's a loving grandmother.

I don't ring on Mother's Day, knowing it's the hardest day in her calendar. Of her three surviving children, I'm the only one she hears from. She is, after everything, my mother, and we have, somehow, always found our way back to each other. And there is love there. I'm sure she has much to teach me about being a survivor . . . if I can ever unravel her story.

I'm glad my mother left.

There, I said it.

My life was better because she did. And not only because she says she was planning to murder my father with the knife she kept under her pillow or, if she could handle it, one of his hunting guns.

'Oh God! I'm glad I went too,' she tells me. 'If I hadn't, I'd probably be in jail or dead. You kids would have been scattered to the four winds. And I've thought this through, constantly. You wouldn't have grown up to be the people you are.'

Finally she concedes, 'It's your story; you tell it, darling,' and gives me her blessing.

But even now I wouldn't put it past her to recant the lot of it.

*

I began a lot of sentences with 'Dad says . . .' back then.

And I admit that, for all the time he was alive, I always deferred to him as the final authority on almost every fact, to the frustration of boyfriends and husbands. My father was what you'd call a 'know-it-all'. Thing was, he did know more than most of us.

I treasure those recordings I have of Graham Frederick Brown, when his mind was a bright and brilliant whirring thing, before it was thieved by Parkinson's disease and dementia. He was a teacher with Victoria's Education Department for more than forty years and events and names are retrieved from the exact place and time. In the recordings, his memories are almost photographic in their detail. A car numberplate; the prevailing weather; the number of fish he caught or rabbits he shot; the names of his many dogs; the hair colour of a student he taught who sat in the second row from the back half a century ago. His deep knowledge of the natural world, as a man who'd lived most of his life in the country, was astounding.

The original self-starter, an autodidact with an adamantine belief in his own abilities, he revelled in the title of 'The Professor' bestowed by his mates at the pub. 'Ask Graham, he'll know,' was possibly his favourite phrase.

My father's fatal flaw was vanity.

And beer.

And *way* too much footy.

I swear, my father was one of the most unsentimental men who ever lived. Birthdays and anniversaries were ignored or forgotten. Father's Day was 'bullshit'. Presents thoughtfully chosen for him were either given away or never used. His gifts to us sometimes came in brown paper bags and were bought from the local petrol station.

What we might see now as a 'lack of empathy', he would have defended as the correct, clear-eyed response to an unvarnished reality.

What he thought of as the rigorous application of logic to encourage risk and learning through failure or success we called 'building resilience' not so long ago. Now we might call it 'neglect' or, worse, 'emotional abuse'.

When I was a teenager, sometimes Dad would come home worse for wear from the pub, rouse me from bed, sit me at the kitchen table and ask me to advance some random topic for debate. He'd take the opposing view. *Have you supported your premise here? Is this a rash generalisation? Have you inferred or assumed? How does this statement support your conclusion?*

Damned if I knew. I just wanted to go back to bed. Imagine going to the children's services and complaining that your father had bludgeoned you with a lump of midnight logic? But I knew it was an expression of how much he loved me, even if, reading this now, you cannot.

Graham Frederick was a practical man who could fix anything—from a car engine to a toaster. 'Function' was the main criterion of worthiness he applied to an object. If it stopped working, could it be dismantled and repaired with stuff scavenged from the local tip? Re-wired?

He applied this principle to humans too. If the application of pure 'logic' hadn't done the trick? You might sputter and fail. Too bad. Mistakes would be made. You would learn from them—no matter how painful the lesson.

It sounds so harsh, and I've often been asked: Where was the kindness? Where was the love?

I can only answer for me.

The missteps I made were never judged. There was never an 'I told you so', even when I would have much preferred him to have stopped me from going ahead with some foolishness or other. He offered a deep, uncritical acceptance of the choices I made in life. His only direction: 'Whatever you choose to do, *do it well*. To the best of your ability. I don't care if you decide to collect rubbish. Just be *the best* rubbish collector you can be.'

My father did not ever raise a palm in anger or shout at me. There were no quarrels. I mean, *not ever*. Conflict was not in our shared vocabulary.

He remained supremely confident and steadfast in his belief in my abilities and he pushed me way beyond my imagined boundaries.

As a young boy, he had always dreamed of attending university. He sometimes spoke of how different his life would have been if his family had enough money to send him. Sir David Attenborough was the man he most admired and, as he sat us down to watch interminable documentaries on nature, archaeology or history, I came to understand that his was a brilliant mind, thwarted. That's why he revelled in the title 'The Professor' at the pub.

When he was an old man, he mellowed and was more comfortable in expressing his loving nature. Doted on his grandchildren. His biggest regret? 'I thought that the best thing in life would be to be a successful husband. And that's one area in which I feel I've failed the world because I've lost two wives and I really don't understand women'.

He told me that the secret to a happy life was 'to be resigned to your position'. Surely that couldn't mean 'giving up' or 'giving in'? I was certainly not about to do either.

But 'resignation' can also come at the end of a beautiful piece of music or a prayer—a calm, peaceful state. I came to realise that my father had long ago come to an acceptance of life's vicissitudes; had let go of a resentful battle against the tides.

I still struggle with this lesson.

It was one of his many gifts to me and it has taken a long, long time to unwrap the layers and decipher the profound effect of his legacy.

As they say: it's complicated.

I adored my father. Loved him more than he probably deserved to be loved, as that geography teacher knew so long ago. When we knew he was dying, I asked him what he was most dreading: 'I don't think I'll have everything finished', he said. 'I don't think I'll be ready.'

Always a declared 'humanist' with no need for a god, I wonder if instead he was thinking of the spectre of the school inspector coming to assess him as either 'fair', 'good', 'very good' or 'outstanding'. He never did achieve an 'outstanding'.

But then again, he also proudly declared, 'I have not lived by the rules others followed.'

As he lay on his deathbed, there was just the two of us, holding hands. His last words to me were: 'I love you too.'

*

I had abandoned my brothers and sister to seek shelter from the storm raging in the derelict schoolhouse at Freshwater Creek. I've always felt bad about that, especially when, much later, I learned of what Phil endured.

After a violent confrontation with Alison, in defence of his little brother, he was evicted from home, left behind to find his own way when Dad uprooted what was left of the family and took the headmaster's position at Lucknow.

In his turn, Phil deeply regretted leaving Noel. They were close in age. At this time they were sixteen and fourteen—almost like twins, and with a deep, loving bond.

Without the influence of his big brother, Noel started drinking heavily in those years. Could Phil have saved him from this ruinous path? None of us are sure.

'I don't think we ever understood how deeply hurt he was, losing Mum when he was seven, and then you and me in his teens,' says Phil.

Back then it was everyone for him or herself.

The anger of my siblings ran very deep. Still does. They have their own good reasons, and their stories are not mine to tell.

Noel died from alcoholism in 2013, at the age of fifty-four. His widow, Wendy, sent me a letter after his funeral: 'There was a lot of harshness in our marriage that was caused by the hurt from childhood which led him to drink himself to death. Unfortunately, Noel could not let go of the hurt and pain that so destroyed him.'

Noel's cleft lip was repaired at birth, but he was always insecure about his appearance. As Wendy tells me, he would spend hours in front of the mirror but always came away thinking he was never 'good enough'. 'He had such low self-esteem,' she says.

At his funeral, his two daughters, Stephanie and Gabriella, spoke of his 'get tough or die' mantra. 'To truly laugh, you must be able to take your pain and play with it' was the message they received from their father.

Maybe it was Noel who understood me better than anyone.

He certainly always thought he was a lot funnier than me, and it was only a trick of fate that *I* was famous and he *wasn't* . . . and didn't mind telling me so.

He is remembered by his daughters as a man whose heart remained a 'mystery'.

Same for me, his Big Sister.

I had always brought Noel home . . . even after a day mucking around down the creek or roaming the sunburned paddocks with the ferrets. He would run off and hide, just to tease me, because he knew I'd be searching frantically for him. 'Noel. *Noel*. Come back! We have to go now. It's getting dark. I know you're hiding. This isn't funny, Noel.'

He'd swing down from a branch in a gum tree or leap out from behind a big rock, and then tear away.

I'd run after him, sobbing with relief and threatening to kill him. Phil and Helen would come tumbling after and, by the time we made it through the back gate, we were all crying with laughter at the joke.

And then I went and lost him, and now we are just a rickety, uneven three. We are, forever, incomplete.

*

My sister Helen settled with her husband and their three children on a farm in the Yarra Valley which produced poultry, cattle, grapes and award-winning olive oil. She has been estranged from my family for some years now. Something I could never have envisaged after so many years of intense closeness. For me it's been almost like losing a child. But, again, I'll leave her to write the pages of her story.

I search for so many people I loved dearly in the rear-view mirror.

But, the times I spent with my beloved companions can't be found in any looking glass. They are a smell, a touch, sounds and words which cannot be framed and hung on any wall.

We see only our own faces when we look into a mirror.

*

I cannot recall how I found my way to the story of Prudence Sarn or how she came to me. A wise old owl of my acquaintance must have put the book *Precious Bane* into my hands just at the time I most needed to read it.

I'm thinking it was around time of my operation as a teenager—just before or after—when I was falling in and out of unrequited love with movie stars, handsome musicians or boys who lived up the road.

Written by the English author Mary Webb and published in 1924, it's a tale put down with exquisite eloquence and, hailed as a masterpiece in its day, regarded as equal to anything written by Thomas Hardy or Emily Brontë. Webb is lately resurrected as a 'forgotten genius'.

Set in the remote farmlands of Shropshire during the early 1800s, and written in local dialect, the tale is narrated by Prudence, who has a 'hare-shotten lip'. (The word 'shotten' meaning 'worthless' or 'undesirable'.) Her mother, berated by her husband for birthing a cursed child, cries: 'Could I help it if the hare crossed my path—could I help it?'

Prue is persecuted not only for her obvious affliction, but also because she can read and write, which marks her as 'uncommon' and a target for superstition and fine cruelties.

On a trip from her family farm to the village marketplace, she feels every eye upon her, 'as young owls will stare and turn their heads, watching you over their feathers'.

'Here's a queer outlandish creature.'

'Here be a wench who turns into a hare by night.'

'Her's a witch, an ugly, hare-shotten witch.'

'Her'll put the evil eye on you. You'll dwine and dwine away.'

Prue dreams of the handsome weaver Kester Woodseaves, although she's often told she'll never have a lover. In a triumphant ending (spoiler alert), Kester rescues Prue from the ducking stool (she is about to be drowned for sorcery) and hoists her onto his horse.

'Tabor on, owd nag!' says Kester, and we were going at a canter towards the blue and purple mountains.

'But no!' I said. 'It mun be frommet, Kester, You mun marry a girl like a lily. See, I be hare-shotten!'

But he wouldna listen. We wouldna argufy. Only after I'd pleaded agen myself a long while, he pulled up sharp, and looking down into my eyes, he said—'No more sad talk! I've chosen my bit of Paradise. 'Tis on your breast, my dear acquaintance!'

And when he'd said those words, be bent his comely head and kissed me full upon the mouth.'

'Here ends the story of Prudence Sarn.'

I knew *Precious Bane* was written for me and me alone. Ever since, I've kept it close as my talisman.

And *Here* (not quite . . . not for a while now . . . hopefully) *ends the story of Wendy Brown.*

Acknowledgements

I often advise anyone thinking of writing a memoir to do it early and often . . . even if it takes a set of volumes to get the story down. In that way their memories will, hopefully, be reliable.

Perhaps there should be a new name for a book like mine. Not so much a 'me'moir as a 'they'moir.

Almost every anecdote related here has been included after lengthy phone and video calls, texts and emails to corroborate my recollection of events. All I have been in contact with have been patient and accommodating, even as I have queried, 'Are you sure?' when their memories and mine didn't tally.

That's the old journo in me, seeking eyewitness accounts and revelling in the re-telling of it through a new perspective, even if it proved my memory to be spectacularly flawed and more so as the years pass. I shan't thank all my correspondents here individually because you will see their words on the page.

My task has been further complicated by my peripatetic wanderings through relationships, workplaces and creative endeavours both big and small, successful and less so. It pains me to omit so many partnerships and projects worthy of inclusion. (A few more volumes should do it!)

I am so grateful for the forbearance and generosity my friends have shown. My bestie Mary Finkelsen and her husband John were especially supportive as they read early pages and were encouraging. I could always pick up the phone to Meredith Jaffe, Lee Tulloch, Caroline Baum, Helen Thomas, Tory McBride, Dasha Ross, Catharine Lumby, Kaz Cooke, Jean Kittson and Kayte Murphy to have a moan when the whole enterprise looked daunting and I felt inadequate to the task. They urged me to keep at it!

Thank you, one and all.

As for the wordsmiths and editors at Allen & Unwin who have shepherded me though the tangled thickets of memory?

Almost twenty years ago Richard Walsh commissioned me to write my first novel. In the acknowledgments, I hailed him as 'good tempered, frighteningly erudite, witty, constructively critical, always available and up for a fabulous gossip.' In this new venture I must add 'compassionate' as Richard waited eight years after I signed a contract for me to write this book and he nursed my considerable fears and insecurities along the way. That he is still here, holding my hand, is a blessing.

Editors Annette Barlow and Ali Lavau have also been with me since the early days and, with Samantha Kent, have been diligent and forensic—their constancy and unwavering support have been a balm. Likewise all the staff at my agency, HLA, where Kate Richter has been a name I've trusted for three decades.

I thank my brother Phillip for our long conversations from New York and for the recordings he made of my father which I have on my desktop and allow me to see Dad's face and hear his voice whenever I choose. Also, all my love to my dear Aunt Elise for our long phone calls when we laugh and laugh as the eras unroll. And I'm also grateful to my mother, Margaret, who has fielded many questions from me about events long ago.

To my little family—Brendan, Marley and Maeve. I wished for you. And here you are. More than anything I could have hoped for. We are the new Famous Four.

Finally, to my best of friends and confidantes, now lost to me—Hilary Linstead, Mietta O'Donnell, John Pinder, Pete McCarthy, Dale Langley, Nigel Triffitt, Patsy Earnshaw—I miss you *all the day*.

How I would have loved you to be here and tell me that every memory I have recorded is quite mistaken and that you remember the *true* story.

With you gone, I write these words as best as I am able.